Resurrection

A War Journey

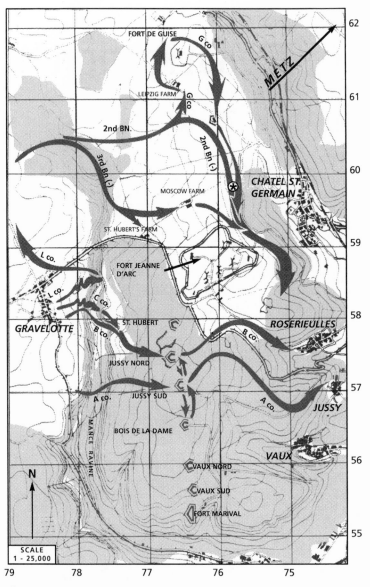

FORT DE GUISE

G CO.

METZ

LEIPZIG FARM

G CO.

2nd BN.

2nd Bn (-)

3rd Bn (-)

MOSCOW FARM

CHATEL ST. GERMAIN

ST. HUBERT'S FARM

L CO.

FORT JEANNE D'ARC

L CO.

C CO.

GRAVELOTTE

B CO.

ST. HUBERT

ROSERIEULLES

B CO.

JUSSY NORD

A CO.

JUSSY SUD

A CO.

JUSSY

MANCE RAVINE

BOIS DE LA DAME

VAUX

N

VAUX NORD

VAUX SUD

FORT MARIVAL

SCALE
1 - 25,000

79   78   77   76   75

62
61
60
59
58
57
56
55

* Site of wounding.

Resurrection

A War Journey

A Chronicle of Events During and Following
the Attack on Fort Jeanne d'Arc at Metz, France,
by F Company of the 379th Regiment
of the 95th Infantry Division,
November 14–21, 1944

Robert E. Gajdusek

UNIVERSITY OF NOTRE DAME PRESS
Notre Dame, Indiana

P. vii, excerpt from "Credences of Summer"
from *Collected Poems* by Wallace Stevens, copyright
1947 by Wallace Stevens. Reprinted by permission
of Alfred A. Knopf, Inc.

Copyright © 1997 by
University of Notre Dame Press
Notre Dame, Indiana 46556
All Rights Reserved.

Designed by Wendy McMillen
Set in 10.5/12 Meridien by The Book Page, Inc.
Printed in the U.S.A. by Braun-Brumfield, Inc.

The author and publisher are grateful to the following for permission to reprint:
- The National Archives for the use of photographs, nos. 337948, 196711,
  499053, 411773, 196758-S, 200712, 204244.
- Department of the Army, publisher of *United States Army in World War II:*
  The European Theater of Operations, The Lorraine Campaign by H. M. Cole,
  Historical Division, Department of the Army, Washington, D.C., 1950.
- Anthony Kemp, author of *The Unknown Battle: Metz, 1944* (New York: Stein
  and Day, 1981).
- John E. Loomis, PCF, F Co., 379th Infantry Regiment, 95th Division.
- Image of the bird on the cover courtesy of UniPhoto. Photo by Dilys King.

On the cover: April 12, 1945. A mortar section (Company M, 3rd Battalion,
378th Infantry Regiment) of the 95th Infantry Division, Ninth U.S. Army,
moves through a rubble-littered underpass as they advance toward their
objective, Dortmund, Germany, visible in the distance.

Library of Congress Cataloging-in-Publication Data
Gajdusek, Robert E.
    Resurrection, a war journey : a chronicle of events during and
following the attack on Fort Jeanne d'Arc at Metz, France, by F
Company of the 379th Regiment of the 95th Infantry Division,
November 14–21, 1944 / Robert E. Gajdusek.
        p.   cm.
    ISBN 0-268-01657-7 (alk. paper)
    1. Gajdusek, Robert E.   2. Metz, Battle of, 1944.   3. World War,
1939–1945—Personal narratives, American.   4. United States.   Army—
Biography.   5. Soliders—United States—Biography.   6. United
States. Army.   Infantry Division, 95th.   Regiment, 379th. —F
Company History.   I. Title
D756.5.M39G35   1997
940.54'2143825—dc21   97-6150
                                                                        CIP

∞ *The paper used in this publication meets the minimum*
requirements of the American National Standard for Information Sciences—Permanence
of Paper for Printed Library Materials, ANSI Z39.48-1984

This book is dedicated to

―――――➤●◄――――

"Josef and Hartmund,"

and to
An unknown German air force sergeant

and to
"Jo Poz," John, "Tex"

and to
Those who in the midst of battle and war were able to make
their own gestures, to speak with their own voices,
and to choose sacrificially and generously to
express themselves—in often self annihilating decisions
for which they alone were ultimately responsible,
keeping their destiny and morality
in their own hands.

. . . Let's see the very thing and nothing else
Let's see it with the hottest fire of sight.
Burn everything not part of it to ash.

Trace the gold sun about the whitened sky
Without evasion by a single metaphor.
Look at it in its essential barrenness
And say this, this is the centre that I seek.
Fix it in an eternal foliage

And fill the foliage with arrested peace,
Joy of such permanence, right ignorance
Of change still possible. Exile desire
For what is not. This is the barrenness
Of the fertile thing that can attain no more . . .

"Credences of Summer"—Wallace Stevens

. . . The war occurred half a lifetime ago, and yet the remembering makes it now. And sometimes remembering will lead to a story, which makes it forever. That's what stories are for. Stories are for joining the past to the future. Stories are for those late hours in the night when you can't remember how you got from where you were to where you are. Stories are for eternity, when memory is erased, when there is nothing to remember except the story.

The Things They Carried—Tim O'Brien

Contents

———➤●◄———

Preface

The account you are about to read is my personal account of my experiences as a foot soldier in F Company of the 379th Regiment of the 95th Infantry Division while part of The Third Army in its assault on Fortress Metz, in France. During this general attack, which began at 0600 on 14 November, 1944, my Battalion, the 2nd, was one of two proceeding against the forts surrounding Fort Jeanne d'Arc in the hills west of Metz.

We nominally "attained our objective" by noon of that day, but were subsequently pinned down and surrounded by the Germans, so that after I was wounded on the field and found shelter in a shell hole, I subsequently remained hidden there behind German lines until the third day when I made my escape. This account tells of the attack, my wounding, my days wounded on the field, my subsequent hiding out behind the lines before being taken prisoner, my treatment and interrogation by my captors, my being taken into Metz and then on to Saarbrücken for further interrogation and then back into Metz where I was placed in a hospital cellar with other wounded American captured GIs until the building was taken by storm by the American Fifth Division.

Since my account is the very incomplete one of an infantryman engaged in a battle where his perceptions were always limited, lacking in information, and distorted by the inescapable bias of his constrained situation, I *very* strongly urge those about to embark with me on this reclamation of that past to read the "official" documents that I here place throughout my tale. These include a military description of Metz and its fortifications and defenses, particularly of the forts that we in our battle were attempting to subdue; an account of the Battle of Gravelotte, fought in the Franco-Prussian War, 1871, on the very field where I was wounded; the US Government report of the first assault on Fort Driant; a military historical account of our battle for Fort Jeanne D'Arc; and finally, the account of John E. Loomis, a GI who fought beside me and saw me wounded.

I place them here because I feel they are condensed necessary background reading, for not to understand the nature of the field, and its defenses and defenders, on which and among which I was maneuvering and attempting to stay alive, is to lack too much, to be unaware of what exactly was informing and creating my fears, reactions and my state of mind at that time. The official accounts are also vital to an understanding of the vast distance between the perception of the soldier fighting as one minute element in a vast scheme, and the larger picture. Without them many ironies will go unseen. For example, without the official account of the first assault on Fort Driant, the reader may well be unable to assess our unique state of mind as an outfit, for we in the 379th were, in the misinformation that goes for truth at the front, aware of that battle and its many casualties and seeming absurdities and insanities, as we were ordered to yet another assault on those same forts. Without this history, how can a disengaged reader understand the forces that might bring an infantryman to shoot himself on the eve of a battle, to write last letters and give away what is of value on the morning before an attack?

I invite most of you to a place you have not been, that, being there, you may at once find the compassion and understanding that help make wars avoidable, while simultaneously perhaps discovering what of value can be resurrected from that dying and suffering—that they not "be in vain." Others, who may have been there with me, knowing how every battle comes down finally to its focal point in the individual soldier, may be reminded again of what they know, that every man's war is his own private war in which the discovery is at last a double discovery, of life and death, spirit and flesh, society and man, the earth and himself.

Introduction

Finally, fifty years after the events I describe came into the world as real and vivid facts, I set down the chronicle of their life. It has taken me this long while to get them out and defined. As I here and there will reveal, I have occasionally been either driven or enticed towards this account, but ever in the past an urge towards definition would end with a barely glimpsed glance at one "event" or a fictionally enclosed treatment of another. Never was I able, until 1987, to mount a sustained attack on the recalcitrant material to bring it to surrender its important secrets and hidden defenses. I have always, at some indefinable level, wanted to reduce the mysteries of those days to objective truths, to find the heart of the reluctant matter, but my sporadic forays were frustrated of their goal.

After the partial success of 1987, when I had managed to repossess the ground we gained in an assault in November of 1944 on Fort Jeanne d'Arc that defended Metz, I had held that position but advanced no further. That is, until 1995, which, marking the fiftieth anniversary of those events, signaled to me that the best celebratory act would be a final attack and capture of those positions in the mind that still held out, like surrounded and dangerous outposts in enemy territory.

It hasn't been easy. I have written against still active resistances and reluctances behind my lines, but managed to fight my way through to some clarity and then to further and further freedom on fields where the engagements have been hard and occasionally bitter, reviving old wounds. I have at last taken positions I didn't dream of being able to take, and I finally find myself in momentary possession of a newly won city, a city of Mystery whose keys were never in my hands until Time placed them in my hands.

This isn't the whole story, nor is it yet a complete victory—I only tell of my battle, my wounding, my capture and my interval behind German lines before recapture. There is so much more that leads up to the battle and so much more that follows my return into American hands, when I was moved back to hospitals in Paris, and in Oxford, England, before being ZI-ed—sent to the Zone of Interior, the US—to a further year in hospitals in the United States. What is studiously neglected in this chronicle is the larger picture of the war being fought, the armies engaged—the historical overview. It only exists here in fleeting references because my fascination has been from the beginning with MY War for this work. I am always intrigued here to note whatever discrepancies I can unearth between the official accounts and my perceptions, between statistics and certified facts and my impressions of reality, but my concern has ever been with my own sense of what was happening to me and about me and within me. And, as I have severally engaged this adversary—the unknown past—I have again and again been brought to recognize that I have had to fight against myself to gain whatever partial victory. It has always been the recalcitrant mind, the false memory that has had to be brought to account; and the most fascinating of all revelations during this writing have been the strategies of evasion of the mind that has apparently had a vested interest in *not* telling, in not revealing, in continuing to conceal from itself part of its rich, fecund, and unconfronted past.

I learn from official accounts now what I never knew then, the actual fates of battalions and others, for I was, after my wounding, a solitary GI alone behind German lines until captured and never again in touch with his outfit. I learn that the German Commanding General, General Kittel, in charge of the defense of Metz, was found on the 21st of November in an "underground field hospital badly wounded (he had been fighting in the line) and under morphine." I therefore wonder whether November 21st was the date when the Fifth American Division stormed the building in whose cellar several of us lay wounded, for it might have been that same cellar hospital where I was held. I learn that Fort Jeanne d'Arc, the center of our attack, was the last of all the forts defending Metz to finally fall, on the 13th of December(!) long after the city itself fell, on November 22nd. These facts, however, are not my subject. My subject is one man's war: what he saw, how he saw it, how he endured it, how he survived it. And my fascination throughout is with the mind and sensibility undergoing that encounter, both then, and now.

I have learned how a fictive device may be a means towards truth, and as I have forced a blank space in memory to recover what was once printed upon it, to seem again to be what it must have been, I have retrieved from it, and discovered by means of it, the real facts that were hiding and mute within it. It has occasionally seemed that I was in a darkroom, where in the developing tray, aided by the addition of chemical additives that I brought to the process—need, desire, fascination with the unknown truth hidden there—images have gradually emerged from nowhere and begun to declare themselves. These I have seized and here fixed that they may not again escape.

Vast parts of this narrative and chronicle seem to yield themselves into my hands, to surrender themselves without struggle, while others are too well concealed within time and strategy to be revealed. As I tell in this tale, I have no valid memory of what I met with as I entered the actual city of Metz on my first arrival there, and I must speculate and label my speculation such. Similarly, I cannot retrieve the actual names or identities of the GIs who shared my cellar hospital room in the last days before that building was taken, for strangely, the cellar room experience is far less accessible to memory than the days on the fields and hills and in the woods of battle. This is, I believe, partly due to the relaxation and sleep I was able to fall into once I knew I was truly a prisoner and not still struggling to survive. I think I must have given way utterly and "let go" once I felt at last that I was reasonably safe and cared for, no longer recording and guarding myself with the heightened perception that characterized my several days after my wounding.

The cellar account, therefore, has had to be written with a fidelity to the *sense* of what I there felt and underwent, and unlike the scenes preceding, to a degree fleshed out fictionally where it lacks specific detail. The memories there of the

German doctors, nurses and orderlies and what happened to them are precise; what I have lost is a clear sense of my inter-action with other GIs in the room. So I have there fabricated names and identities (as I have occasionally done elsewhere in this document) as I have in an expressionistic way found a form to reveal my *sense* of what there took place. In this way, as I reenact in idols and masks the story, I may bring to life authentic spirits and voices of the past. Most of the rest is re-captured objectively to the best of my ability, or my disability is confessed.

Many details still elude capture. I cannot tell how many of us were trapped on the upper field, how many "made a run for it," and how many made it. I cannot really know how many strikes and salvos were fired from our artillery and TD (Tank Destroyer) batteries and precisely when, just as I cannot now recapture the hours of rain and the hours of sun, though the weather I record is as much as it was as I can recover. I am vague about just where it was that we were against the wire and had to go on over, but I describe what, to the best of my memory's ability, I experienced and saw. The improbable en-counter with the Waffen SS soldier in the road was, in all my early memories of him, two Waffen SS soldiers walking to-gether. I have here made them into one because now that is how I see it. The almost identical repeated remarks of the two sergeants after both had similarly carried me across an open space under fire, are there because they actually, however im-probably, were so spoken, and amazed me at the time by their repetition. But enough of this explanation and justification. It is all to say, simply, that my concern is to retrieve as much of the actual as I can while not falsifying the record of sensations and perceptions.

When I speak of the process of my writing, this explora-tion for retrieval and resurrection of that lost or unexamined part of my life, I speak of my need now to find the actual, to recover again the precise factual details of what was then an almost fatal journey. Once, many years ago, I found myself seeking recourse to my history, not as an historian but rather as a mythographer, sensing rather than knowing that in its depths lay healing and medicinal waters. I had never told my "tale," but one day, confronted by the suicidal despair of Diana, a very dear friend, I spoke into a tape recorder to send to her the story that I have to tell. That story exists as I then told it spontaneously into a tape recorder while I myself lay ill in bed in California. I knew then that its value was profoundly psychological and that, if anything, it might, it just conceivably might, help. I had never told it, and subsequently, I did not, until now, try to find it fully. I am still convinced that its greatest importance lies in the access it provided and can provide to places that lie too deep for tears.

My temperament and disposition undoubtedly determined who I am, so that at this writing, after having taken degrees at Princeton University and Columbia University, and studied at Kansas, Lausanne, The University of London, and at Berkeley (UC), I am a Professor Emeritus of English Literature from San Francisco State University—where I was named "Outstanding Professor in the Humanities"—having retired after 42 years of university teaching—at The University of California in Berkeley, at Kansas University, at The George Washington University, at Hunter College, and at San Francisco State. I have published books—*Hemingway's Paris* (Charles Scribners)—and had my poetry selected for publication as *A Voyager's Notebook: The Selected Poems of Robin Gajdusek* (Tintagel Press).

The Battle for Metz

Historical Background

Taken from: Anthony Kemp,
The Unknown Battle: Metz, 1944

Metz is an ancient city, deriving its name from that of the Roman city of Mediomatrica. It was fortified by the Romans as the center of an important network of military roads. Prior to the XX Corps attack in 1944, it had only once before been taken by storm—by the Huns in AD 451.

It had, however, been surrounded, besieged and attacked and assaulted in a series of wars and campaigns. The armies of the Emperor Charles V besieged it and bombarded it for two and a half months to no avail. Metz was an important river crossing point and the basis of the defense of the area, and from the Middle Ages on a series of military architects worked successively and diligently to modernize and deepen and perfect the fortifications that surrounded the city. The great late seventeenth century French engineer Vauban radically modified its defenses, and Cormontaigne, between 1728 and 1752, extended these, one of his forts, Fort Bellecroix, figuring in the fighting in 1944. Vauban wrote to King Louis XIV, "Each of your Majesty's fortresses defends a province. Metz defends the State."

The developments of artillery determined the alterations and changes in the forts. The military strategy was to ring the city with a connected ring of forts. By the time of the 1870 siege during the Franco Prussian war these were located 2 to 3 miles from the city on the hills about it, where they now stand—but even by 1860 the range of siege guns was up to 9 miles. Although detached from one another, each individual fort could put up a

powerful resistance while being supported by fire from its neigh-
boring forts. In 1867, Séré de Rivières, just before the Franco-
Prussian war, started work on four new forts, and after the
German victory in the war, when Metz was ceded to Germany as
part of the province of Alsace and Lorraine, the four were com-
pleted and five new ones were additionally built to complete the
ring of fortresses surrounding the city.

Preface to Another Battle

Land is sacred. War is an attestation to this, its holy high imperatives within the sensibilities of men, so that it is pur-
chased and maintained with blood. It is almost as though the
bond between Nature and man is expressed in the fatality of
this alliance, as though the fertility the earth implies were
guarded with the energies and life resources of those who
in turn depend upon its life giving resources for their lives.
Armies by their presence and even the unique individual soldier, by his placement on it, affirm an ownership that must be
stated. The territorial imperatives of birds, of insects and animals lay down a fine and intricate set of signals and signs that
define possession. It is not alone the claim and the presence
that lay out the identity of a landscape, but its history reso-
nates, and what is done with it and upon it becomes part of
its meaning. Emerson carefully enumerated the resonances
that accrued as the deeds of men in a place and upon a specific
spot of ground incrementally bring ghosts to inhabit, legends
to establish themselves and resound, and history to imbed
significant wonder. The times and occasions of men are impressed more or less deeply in different places. Cities on rivers
and in harbors and at the juncture of geographically predictable trade routes deeply gather multitudes and their dramatic
and urgent intensities. There is a sense of spell that resides
about a place where the wonderful has transpired, where the
god's foot has touched earth, where Zeus met Io, where the
significant happened. Sinai, Ararat, the Acropolis, or Mont-
martre define loci where the passionate engagements, human
and superhuman, were consummated. One man placing himself or placed significantly for monumental encounter begins
to establish an aura in a landscape, a set of perhaps enduring

presences which initially existing as identifying markers, subsequently exist as memory, finally gathering the memories or thoughts of others to this increasingly radiant center. Thermopylae or Waterloo, Kitty Hawk or Gettysburg or Mt. Segur or Camelot—places saturated in the events that determined their future, places of imperative and significant living and dying—do more than effect the imagination: they seem to take unto themselves the holiness or horror of what there occurred, the passionate intensities of the lives of men and women who were there. Hemingway wrote in *The Spanish Earth* of those who, going forward into battle, declare by their presence upon the land they walk over their possession of it, and say this is mine, investing it with their energy and commitment.

Not long ago and after I had written this chronicle of "my" war, I came by fortuitous accident upon a book stalled and alone and probably, until my eye fell upon it, attracting little attention: *Gravelotte–St. Privat 1870: End of the Second Empire,* No. 21 in the Osprey Military Campaign Series, and written by Philipp Elliot-Wright. I say "fortuitous" to bring Fortune into the picture and to so suggestively assert that such accidents are meant to happen. I recognized at once that Gravelotte was the nearest village of any size, though little more than a crossroads town, that I had passed through as I came into the line outside Metz before Fort Jeanne d'Arc. I had passed through it in a jeep that brought me as an Infantry replacement to join my new outfit, the 379th infantry Regiment of the 95th Infantry Division—part of the Third Army—to take my place in the woods bordering the fields leading up to the forts where the German army waited. It was in the edge of a small field in those woods that I was first startled to come upon a large monument, looming like an obelisk before me, a monument—I learned as I read its nearly effaced message—to those soldiers of the Franco Prussian war who had there died, precisely where we now, in another century, were assembling for our own patrols and attack—before, equally, dying or surviving. The irony seemed to me major. Later, in other years, as I had explored the fields where I had fought and been wounded, I came upon other markers, to graves or battles relating to the Franco Prussian War fought there. These startled me and stirred me and bewildered me—for there were no monuments nor markers to locate my own battle or even "our" war—but they essentially did not break my fixation on my own battle and my attempts to retrieve my own history. I thought of them as testaments to that earlier war that had been fought in that vicinity, a contest of footsoldier and cavalry, one remote from me in time and significance.

Only as I read the volume I had so circumstantially found was I finally further shocked into attention, for in the many maps that were scattered through its pages I saw what I could hardly believe, that perhaps the greatest battle of this great and major engagement, one of the great battles of its kind in the history of the world, had been fought NOT in the vicinity of my own field of battle but precisely and exactly UPON IT! I was therefore dealing—in the geography of my war experience that I was attempting to retrieve—not with my own experience but palimpsestually trying to make out the features of a landscape that could only be understood in its overlays of life and death that it kept in record and legend and fact among the ghosts of others that there inhabited. There had been there a vast, incredible bloodletting—that field had been literally drenched, soaked in blood, the air above it filled with the cries and sounds of struggle and pain, and we who innocently and illiterately came there, in a new age, from a different culture, seeking our own defilade and cover, were in fact reenacting rather than acting out a German/French debacle we scarcely understood. We were merely, like the foreign elements of the German army that came together on that field, only allies and almost mercenaries in their century old feud. We had no sense, no inkling that our blood was soon to flow into an earth already so liberally made fertile in their deaths.

As I come upon the metaphor of death fertilizing life, I remember vividly my first return to that, my field of battle, on which I had been wounded. As I walked again across it, the grain blowing soft against my body as I now unopposed moved forward across the land we had fought so hard to be able to stand upon, I was walking across the abundant wheat fields attached to the farms whose names dictated our movements on that day in November 1944: Moscou Farm, St. Hubert Farm, Leipzig Farm—fields that, bare in our late autumn, had offered little cover and increased our exposure and danger. When I finally had found the place of my wounding, the shell hole indentation where I had lain for three days, and, later, as I was returning across that same field, I was brought up suddenly before a man in a German uniform—the very same uniform I had fought against—blocking my way in a lane through the wheat, like an apparition from my revived past. "Grüss Gott!" Startled, both of us, we sized each other up, met and talked, to satisfy his curiosity as to why I was there, upon *his* land. His land—Dear God!—HIS land. I learned that I had indeed fought against him, for he had been there and, stationed there before our armies moved to question his possession of where he then was, had met a girl, a daughter of one of the farms, whom he had returned after the war to marry. It was now, indeed, *his* farm, and he was working that soil that my blood—a few yards from where we stood—had fertilized. This exchange of favors was a soft acknowledgment of the hard truths: I can remember how gently we talked, finally, as he understood my mission; and in the conversation, I remember coming upon a great peace, a sense of extraordinary ease of heart, so that while talking I could note the drift and rise and fall of swallows about us above the wheat, could note their song and the clouds in the otherwise clear blue sky above us.

Truly to understand all this, however, I need to go back a little way further into the past—not all the way back to the Romans who struggled there against the Gauls, but only to a day or two in August of 1870, days on which that field was prepared for our meeting.

The Franco-Prussian War: An Account of the Battle of Gravelotte–St. Privat

The Osprey Military Campaign Series No. 21:
Gravelotte-St-Privat 1870: End of the Second Empire,
by Philipp Elliot-Wright

In the early days of the Franco-Prussian War, General Bazaine's French Army of The Rhine, retreating from Saarbrücken, fell back to Metz and began its retreat through Metz back to Verdun. At sunrise on August 16th 1870 Emperor Napoleon III bid good-bye to Bazaine at the Gravelotte crossroads just outside of Metz, as he departed for Verdun and thence on to Châlons. Bazaine, in-

stead of hurrying his troops' departure after the Emperor, decided to halt to await events. This was possibly the fatal decision of the campaign because with every passing second the avenue of retreat was being closed by General von Moltke's troops. Therefore, later in the day, when General von Alvensleben made contact with the French at Vionville, believing them to be the French rearguard, covering their retreat, he suddenly realized that he was facing the entire French Army, which was spread across the hills to the West of Metz in an almost static arc. In the resulting battle and the series of engagements that continued to spin off between the meeting armies on those plains outside Metz, the vast superiority of the French bolt action Chassepot rifle determined many victories as equally did the vast superiority of the German breach-loading artillery. At that time each army corps consisted of two divisions of infantry and one brigade of cavalry. On a war footing this meant 12,777 officers, 543,058 men, 155,896 horse and 1,212 guns in each corps.

Alvensleben, partly to convince the French that they faced the entire German army, not just a corps, launched General Stupnagel's 5th Division forward, only to see it suffer heavily, and then he committed his remaining division to attack Vionville. He had quickly established 15 German batteries on the heights south-west of Flavigny which dominated the whole French position. More and more guns were massed in an arc from Mars-la-Tour to the Bois de St-Arnould until by evening 210 guns were engaged. Under such fire, the French General Frossard, considering his own situation desperate, launched the Cuirassiers and lancers of the Guard against the unbroken lines of German infantry formed up before Flavigny. Within minutes both splendid regiments were reduced to bloodstained heaps. By noon Alvensleben was desperate: with only one infantry reserve, he called upon General Bredow of the 5th Division to win time. At 2 p.m. six squadrons of the 7th Cuirassiers and the 16th Uhlans swung out north from behind Vionville and, using a depression for concealment, were able to charge into the center of Canrobert's gun line. The charge poured over and through guns and infantry until halted by Forton's Division which chased the survivors back to the German lines. "Von Bredow's Death Ride" cost 380 of the original 800 or so. As other German divisions arrived to assist Alvensleben, the 20th shored up the line at Tronville, while the 19th, emerging blind from Mars-la-Tour in company column, *marched into the heart of Ladmirault's line. Now, in extended order, the leading brigade, Wedell's, drove on only to be brought to a bloody halt by the ubiquitous Chassepot; the two regiments, the 16th and the 57th, lost 2,000 out of 4,600 men within a few minutes. Then the infantry of Greniers' division countercharged and swept the shattered Germans back. At that moment it appeared as if the whole German left would collapse. Meanwhile, the commander of X Corps, General Voigts-Retz, launched the 1st and 2nd Regiments of Dragoon Guards in yet another desperate, time-winning charge. While they were inevitably shot down, they successfully disordered and halted any further French infantry advance. On the open grass to the north of Mars-la-Tour, the German cavalry under Rheinbabben sought to move around Ladmirault's right flank. Three French cavalry divisions countered this and a massive mêlée developed between more than forty-nine squadrons of dragoons, Uhlans, hussars and chasseurs. In this battle on the 16th, the fighting had been desperate for the Germans with two corps holding the entire French Army at a cost of under 15,800 against some 17,000 for the French. Yet they had successfully held the Verdun road thereby cutting the line of French retreat. This was but the first of two major battles within three days that had to be fought on those fields*

Reconnaissance on the 17th of August did little to correctly assess the enemy's plans and positions. Von Moltke was seeing sure signs of the French army falling back on Metz, and was rendered unaware that Bazaine's army had settled on a strong defensive position between St. Privat to the north and the Rozérieulles plateau overlooking the Moselle to the south. The Battle of Gravelotte–St. Privat was fought on the morning of 18 August 1870 and began as almost 200,000 German troops marched across the front of 120,000 French troops, not knowing that what they took to be rear guard elements of the French Army now retreating towards Verdun was actually the whole emplaced French Army of the Rhine.

A third of the way down the Mance Ravine the Gravelotte–St. Hubert road crosses the ravine on a raised causeway; to the east of the Mance Ravine is the Rozérieulles plateau whose slopes swing round to the south-east just above the river Moselle; at the southern end, the Bois des Ognon and Bois de Vaux cover the west and east banks of the Mance respectively, the Bois de Vaux also covering the south-eastern slopes of the Rozérieulles plateau.

On the morning of the battle, sitting above the Mance Ravine were three walled farms: Moscou, Leipzig and St. Hubert. The solid walls of these provided natural fortresses with which to anchor the French line. Finally, the farmstead on the heights of the Point du Jour overlooked the south-eastern slopes down to the Mance. [This described landscape was approximately the center of the great action of the 1870 battle as well as for the 1944 attack of the 95th Infantry Division upon the forts on the plateau and the heights.]

On the morning of August 18, from 7 to 8 a.m., a solid phalanx of more than 200,000 men was advancing on the French positions. Just before noon, the commander of the German IX Corps, deployed east of Verneville without infantry support, opened fire with a battery of 54 guns. He was immediately answered by the full weight of Ladmirault's Corps artillery from less than 1000 yards. With his artillery within Chassepot and mitrailleuse range, his gunners were devastated, and he had to fall back. A desperate charge by the fusilier battalion of the 85th regiment saved some guns though it lost 12 officers and 400 men within a few minutes. At noon the German First Army sat astride the Mance Ravine in the woods covering each side. The French General Frossart's position was a veritable fortress: the crest dominated the plain below with the Mance Ravine acting as a moat, and further slopes up to the crest were bare and a natural killing ground. The crest was criss-crossed by a series of trenches, rifle-pits, gun-emplacements and loopholed walls.

General Steinmetz on his own initiative decided to initiate a full-scale attack by the first Army. By 1 p.m. he had deployed the 150 guns available to him. Weltzien's 15th division drove forward to clear the Bois de Genivaux and were met with a wall of Chassepot fire. Simultaneously the guns around Moscou and St-Hubert poured fire onto them and the leading battalions were brought to a halt. At just before 2:30 p.m. Steinmetz ordered his VIII Corps forward across the ravine. The objective of the VIII Corps' assault was the farm of St-Hubert which would provide a foothold on the Rozérieulles plateau. The whole of the 15th Division and the 31st Brigade of the 16th Division moved forward frontally to assault the farm. Steinmetz was able to bring his 150 guns from around Gravelotte to the western edge of the ravine by 3 p.m. Within a minute the farm of St-Hubert was a blazing ruin and the garrison was slaughtered. By 3:30 the survivors of the 80th defending had to retire to the main trench line just above the farm, and the German units dashed forward to seize the farm. Steinmetz was elated and reported that he had seized the heights. The reality was that the farm of St-Hubert was a death-trap overlooked by a complex of trenches and the massed guns of the two French corps. From Moscou Farm on its left and the Point du Jour on its right, all avenues of advance were covered. All attempts by the men of the VIII Corps to move beyond its walls were met by a wall of bullets and shells.

Just before 4 p.m. the 25th and 28th Brigades moved on the Point du Jour. As the skirmishers emerged at the wood line, they were immediately hit by a wall of Chassepot, mitrailleuse and artillery fire. The bulk of the two brigades were meanwhile advancing in dense company column, but before they could close the tree line their ranks were swept into confusion by the broken remnants of the skirmishers. Within a few minutes utter disorder reigned at the base of the ravine as both brigades joined the previous survivors. Steinmetz now capped his folly by launching an entire division of cavalry forward to throw themselves on what he blindly took to be a retreating enemy. Characteristic impetuosity and reckless disregard for losses blinded him to reason. Just after 4 p.m. I Corps' First Cavalry Division was ordered forward. It was to move up through the steep and narrow defile to reach the Rozéreuilles plateau. The cavalry were to be followed by the entire VII Corps artillery. All this was to be executed in clear view of the French on the Point du Jour; folly hardly seems to sum up this action.

It is doubtful if the German infantry crouching in the ravine could believe their eyes as in column of fours the cavalry trotted down the road and then attempted to thread its way round the wagons, limbers and bodies covering the causeway while the French guns found their range. Only one cavalry regiment, the 4th Uhlans, managed to thread its way through the debris on the causeway and dash up to deploy on the plateau to the right of the road. Within minutes half their number were shot down and the survivors streamed back to seek what cover they could in the gravel-pits. Meanwhile, of four artillery batteries that managed to reach the edge of the plateau by 4:30 p.m., two were shot down before they could unlimber, a few survivors joining the jumble at the bottom of the ravine. Steinmetz asked the king for permission to launch his only two surviving reserve formations.

He insisted that his tenuous hold on the plateau St. Hubert was in fact a major lodgement and that the French were on the verge of collapse. The king accepted this fiction. Just after 6 p.m., this pointless action began as two brigades plus three other uncommitted battalions crossed the floor of the ravine. Amid the debris and confusion there, a few other units gathered together in some sort of order and joined the advance up the wooded eastern slope. As they emerged at the wood line, they were met by point blank fire and within minutes were reduced to a bloody shambles. As the men poured back into the ravine, the survivors of the earlier assaults assumed that the French were in close pursuit and joined the flight. Just after 6:30 thousands of men and horses emerged on the western side of the Mance Ravine in total confusion and panic. With French shells landing in their midst, the mass of men and matériel could not be halted much short of Rezonville, even the presence of the king and General Staff being ignored as the multitude fled through Malmaison.

While the remaining wreckage of the VII and VIII Corps milled around the floor of the Mance ravine, Fransecky's II Corps arrived at Gravelotte at about 7:00 p.m. Knowing nothing of the afternoon's slaughter, Fransecky obeyed orders from Steinmetz to continue forward. Neither Moltke nor the king intervened even now as yet another German formation prepared for disaster. Fransecky's leading unit, the 3rd Division, began the ascent of the eastern slope only to be met by the now familiar hail of French fire which tore the columns to pieces, inflicting more than 1,300 casualties in a few minutes. At this point the surviving German troops at St. Hubert mistook the leading units of the 3rd Division for French and both they and 3rd Division exchanged fire in the dark and confusion. This tragic and pointless slaughter lasted until just before 8 p.m. when the survivors at St. Hubert finally broke and fled back down the slope. The French on the plateau had no orders to move forward and the bulk of the German forces before them were mostly shattered fragments, either lying dead on the eastern slope or heading west in chaotic panic. The next day dawned to reveal that the French had abandoned the plateau during the night.

This part of the great battle being fought on August 18—in attacks by the German Army on the French Army, through the Mance Ravine and onto the Rozérieulles plateau—was in large part a first model of our attack, the attack on November 14, 1944, by the American 95th Infantry Division of the American Third Army, against the entrenched German Army encamped on that same plateau. There is great irony in the reversal: we, in our century, assuming the positions and attack of the Germans, on almost precisely the same ground, but attacking not French but Germans. And, exactly as the Germans, we seemed to be largely defeated in our immediate attack, and like them again, were ultimately successful in our objective. In 1870, the Germans were here defeated, their whole Army's general attack, however, ending in a French rout by virtue of the absolutely unpredicted success of German units that broke through at St Privat to the west, in equally bloody and costly fighting that turned the French flank. The Germans there lost 20,160 dead and wounded on the slopes of the French position, while the French lost 12,275.

World War II: Fall 1944

━━━━►●◄━━━━

Hitler and Patton on Metz

General George Patton:
"We're using Metz to blood the new divisions."

General George Patton to General Walker:
"If it takes every man in the XX Corps, I can not allow an attack by this army to fail."

General George Patton to General Walker:
"The workmanlike manner in which your Corps accomplished the capture of the heretofore impregnable City of Metz is an outstanding military achievement."

Hitler:
"Metz must be held . . . to the last man."

General George Patton:
Code words transmitted to begin the November 8th attack:
"Play Ball!"

Military terminology for attacks by an outfit that has not earlier seen combat:
"Baptismal attacks."

Historical Background to the Modern Battle

Taken from: Anthony Kemp,
The Unknown Battle: Metz, 1944

In 1899, five more forts were built, two of which were Driant and Jeanne d'Arc. Five more were built in 1906. When war broke out in 1914, the Moselle position was immediately garrisoned by 85,000 men armed with 600 guns, 100 of which were under turrets. Metz was at that time considered the strongest fortress in Europe. It is estimated it would take an army of 250,000 men to reduce the works.

With the introduction of high explosive filling for shells by 1885, changes had to be made. In 1889 and 1898, numerous gun batteries were rebuilt at intervals between the forts. The concept of the fort altered, so it was now conceived as a turret to a vast army complex located below ground which garrisoned great numbers of troops, the whole backed by a network of strategic railways. Forts began to resemble battleships on land. There is a term in military literature, "the battlefield prepared in peacetime," which perfectly describes Metz: every foot of land to be defended intricately studied for defense, every vulnerable area strengthened, and maximum firepower provided to every spot of ground, each space locked into a grid plan in anticipation of possible attack. The forts to the West of Metz and the Moselle were organized into the Moselle Stellung, and in the Schlieffen Plan of 1899, this position was to form the pivot about which the whole German army would wheel in its attempt to take the French in the rear.

These forts were all joined up to one another or connected by defensible lines to form a vast fortified complex. This was the Feste concept, in which each fort could support its neighboring forts and terrain with artillery and supporting fire and yet be a strongpoint for the troops operating in the intervals between the forts. Each fort was part of the whole complex of supporting forts and yet each was independent and could hold out for months if besieged. When attacked in 1944, there were the original fortifications, which consisted of an inner ring of 15 forts, and also an outer perimeter of 28 steel and concrete bastions that had been built in 1912. In 1941, the forts were reinforced with 210-mm guns and 105-mm guns placed in revolving steel turrets which could withstand fire from high velocity direct-fire weapons.

Each fort included infantry trenches, shell proof bunkers and guardrooms, outlying strong points and observation posts. 120-mm guns were mounted individually in rotating turrets with all-round fire capability. 150-mm howitzers were installed *for dispersing attackers. Each gun battery mounted between 2 and 4 guns and had its own independent barracks and forward observation posts, with telephone and speaking tube communications and elaborate tunnel connections which could be easily demolished. If any unit was penetrated, it could be instantly sealed off. Each Feste was surrounded by multi-strand barbed wire entanglements, with ditches and palisades. Each German unit of infantry and artillery had its own wire surround to make it an independent unit on the surface. Each fort had one or more main barracks, which were multi-story blocks equipped with sleeping quarters, bakeries, kitchens, hospitals, and central power stations for generating electricity and providing heating. Forced feed ventilation was installed that could be operated by hand in case of power failure. Each fort covered a great deal of ground. Driant occupied 355 acres. They were well camouflaged, virtually impossible to spot from the air, and each one presented a different problem to an attacker.*

The 379th Infantry attacked and "contained" seven of these forts until, after turning them over to the Fifth Division, they subsequntly fell. I give the dates on which each eventually was taken.

Fort Bois de la Dame, November 26
Fort Marival, November 26
Fort St. Hubert, November 26
Fort St. Quentin, December 6
Fort Plappeville, December 7
Fort Driant, December 8
Fort Jean d'Arc, December 9

US Army Report of the First Assault on Fort Driant

Taken from: *United States Army in World War II: The European Theater of Operations*, The Lorraine Campaign, by H. M. Cole, Historical Division, Department of the Army, 1950.

The code name "Operation Thunderbolt" designated the Third Army assault on Fort Driant. Each phase [of the attack] consisted of: preparatory attacks by heavy bombers; advance by the infantry to the line of departure under cover of a bombardment by medium bombers and artillery fire; then the final infantry as-

*sault, supported by direct-fire weapons and artillery. . . . [The
attack plans] contained one extremely important proviso: "The
assault will be based on the attack of the medium bombers and
will not take place until weather permits their use."*

*By 26 September . . . General Walker, more and more impa-
tient with the delay at Fort Driant, ordered the attack to begin the
following day—with or without support from the air . . . [yet]
virtually nothing was yet known of the detailed construction of
Fort Driant, or the field fortifications around it. American patrols
had made numerous attempts to work their way into the fort
area only to be stopped each time. [There was an intense] search
for detailed plans of the fortification. The trail led from Verdun to
Nancy to Lyons, where engraving plates, hidden by a French officer in 1940, were uncovered. Unfortunately, the detailed ground
plans did not reach the 11th Infantry until 29 September, and
the troops making the first assault received only a vague briefing
on the basis of inexact sketch maps of Fort Driant and its surrounding terrain.*

*[Fort Driant's] main defenses consisted of four casemates,
with reinforced concrete walls some seven feet thick and a central
fort in the shape of a pentagon, the whole connected by underground tunnels running into the central work. Each casemate
mounted a three-gun battery, of either 100 or 150-mm. caliber,
while the southern side . . . was covered by a detached battery . . .
of three 100-mm. turret guns. The interior of the works seemed
almost a flat, bare surface, for the casemate roofs were built flush
with the surface of the ground, leaving only the gun turrets, four
concrete bunkers (each providing shelter for 200–500 men), and
some armored observation posts and pillboxes above the surface. . . . its main batteries were sited so as to provide fire through
360°, with a frontage of 1,000 yards and a depth of 700. The
central fort was surrounded by a dry moat, 60 feet wide and
as much as 30 feet deep, with wings extended to either flank.
Barbed wire to a depth of 60 feet encircled the entire fort. . . . It
is not known how large the Fort Driant garrison was at the time
of the first American assault.*

*The 3rd Battalion of the 359th . . . commenced a fight to
seize the road between Gravelotte and St. Hubert's Farm as a
jumping-off point for the projected large-scale attack. Repeated
attacks by the 359th made no headway, even after the entire regiment was committed. On the evening of the 27th September it
was clear that the 359th had shot its bolt. . . . Although General*

Patton and General Walker disliked giving up any ground it was apparent that the 5th Division by itself could not hold the existing line east of the river and mount an assault on Fort Driant at the same time.

The ground commanders and the troops around Metz were . . . as one in their conviction that air support was essential if Metz was to be taken . . . [since] the infantry-artillery team could not breach the fortress ring alone. [The Ninth Air Force, which was to support in the Metz area, however described its attempts to bomb in the Brest port area: "The reports of the bombing of modern reinforced concrete emplacements were negative. These structures proved practically impervious to air attack, and there appears to be no authenticated report of one being destroyed." They would be equally frustrated at Metz: "the fighter-bomber efforts had little effect."]

After the attack on the fort began, P-47's dropped 1,000-pound bombs and napalms as a starter, coming in as low as fifty feet to make their strikes on the fort, but with negligible results. Other squadrons of P-47's failed to damage Fort Driant. The artillery, which fired two concentrations prior to H hour, seems to have had no better luck. . . . Fire from the 1550-mm. howitzers [of Field Artillery units and tank destroyers] when directed against the pillboxes dotting the forward slopes, failed to penetrate or destroy these outworks. The tank destroyers . . . engaged the outer German pillboxes and then machine-gun embrasures in the main works, but, despite what appeared to be accurate laying, could not put the enemy crews out of action. The mass of wire entanglements, fire from numerous and previously undiscovered pillboxes surrounding the fort, and the inefficacy of tank destroyer fire against reinforced concrete works forbade a continuation of the action.

Plans went ahead, after this defeat, for another assault on the Fort, to begin on 3 October. On 20 October an 8-inch howitzer got 8 direct hits on one of the turrets at Fort Driant only to have its fire returned fifteen minutes later by guns in the same turret. . . . What the 500- and 1,000-pound aerial bombs failed to accomplish by direct hits could hardly be expected of a 286-pound shell. . . . Air support had been promised by the IX Bombardment Division for the morning of 3 October but because of bad weather the bombers did not arrive, and finally at 1200, unwilling to wait any longer, General Irwin gave the order for the attack to begin.

Snakes [to blow a way through the wire] broke up almost immediately . . . [and the] tankdozers were halted by mechanical failures. . . . Company B had four flame throwers but only one functioned. . . . Company E was stopped at the wire by intense German artillery fire and entrenched enemy infantry. . . . [When they fought their way to the bunkers,] the heavy walls were as impervious to TNT as to shells and bombs. The first attack failed: the platoons were badly shot up and forced to withdraw when the Germans came up from the tunnels and filtered into their rear. All through the night small groups of the enemy continued forays into the American positions. Four American tanks were knocked out by bazooka men, and by dawn the Americans in the fort were badly disorganized. [Company E dug in on the glacis and held there under constant fire for four days; when the company withdrew, it numbered 85 officers and men.]

German snipers systematically picked off the men carrying flame throwers and explosives. The few who reached the large steel doors at the rear of the fort found them covered by protruding grillwork that made it impossible to put the charges against the doors themselves.

When the second night came, attempts were made to reorganize the troops who, during the day, had scattered wherever they could find shelter from the enemy fire—in abandoned pillboxes, ditches, shell holes, and open bunkers. During the night, however, the Germans again came out of the underground tunnels and threw the attackers into confusion.

*As daylight came on 5 October, the guns of the surrounding German forts opened a heavy fire on troops in and around Driant. American artillery observers crawled forward and tried to locate the enemy guns, but a thick haze lay in the Moselle valley and counter battery work brought few results. . . . Two German howitzers finally were depressed so as to give bursts in the trees fringing the fort. Their effect was deadly. By mid afternoon B and G companies were reduced to a combined strength of less than one hundred men; K Company also was growing weaker.**

---

* *In the late afternoon of 5 October the S-3 of the 2nd Battalion, Capt. Ferris Church, sent back a message with a graphic report from an infantry captain on conditions at the fort:*

"The situation is critical a couple more barrages and another counterattack and we are sunk. We have no men, our equipment is shot and we just can't go. The trs [trainees] in G [company] are done, they are just there whats left of them.

Somewhere about this time General Patton told General Walker to take Driant, saying that "if it took every man in the XX Corps, [he] could not allow an attack by this army to fail." During the night of 5–6 October the 1st Battalion, 10th Infantry (minus A Company), went in . . . to relieve B and G Companies . . . many of the original assault force having to be carried down from the fort on stretchers.

General Warnock gave orders for a resumption of the attack on 7 October. . . . At 1000 on 7 October the 1st Battalion, 10th Infantry, opened the attack. One rifle company slowly worked its way east and in four hours succeeded in inching forward about two hundred yards, taking three pillboxes in the process. This advance brought the lead infantry into a deadly cross fire coming from the southern casemate and Battery Moselle. Orders were given for the company to reorganize and hold onto its gains, but the ground was too hard for digging and the captured pillboxes were open to the side now exposed to the Germans. About 16:15 the Germans came to the surface and counterattacked. The company commander and two forward platoons were cut off and lost. The survivors fell back to the original positions.

One platoon had been sent into the tunnel, entering at a concrete bunker which was already in American hands. The passageway was very narrow . . . and was barred close to the entrance by an iron door. Engineers blew a hole in the door, but found the other side blocked with pieces of machinery and old cannons. This block could be moved only if the wrecked iron door was cut away, an operation that would require an acetylene

---

Enemy has infiltrated and pinned what is here down. We cannot advance nor can K Co., B Co is in same shape I'm in. We cannot delay any longer on replacement. We may be able to hold till dark but if anything happens this afternoon I can make no predictions. The enemy arty [artillery] is butchering these trs until we have nothing left to hold with. We cannot get out to get our wounded and there is a hell of a lot of dead and missing. There is only one answer the way things stand. First either to withdraw and saturate it with hvy bombers or reinforce with a hell of a strong force. This strong force might hold here but eventually they'll get it by arty too. They have all of these places zeroed in by arty. The forts have 5–6 feet walls inside and 15 foot roofs of reinforced concrete. All our charges have been useless against this stuff. The few leaders are trying to keep what is left intact and that's all they can do. The trs are just not sufficiently trained and what is more they have no training in even basic Inf. Everything is committed and we cannot follow attack plan. This is just a suggestion but if we want this damned fort lets get the stuff required to take it and then go. Right now you haven't got it. Gerrie, Capt., Inf."

torch. *On such seemingly small items the fight now turned. During the night an acetylene torch was brought up to the fort and the tunnel door was cut down. By the middle of the morning of 8 October the rubble and debris had been cleared away. . . . A 600 pound beehive charge was [rushed in and] exploded. This detonation released carbide fumes and for the next two hours no one could re-enter the tunnel. Ordinary gas masks were tried but failed to protect the wearer. An engineer officer finally groped his way through the tunnel and found that the first charge had made only a small hole. When the fumes began to clear, more explosive was brought in, but the Germans opened fire with a machine gun and rifle grenades and there was nothing left to do except hastily erect a parapet of sandbags, mount a machine gun, and engage in an . . . exchange of shots. The Germans set off a counterblast in the tunnel, killing some men of Company C and driving the rest into the barracks. . . . With many of the troops* hors de combat *and a general state of confusion prevailing, the attack against the two southern casemates scheduled for the night of 8–9 October was canceled.*

By 9 October the situation at Fort Driant was confused beyond belief. . . . Daylight attack had proved too costly in the face of the cross fire sweeping the surface, and night attacks had quickly become disorganized when the Germans erupted from the tunnels onto flank and rear. The American troops were jittery and in some companies their officers believed it questionable whether they would stick much longer. Losses thus far had been relatively high: 21 officers and 485 men killed, wounded, and missing.

General Gay ordered the fort to be evacuated and the operation abandoned, although he gave the corps commander permission to make one more attempt to blast a way through the tunnel. This attempt was not made; on the night of 12–13 October the last American troops left the fort without a shot being fired by the enemy.

This battle was the first publicized reverse suffered by the Third Army.

The Larger Picture: Metz, November 14, 1944

Account of the Battle in Which I Was Wounded

Taken from Anthony Kemp:
The Unknown Battle: Metz, 1944, "The Closing Jaws"

Anthony Kemp, the military historian on the Battle for Metz, November 1944:

"The battle for Metz represents the last time in which extensive use was made of permanent fortifications to fulfill their traditional purpose of delaying a superior force."

"The Battle of Metz . . . would seem to be the only instance in comparatively modern times of two battles having been fought over the same ground and with the same tactical problems— in 1870 and 1944."

"Suffering from appalling weather conditions, the infantryman reverted to his primeval role as a one-man fighting unit, robbed of much of his 20th Century technical support."

"In fighting reminiscent of the First World War, the Americans hurled themselves repeatedly against determined enemy well protected by concrete and armour plate. Gains were measured in yards."

"One can really say the final doom of Metz was determined on 14 November, when the 95th Division, the bulk of which had been guarding the western fortifications, was committed to an active role. . . ."

The original mission assigned to General Twaddle's division [the 95th] was to attack frontally into the city once the pinchers had been closed by the 5th and 90th Divisions. . . .Therefore, on 14 November, Twaddle requested permission to start his attack before the pinchers were entirely shut, and instead of the simple attack from the west, to assault astride the river.

The 379th Infantry occupied a line running southeast from Gravelotte to Noveant on the Moselle, facing the main forts at Driant and Jeanne d'Arc, plus the so-called Seven Dwarfs and a maze of fieldworks. This sector was garrisoned by the 1217th VG Regiment. . . .The Division . . . confronted . . . the same problems that had defeated the XX Corps in early September, a lengthy front held by comparatively few troops faced by an enemy in well-fortified positions. . . .The mission assigned to the 379th Infantry was to penetrate on both sides of the Jeanne d'Arc group. The attack was to commence on 14 November. . . . Support consisted of two field artillery units and a company of tank destroyers. . . . As the shells from the latter repeatedly fell short, their use was soon discontinued.

The mission of the 1st Battalion was to force a way over the infamous Mance ravine and to clear the Seven Dwarfs. . . . The 2nd Battalion was to move along the road leading between the Jeanne d'Arc group and Fort de Guise. . . . [The] 3rd Battalion was in reserve, thinly spread along the whole of the regimental front as a holding force.

After a heavy (and predictably useless) bombardment of the forts at dawn, the two assault battalions moved off at around 0600. Although shelled by Fort Driant and the Moselle Battery, the 2nd Battalion managed to make its way around to the north of Jeanne d'Arc and by midday were on their objective, 500 yards to the rear of the fort. There they were counterattacked, probably by troops from the fort. . . . These attacks were beaten off, but the American force (two assault companies) was out on a limb. The attackers had been able to penetrate the line held by the 1217th VG Regiment but could not detach sufficient forces to mop up the enemy holed up in the maze of bunkers and trenches. Thus, the German line closed up again after they had moved through and they found themselves cut off. Their reserve company was unable to get through to them and was forced back by heavy fire. The 1st Battalion . . . enjoyed initial success. . . . They captured Forts Jussy North and South but were driven off from Fort Bois de la Dame. At this stage they too were cut off and their reserve company also failed to cross the ravine. . . . It proved impossible [for both surrounded battalions] to evacuate the wounded, who had to be cared for on the spot.

During the night, plans were made to relieve the isolated troops, but in spite of several attempts during 15 November, the bulk of the 1st and 2nd Battalions remained cut off, unable to move forward or backward. The following afternoon, there was nothing else to do but to commit the 3rd Battalion and leave the divisional line more or less denuded of its holding force. They launched their attack along the route taken by the 2nd Battalion—the road between Fort de Guise and Jeanne d'Arc. . . . While forts Driant and Jeanne d'Arc could still fire, movement by road was extremely hazardous. It was intended at this juncture the 1st Battalion would fight their way northward to join up with the rest of the force, but this had to be postponed for a day. It was not until the morning of 18 November that the regiment managed to link up its scattered formations.

US Army Account of Regimental Action of the 379th Infantry: The Attack of November 14, 1944

Taken From: *United States Army in World War II, The European Theater of Operations, The Lorraine Campaign,* by H. M. Cole, Historical Division, Department of the Army, 1950. pp. 433–435.

Earlier attempts by the 2d Infantry Regiment and 90th Division to break through the fortifications west of Metz by frontal assault having proved far too costly, General Twaddle and the 95th Division staff evolved a scheme of maneuver by which the 379th Infantry (Col. C. P. Chapman) would execute a penetration north of Fort Jeanne d'Arc. At the same time it would attempt to overrun the minor works in the Seven Dwarfs chain linking the main German fortifications at Fort Jeanne d'Arc and Fort Driant. The final objective for this attack was designated as the eastern slopes of the heights bordering the Moselle in the sector between the town of Jussy and the edge of the Bois de Vaux. Once the 95th Division had command of this ground, only the river would separate it from the city of Metz.

Before dawn on 14 November the 359th Field Artillery Battalion opened up on the German works with its 105-mm. howitzers and all battalions of corps artillery within range joined in.

After thirty minutes of this artillery preparation the 2d Battalion, on the regimental left wing, moved into the assault along the road between the de Guise works and Fort Jeanne d'Arc. Fifteen minutes later the 1st Battalion jumped off in an attack to cross the deep draw east of Gravelotte, the scene of so much bloody fighting in September, which lay directly in the path of the advance to the Seven Dwarfs. The 3d Battalion, holding the right flank of the regiment, extended its line to the north but took no part in the initial attack.

Both assault battalions came under shellfire from Fort Driant and the Moselle Battery during the early stages of the advance, but the German infantry in front offered only slight resistance. By 1100, Companies E and F of the 2d Battalion had worked their way around Fort Jeanne d'Arc and were on the wooded high ground about five hundred yards northwest of Rozérieulles, well to the rear of the fort. Here they were immediately counter attacked. The enemy, beaten off, stubbornly returned to the assault twice in the course of the afternoon, only to be driven back with considerable loss.

On the right, Companies A and B of the 1st Battalion found the going slow and difficult. First, the German outpost line on the west bank of the draw had to be cut through. Then the attackers climbed down into the draw and up the opposite side, all the while under a merciless flanking fire from the guns at Fort Driant. The Seven Dwarfs had not been completely garrisoned, however, and shortly after 1400 the three northern works, Fort St. Hubert and the two Jussy forts, were taken. Company A swung south and about 1600 launched an assault at Fort Bois la Dame. Some of its men reached the top of the enemy works, but were driven off by fire from Fort Driant and a counterattack before they could pry the garrison loose.

By late evening, however, the situation of the 379th Infantry was critical. The two companies of the 1st Battalion were cut off by a large party of the 462nd Fuesilier Battalion that had filtered back into the draw east of Gravelotte. The force from the 2d Battalion was somewhat disorganized as the result of the loss of the battalion commander, Lt. Col. J. L. Golson, who was seriously wounded. Both battalions had incurred a high number of casualties during the day. The only supply road leading to these forward units was interdicted by Fort Jeanne d'Arc, and although artillery liaison planes had dropped ammunition and supplies just before dark, such air service provided a very thin link with the rest of the regiment.

During 14 November the Germans had been able to concentrate their reserves in the west bank sector to meet the single-handed attack of the 379th Infantry. But on 15 November the 95th Division committed elements of he 378th on the west bank in a co-ordinated advance against the north and northwestern sectors of the Metz bridgehead, easing slightly the pressure on the two isolated battalions of the 379th. At 0900, companies C and L, led by Lt. Col. Tobias R. Philbin, began to fight their way across the draw in an effort to pass through the two companies of the 1st Battalion. Once more the enemy took advantage of this natural defensive position to make an obstinate stand, but just after midday Company C reached the 1st Battalion. An attempt to push on to the final regimental objective was held in check. Company G, the 2d Battalion reserve, was less successful when it attempted to resupply and reinforce the troops southeast of Fort Jeanne d'Arc. While moving along the road north of the fort the column was brought to a halt by small arms fire from concrete field works commanding the road. No approach to these works could be made in daylight without high losses. After dark, demolition details tried their hand but the charges failed to blast open the concrete. However, this experience seems to have shaken the German lieutenant in command, for he allowed the Americans to talk him into surrendering.

The supply situation still was uncertain on this and the following day. The weather grew progressively worse as snow alternated with rain. The only road to the forward companies, that between Fort de Guise and Fort Jeanne d'Arc, was impassable for wheeled traffic—even if it had not been still under interdictory fire. Air supply was increasingly difficult and each time a pilot took off in one of the flimsy liaison planes he risked his life. Furthermore, the entire area was a rabbit warren of tunnels connecting the forts and outworks; the Germans could constantly reappear to block the paths and trails leading to the forward companies of the 379th. It was increasingly apparent that the 379th could not push on to its final objective until a main supply road was cleared. Therefore, on 16 November the 3d Battalion was committed in the zone of the 2d Battalion, where it captured the large bunkers at St. Hubert Farm and Moscou Farm, then blew the tunnels leading back to the main forts. South of Fort

Jeanne d'Arc the 462nd Fusilier Battalion *continued to fight to hem in the 1st Battalion of the 379th. General Walker sent word to the 95th Division commander, as well as to his other commanders, to step up the attacks towards Metz. But the 379th had been badly mauled, still lacked sufficient supplies, and could not yet reassemble for a final coordinated assault.*

Divisional Account of Action Seen by the 1st and 2nd Battalions of the 379th Infantry between November 14 and 18, 1944

"Ninety-Fifth Division History 1918–1946" by George M. Fuermann & F. Edward Cranz; maps & drawings by Jerome R. Gibbons & David M. Landis. Publisher: Albert Love Enterprises, 1080 Capitol Ave. S.W., Atlanta, GA. No publication date, but it was shortly before 1950.

When the 95th Division was relieved by the 5th Division in the Pagny bridgehead and moved north to a position before Metz in the first days of November, the 379th Infantry had originally placed only one battalion in the line. This was its 2nd Battalion which relieved a battalion of the 359th Infantry Regiment of the 90th Division in the Gravelotte sector. Facing the regiment in this new position were the great southwestern fortifications including Forts Jeanne d'Arc, de Guise and Driant as well as innumerable smaller defensive works such as bunkers, concrete dugouts and fortified buildings.

[For the attack ordered for 14 November] the 3rd Battalion was stretched north to cover the entire regimental front, and the 1st and 2nd battalions were regrouped in assembly areas in preparation for the attack. The 2nd Battalion was to attack on the left (north) to capture an initial objective southeast of Fort Jeanne d'Arc. The 1st Battalion on the right was given as initial objectives a group of forts south of Fort Jeanne d'Arc (from north to south these were Forts St. Hubert, Jussy Nord, Jussy Sud, and Bois de la Dame); on order, it would continue the attack to its final objective, the high ground northwest of Vaux. In other words, the 379th Regiment planned to by-pass the tremendous Fort Jeanne d'Arc from both north and south; its two attacking battalions [the 1st and 2nd] would work their way through the line of western forts and would eventually gain control of the high ground east of these forts.

The 2nd Battalion jumped off at 0545 November 14 with Companies E and F attacking, Company G in reserve. By 0850 the attacking companies had reached their first objective and had captured a number of pillboxes, and by 1100 they were on the final objective. During the afternoon, three German counter-attacks were directed against [E and F] Companies but all were successfully repulsed. Meanwhile, however, the German lines which had been breached in the assault closed behind the attacking E and F companies. When Company G, in battalion reserve, attempted to move forward to join the cut-off companies, it was turned back by tremendous concentrations of artillery and mortar and by deadly small arms fire coming from the complex system of bunkers surrounding the great forts.

The 1st Battalion 379th Infantry jumped off in the attack at 0600. . . . The attack ran into heavy small arms, mortar and artillery fire. . . . As in the case of the 2nd Battalion, the attacking companies of the 1st Battalion were isolated at the end of the day.

By late evening of November 14, the position of the 1st and 2nd Battalions was critical. . . . The two assaulting companies of the 1st Battalion were separated from the remainder of the regiment by a wooded draw approximately 300 feet deep and 800 yards wide. The two assaulting companies of the 2nd Battalion were similarly cut-off from the remainder of the regiment. . . . . As early as the afternoon of November 14, the first day of the attack, ammunition, radio batteries and much needed medical supplies were dropped to the 2nd Battalion. On November 15 the liaison planes began to supply the 1st Battalion as well. Meanwhile, the night of November 14–15, plans were being made to effect relief of the isolated 1st and 2nd Battalions. . . . Company L was . . . directed to join Company C in an attack across the draw southeast of Gravelotte. . . . The attack jumped off at 0900. The Germans had brought up reinforcements from Fort Driant during the night and resistance in the draw was extremely heavy. . . . Company C . . . suffered heavy casualties and was unable to continue the attack. . . . Company L was withdrawn.

During the day of November 15, Company G made repeated efforts to open a route to the remainder of the 2nd Battalion. It was unsuccessful, primarily because of concentrated fire coming from a fortified area midway between Forts de Guise and Jeanne d'Arc. The morning of November 16 found the 1st and 2nd Bat-

*talions in the same position. Meanwhile, plans were being made
to have the 3rd Battalion launch an attack through the zone of
the 2nd Battalion. . . . The attack jumped off at 1400 . . . but ran
into heavy resistance. . . . At 0645 November 17, it resumed the
attack . . . and drove towards the 2nd Battalion and by 1245 they
had joined with it on its final objective. . . . The 1st Battalion, isolated for three days, was ordered to attack and join the 2nd and
3rd Battalions. . . . It jumped off before dawn November 18 and
by 0930 had made contact with the 3rd Battalion.*

*By November 18, consequently, the 379th Infantry had suc-
cessfully united its forces behind the German line of fortifications.*

An account by John Loomis, of F Company, who had been
surrounded with the remains of the 2nd Battalion, says that
"when the 3rd Battalion finally broke through to us on the
18th . . . we had some 60 men left."

My Battle

My Battle,
My Wounding, and
Life and Death in a
Shell Hole

The story that I here wish to tell is not so much a story as a chronicle of events, things that happened to me as I experienced them during the last great war. Though wars have multiplied since the Second World War, none—not the Korean and not the War in Vietnam—can conceivably be called The Great War. Even as I write "the last great war" I hear the reprimand of history, that anyone alive after 1918 and until 1939 would have heard, a reference rather to the First World War, which was, if any war deserved that title, the Last Great War. The irony of this is accurately heard here by me, for one of my purposes in this writing is to acknowledge that what seems our own and irreplaceable irreduplicable experience is and has been but the recapitulated experience of men, and that no matter how "great" a seeming event, it lapses back in time against other enormities that it may be informed of its place in human history. It was therefore but another dismaying fact that the battle in which I was wounded was fought on fields long famous for the battles already there fought in earlier wars, and that even as we filed down for attack from our hillside foxholes, it was to pass a standing monument to the heroic dead of the Franco-Prussian War who had there given their "last full measure of devotion."

I ask you to let this time of your reading be time of your life absented from your life, a life apart as it were—as all good reading is: you are "the music while the music lasts"—it becomes the metaphor for all possible living that can be done within the mind, whether you be enchanted by Catullus or seduced by Ovid, working on your income tax or making your will. I suppose these retold incidents have much to do with the origins of the mind, and how the mind has a matter at all to deal with; they have to do with the sources of that "stuff" on which the imagination builds skywards and away from its delving root in the darkness. And yet these are but tales, tales of "events" within a war, a war that was "my" war even as it seemed everyone else's. That, I suppose, is the important thing about wars, and certainly that is what makes the soldier a solider citizen than most, finally, for his values stem from what he knows, and he knows that by virtue of his own experience, yet it is an experience that he ever and always largely can only refer to the "larger picture," the greater historical ethos which includes him. He is therefore welded to, bonded to, history and time and his country in ways that many cannot imagine: the battle on the page of the history book was his battle, the major social or political abstraction was his minute particular passion. Citizens who are not soldiers make do as they can with what they may be given, as history is pressed occasionally if seemingly rarely close to them so that they can see themselves "in" it. That is what Kennedy's assassination meant to most—not what happened to Kennedy but where they were in their lives in relation to his death which was not theirs to suffer. Well, then, citizens, says the old warrior, with that undisguisable note of condescension in his drama-saturated voice, do the soldier the bit of grace of understanding that his service in combat may be an almost unbroken series of such assassinations. Ask yourself how you might serve under the impact of such electrically stimulated ganglia.

No, I will not go back to the beginning of "my" battle— that story is a book—but rather into the midst of it, without any attempt to explain in detail its truly inexplicable dimensions and coordinates, for from it I wish to extract finally only a few incidents, and especially, only one moment. But a moment is most often prepared for by a million coordinated and related events, which are the filaments and fibers that lead to it, the pebbles or crumbs dropped in the forest that connect us to it. For me, and therefore for you, most of the crumbs are always already eaten by the birds or beasts and the best one can do is recover the place, find it out by whatever logics or illogics or circumstances one may, to get and be again there, in whatever quandary.

And there I was: Infantry soldier in Patton's Third Army, part of an American division stalled in the forests confronting the forts defending Metz, one of those wounded in the battle, coordinated assaults to penetrate both sides of the Jeanne d'Arc group of forts, so incomprehensible a tactic that several, the rumor ran, shot themselves on the night preceding battle, and officers, so some told us, refused to lead their troops into such obvious and unavoidable defeat and carnage. The mythos is not the fact, but it is what line infantrymen hear and enlarge. The evidence on which an uninformed soldier builds his hyperbolical "total picture" is slight, misinformed and partial, and before we know better and guessing on the evidence of our senses, the attack was a failure, squads wiped out "to a man" (as soldiers say, knowing well how all battles are personal and all come down at last to that single one), platoons were shattered and battalions lost, a whole exposed hillside filled with irretrievable wounded, others unprovided and surrounded, a result exactly and precisely what the infantryman who gave away his letters and possessions on the morning of the battle as light began to break, perfectly knew and had anticipated, predicted and awaited. (How many sacrificed patrols do you have to send out before you believe the information of losses?) "The country cocks do crow, the clocks do toll, and the third hour of drowsy morning name." How do you explain to anyone afterwards, ever, how one can lie on the ground listening to the vague bells of country steeples name the hours towards the pastoral morning that is breaking, on which you will arise, hook up, walk forward and out into and before probed for, established, and determined overwhelming annihilating guns: ring after ring of entrenched, dug in, fortified and pin-pointed machine gun nests whose lanes of fire and killing zones had been intricately laid down over months of preparation for your hoped for but inconceivable stupidity? And yet, there I was.

Another wounded soldier on another battlefield in another age, a parody of the stories of Remarque, Tolstoi, Hemingway, de Joinville and de Hardouin, and resting on the brink of cliche. Even as we "came into position" for the battle, filed in the deep night down from our foxholes on the hills and our intricately imaginatively built dugouts on the mountains behind, to enter the muddy bottom land and the frozen-rutted and foot-and-shell scarred watery bogs of unseen meadows—bumping, falling, rolling in icy water, coming up—and then going down the ravine and through the draw to the tree edge at the lower slope of the lower fields, we passed the monument (there at the dark woods) to the dead who had fallen on that same battlefield outside Gravelotte in the Franco Prussian War in 1870. Lancers, cavalry, artillery, and the same investment with higher purpose—in a war that meant absolutely nothing to a single man among us, that was not even an historical blur on our consciousness.

There we lay like so many dark sacks amidst darkness at the trees' edge on the lower border of the lower field, occasionally looking up and out and towards the immense seemingly inexhaustible open space of the entire hillside seemingly without cover or defillade up which we were supposed to advance, against the entire assembled guns of the entrenched, dug in, fortified, prepared and waiting German army. Our attack directives? Jesus Christ, was any one of us wrong who lay there waiting for morning and wondering whyever they didn't simply by-pass the fucking forts, and Metz if need be, at that stage in the Battle of Europe, with the isolation/encirclement of what German army remained there a foregone conclusion? Who, in what insanity of reasoning still believed in infantry fire against Maginot and Siegfried-line entrenched fortified hillsides? "Ours not to reason why"—and I am philosophical enough by virtue of wounds to refuse to be ironical as I offer you the quote, knowing that ironies often are, like sarcasms, the vanities of weak and unserious minds: they are cheap strategies to gain a sense of intellectual superiority easily, without working. Then why the quote? To suggest that, in ways that history certainly pointed out, ours was not to reason why, but to endure. And if that seems like culpable even criminal acquiescence before immense error and almost certifiable insanity, it also seems to me like the way most of us who came through that debacle gained what unsentimental insight we have into the motivations and ways and operations of history in society and ourselves in their midst. And the cost at Metz? Several thousand bodies. And where has history avoided this cost for such knowledge?

But what is a "battle"? It is like many other moments in war but one where hugely each single man is privately aware he holds his mortality firmly present in his hands, knowing that it is something he cannot alone retain or keep, though his care and cherishing of it may help. And so he may move invested, as men in civilian life are rarely invested, with an overwhelming sense of the presence of such larger forces as Divine Agency, Gods and Angels who may or may not ride on his shoulders, "Luck" as a real phantom, destiny and Fortune and Providence as true companioning presences, and the overseeing goodwill or love of others, such as his Girl, his Wife, his children, his parents—those who especially embrace him in their spirit. His own daemon and self pride and sense of personal immortality are enormously charged with imminence. And, as the forces of the moment force him back upon himself, alone and unaided finally, no matter how backed up and surrounded by his buddies and support groups of armies or flotillas, he feels at once his dependence upon those around him and also his own unaided Self in its isolation and loneliness as he seldom feels them. And then such things as the care of his rifle, the placement of grenades and bandoleers, the packing of his pack, the arrangement of his equipment take on ritual and heightened significance. He is forced back upon the survival knowledge he has, and old soldiers recognize their increasing pride in whatever they have that enables them to survive. Everything comes down to the moment on the field when he performs or does not perform, survives or does not survive, when pride is won, sustained, endorsed, or lost. And that final realization that he is finally going forward into the guns is what makes all the difference. It is no longer preparation or trial run, there are no more blank cartridges, and each bullet "may have his name" upon it. A terrible new beauty is born, for the slightest thing is now monumentally elevated in significance: life in its moments

and incidental details is now fatally lived, so that each movement becomes gesture, each decision complicity in destiny. In
such a prepared "space," language becomes heightened with
metaphor and symbol, so that the slightest word may mean as
it does not ordinarily mean: McAuliffe, when surrounded at
Bastogne and asked to surrender, said "Nuts!" In such situations, profanity becomes almost prayer, and, more importantly, slight gestures become love or life statements. "I'll get
it!" says "John," starting out to find and splice the break in the
line, so that someone else need not go—and no one needs to
tell the rest of us that "going" means crawling several hundred yards across open field exposed to German fire and with
limited chances of making it. "I'll get it" are as good last words
as anyone is ever apt to say. Trying to explain the reordering
of priorities and the forced relocation of values under "battle"
conditions, I wrote a small "essay":

Beauty

When they went into attack they used to wear their
blankets as capes, slit in the middle, plunged over their
heads and blowing out, trailing about them in the wind.
He loved that. That was as close as one came in this war
to an heroic stance, to a banner, to a suggestion of flair
or gesture. Of course, it was not for the sake of image, or
even of warmth that they wore them so, but rather in
the superstition or belief that they so created an indefinite
and distributed target. Often, after an assault or firefight on
patrol, they would count the holes in their blankets and
marvel—how was it possible to remain so invulnerable!
And I suppose that was partly it, a way to press closer to the
myth of immortality, of one's own state of blessedness and
magical survival. Each throw of the dice that left you in possession of the field and unscathed built the incredible and
sacred odds within which you breathed, and walked. The
air was keener, sweeter in your nostrils in that time—each
choice, each insignificant choice, no longer insignificant.

He remembered once, advancing across a field under a
cordon of fire where the sporadic tracers floated like fiery
bees in a soft net in the air about them; and as they advanced in a staggered line up a broad slope of golden field
at a slow walk, firing assault fire, the wind took their capes

and wove them around them from their shoulders in dark
and sinuous veronicas, as though each of them was passing
by his own dark and deadly beast. Afterwards, he would
think that in all his life he had never seen anything quite
so beautiful.

That pleased me enormously when I first wrote it. I think
I rejoiced because it was the first time I had tried to set down
something I feel has been enormously overlooked in battle
accounts, in the memoirs of old soldiers: the exalting and exhilarating and surprising sense of a great and unpredictable
and immeasurable beauty that, strangely, in the stress of
battle and because of the hard placement of life against possible death, is born there on a field of battle. It is perhaps the
signal revelation of an accomplished rite of passage, the sign
of a self affirmation in which man and his fellow men and the
earth and air about him have been eternally bonded. It need
not take place in battle—indeed, for most it does not—but it
can be there that a man first discovers the coordinates of his
manhood, and knows he has unconsciously performed with
care and honor what was there to be performed, for the sake
of life in and against death. That I seemed to find that moment, as I had found it, during the battle itself, was a truth,
but, dismayingly I now see that to tell of it in "Beauty," I had
enmeshed that early account in a fictional apparatus to sus-
tain it: I made myself a participant in an action I had but had
recounted to me from members of a patrol as they had come,
shot up, off that patrol, and as two of them, sitting in the
dugout afterwards had counted the holes in their blankets. I
had not only imposed myself into their experience but I had
made that incident seem to be a mode, a way of being clothed
when fighting—yet what they told me was but hearsay to
which I had added imagery from my own battle, of the slow
walk at something like assault fire with the buzzing golden
bees of tracers about us, and I had joined the exhilaration
of that moment of peace, in which fear seemed to have vanished from my own experience, and bonded it to their de-
scriptions. When, indeed, I saw the fictional truth but the
factual fiction of what I had written, these years afterwards, I
knew that I had to press back the fiction to get further at the
truth—and that is why this book came into being—partly to

reprove the necessary fancies of necessary fictions, and to get closer to the authentic truth.

What do soldiers think about as they lie in dark patches spotted upon the lower slope of a field almost in the wood's shadow? They await a breaking of dawn's early light when they will arise and go now, advance up that long swelling exposed and seemingly unending open field towards where the guns and pillboxes and mines of an alert and expecting enemy await them. Do they indeed think upon their wives, their debts owed, their children left behind, their loved ones? It is hard now to say how clear the thoughts were in minds then enraged with a sense of the idiocy of the order, that all of us were aware of—it was not as though we hadn't probed that hill at the cost of fatally shot-up patrols, that we had little sense of its immense power, fortified actually for centuries as it had been by generations of French military engineers whose only thoughts had been how better to make those specific forts impregnable. We all were perfectly aware of the total insanity of an assault on the forts, and we did not even have the consolation of thinking of ourselves as a valid sacrifice in a diversionary attack, for we well knew, with a precision of reflection that generals may refuse to allow to their troops, that the city of Metz and forts encircling it, at this stage of the "Battle of Europe," could well be by-passed, without losses or interruption in the timetable for the defeat of Germany. (Of course, we were right, for the end result was a partially deci- mated regiment, three shot-up battalions, and platoons and squads that on that field seemed to simply vanish, cease to exist. And, as far as we were subsequently able to note, our one achievement was to have captured the commendation of Patton.) And so we had to ask ourselves whether we were being "tested," whether Patton's vanity demanded the im- agery of gung-ho assault, whether orders of which we knew nothing would countermand or withdraw the attack after it had begun and after it had served to draw German attention to this sector. And we had to ask such irritating questions among the more imperative personal reflections, which had to do with our incidental and seemingly totally expendable lives as those lives were interlocked with others and with in- tricate histories. At our best, I suppose we were mostly aware of one another, of others elsewhere who cared and would care, and of our buddies and our mutual dependencies and love; we were concerned with where each one in the squad was, and how. At our worst perhaps, we were only aware of ourselves.

I, personally, had lost the greatest reliance of all in being a fairly recent Infantry replacement. When casualties on the Western Front had suddenly zoomed, training units Statesside were dissolved or stripped of men to fill lacunae at the front. As a result, I had lost the intimacy and depth of feeling that I had found with those in the squad in the Division with which I had trained—among the greatest of intimacies one may ever know—and now, sent to join an outfit I had not trained with, that love and care and concern, which are the greatest of all stabilizing sustaining forces in an Infantryman, had been stripped from me. I would live if I lived or die among relative strangers, who probably could not spell let alone pronounce my name, for we had not yet had the time to create the bonds that matter, that are forged in training and shared battles. I was consequently necessarily more "alone" than others. Rumors were everywhere, rumors with substance, of who, during the night preceding this early morning, had shot themselves. There was the tale of "The Lizard," who was last seen running screaming towards the German lines; there was the tale of a Captain, somewhere, who had refused to lead his company into this battle. But there was, mostly, a strange and stretched silence in which we dreaded the gradually imposed definitions of first light, as what was hidden in darkness slowly emerged, as more and more clearly we could see ourselves at the field's edge as a mottled speckling of bodies lying about, like black shapes sprouting out of the earth with which we were as infantrymen identified, already like casualties, on this lower perimeter of field.

And lying there, seeing this slow time emerge substantially, altering all, preparing it for its feared changes, we listened acutely to the smallest sounds, those still small sounds which moved, with the slow wind, over us as we lay. As the far/near steeples of the village churches of perhaps Gravelotte and Aars-sur-Moselle almost inaudibly rang the hours and quarter hours, and then, when the first cock arose in the darkness to hideously declare the morning's coming, and then when silence afterwards seemed to reprimand his error, and then as other cocks also chose to wake and to awaken, still in the total darkness but insisting upon day that they were urging on, there must have been, for each of us I think, a sort of wonderfully cynical fantasy, of simply getting up, rising, strolling down (as if to piss in the wood's fringe), and strolling out and on and continuingly on and back towards those steeples and cocks and farmyards whose daily life seemed life eternal, life blessed with sanity and regularity and, certainly, eternity. And the thought was so "sane," so "right" in its way, that I imagine each mind could actually feel the soft and now, in the dream, blessed earth turning our feet under our shoes, accepting and sustaining and supporting and leading our feet down this draw, up this knoll and into this village and so towards another and another and back towards Paris and a world as remote as the astral constellation of Orion above us, as it was above the clouds of soft almost dew like rain, in the night. And there seemed no penalty to decline: I don't think one of us, in such a reverie, thought of being apprehended, arrested by battle police, court-martialed, shot as deserters—walking back towards those bells seemed not only feasible but perfectly possible, the utterly wise and sane and unchallenged thing to do. It was like going home. And all one needed to do was rise on an elbow, get up, and stroll back and out in the darkness, towards the clear and sweet and insanely inappropriate bells of ordinary life.

Then why didn't we? Probably for the same reasons I did not. It simply seemed something one "could not do," not because of penalties, or danger, or even shame—I didn't think of these—but because we were a unit, we depended upon one another, and one could not abandon to another what he could not do, one could not abandon the others. It was not even that one's gun was one gun more—for we didn't (I didn't!) believe the guns would make any difference—but rather that we each needed to support one another, in whatever. I think there are few searing and austere cauteries or therapies as deep as the almost conscious relinquishment of life, should one live. To know that life lies one way, to be almost certain death lies the other, and then to choose the other, for whatever insufficient or absurd or personal reasons, is, I know, therapeutic at the deepest of levels. I just do not want the decision called a "sense of duty," a sense of "serving

one's country." It was an immensely self serving decision, ultimately, although the way to choose for oneself seemed a
way of abnegation and denial.

The situation was this: our regiment, the 379th regiment
of the 95th Infantry Division, was to attack Fort Jeanne d'Arc,
one of the major forts in the Forts Jeanne d'Arc and Driant
complex. The 359th and 204th Field Artillery Battalions were
to support us along with the 607th Tank Destroyer Battalion.
The order for attack was this: it was to be a regimental attack
of three battalions on line; one of these, the third, extended
northwards to cover the front while the first and second were
to attack Fort Jeanne d'Arc from both the north and the
south, by-passing it to gain the high ground east of the forts.
The Second Battalion's—my battalion's—initial objective was
the high ground between Fort Jeanne d'Arc and Fort de Guise.
The First Battalion, to the right of the Second, was to attack
a group of forts—St. Hubert, Jussy Nord, Jussy Sud, and Bois
de la Dame—and to continue onto the high ground northwest of Vaux. In our Second Battalion, Companies E and F
(my company) were to attack, with G Company in reserve. It
was F Company that was chosen to spearhead our battalion's
attack, and our platoon in our company was to spearhead our
company, while our squad in our platoon was to "lead off."

The odds of getting an "assignment" like that are astro-
nomically small: it too much resembled Fate; it was like being
assigned to the Light Brigade at Balaclava at the last minute; it
was like having the sense of probable catastrophe (that so
many had) utterly annulled and moved to inevitable necessity. It was numbing. And—perhaps this is the sort of insight I
write to be able to provide, because it is a "truth" I take from a
place where not so many have been—it was enormously exhilarating. It removed most of the sweat and fear and terror
as it removed the uncertainties: it simply made things "important" in a new way and charged them highly enough with
urgency and drama to make them "significant." It wasn't that
it was thrilling but rather that the importance had been
shifted from the army onto our shoulders, more specifically,
more pointedly, more uniquely; and by "our" I mean the sensitivity of response and honesty of action of our squad, first of
all, for we would meet first fire and take it, absorb it. If this
lessened our chances of ultimate survival in the vast battle

that loomed, it also increased our own ability to deal with imponderables and unknowns: they would not be in uncertain hands but in our own. Do I do too much as I extend my own feelings and thoughts to the rest of my squad? I really don't know. I don't think so. Our tension, our increased sense of interdependency and relationship, was perceptible. It was as though someone had tightened a screw or moved a taut string a notch tighter, and increased the dimension of meaning. First position, as seasoned soldiers know, is not necessarily a fatal one, for we were given the factor of surprise, and even as they would undoubtedly surprise us with first fire, we would be drawing quickly undisciplined if carefully zeroed in, mapped and gridded fire. And by the time the "second wave" approached those first gunners who might still be firing, they would have their aim adjusted and their sense of the reality of what we were better understood. I actually was glad I wasn't going to be in the second wave. I didn't let myself think of where I might be when the second "wave" advanced.

There finally is the moment when you do get up, arise one by one, adjust straps, bandoliers, harness, check your grenades, rifle and pockets, and where you are in the general assembling. And so we "few," we very few, led off, followed by a widening wedge and gradually extending line of sporadically placed men, the squad becoming the platoon becoming the company becoming the battalion. Beyond that, as we well knew, nothing, but somewhere on a hill, a battalion in reserve, those spotted and occasional towns of lyrical bells, and Paris. Before us, several thousand yards of open fields, usually the wheat harvest of the farms we were to cross, and historically, the great cavalry battlefields of several remote and now absurd wars. But in that greyness just emerging from dark in which we moved, where morning was nothing yet but mist in which we were barely distinguishable to one another, we knew that we moved directly up the field and towards the emplaced pillboxes, dugouts, trenches and foxholes of the intricate web of prepared defenses of the forts on the far hill's crests. The question came down only to when, on what instant we would be detected, and whether they would fire at once and in fusillade or sporadically, a sentry's or an outpost's reaction, or wait to let us advance to meet a prepared wall of fire that would erupt on signal. There were really no other unknowns. They would detect us; we would be cut down as they were able to cut us down. Even as we tried for silence as we moved, like dark ghosts approaching a far shore, wading through Lethe, our hearing was unnaturally honed to an exquisiteness, listening for the first sound not our own. And then, halfway up the first field and just across the road we had been alerted to find crossing our way, it came.

There was a small pop, like the almost silent withdrawing of a cork from a very special wine, and we, most of us, hit the ground. Even before the flare burst in the black/grey sky above us, a wall of guns was erupting amidst the cries and outcries of those shot and the hissing-sizzling burning sound of the drifting flare. As I lay there, my face, body, hands, rifle pressed into the ground, and as the roar of guns and cries went on, the flare drifted in its slow descent closer and closer directly overhead until I felt it must land searingly, still sputtering-burning, on my back, drawing the sight and guns of all gunners to me as I lay, as I now saw, behind what I took to be a spiraled tangle of wire. And as it sputtered out, another flare was rising-bursting and the guns went on, and everyone was down and trapped, pinned down, by the incredible wall of gunfire, and nothing but an indefinite darkness out of which it came. There was nothing distinct to fire at, and no way to raise one's head or hand to fire: the cordon of fire was sustained precisely across our backs and allowed little movement. And the longer it went on the more terrible it became, for to the chorus of those hit and crying out "I'm hit! Medic!" or, as one did, "Mother, mother, mother, mother, mother," were added new voices, cries, wails, as the searching guns found another and another and another. Had they brought in mortars at that moment we would have been done for.

But thank God for discipline and training, for experience which gives knowledge to create space in which bravery can exist, for one officer or non-com or another—John, our squad leader first and most importantly—was crying out the commands and advice which made us seem able to withstand. To endure. To survive. To strike back. At first the idea of returning fire at an unseen enemy in a dissolving lifting darkness while seemingly unable to move, let alone raise one's head a fraction of a centimeter, was absurd. How, possibly, could one do so? But, then, it was the urgency of the need, the imperative need, as the cries increased, and the new casualties mounted—Stoddard beside me—and the sense that we were being cut to ribbons without response. And so we began firing—immediately not aiming, not even raising our rifles yet, just firing them forward from their groundlevel position into the whitening morning. Perhaps it was that the sound of our firing reduced the sound of their guns, or that our fire actually was enough to get them to pull in their heads and so reduced their fire—whatever the cause—the occasional lull in their guns gave us the belief that we could raise our helmets enough to peer beneath them and through the sights of our now raised rifles to find the source of their fire, an actual target, the real "enemy," there forward and beyond the wire. And there was no way out but through. John tapped Jo Poz, who suddenly rose and seemed to throw himself full-length and forward on the coils of wire, bearing them down by his weight. Had he been hit? Had he tripped and fallen? Had he chosen, had he deliberately chosen to throw himself on the wire to make our crossing possible? "Robin, go on across!" I couldn't believe that, not that! But there it was. I was to hurl myself forward, precisely towards the German guns and across the wire, and there was Jo Poz as my model, my bridge or holy ladder. An instant, a single searing instant to realize that this may be "it," and I was up, one foot fast forward, another plunged hard down beside my buddy on the wire, where his body bore it down, and I throwing myself face forward and flat out fast down and on the other side, alone beyond, alone there in a roar of renewed machinegun fire. But in an instant, Holmes was lying beside me, and John himself further on, and one, then another of us, pulling pins and with overhand swing throwing grenades far forward and towards where we thought the fire was coming from, giving space, explosive time for others to make it "across" or go forward. And so the break in impotence came. No longer pinned down but moving as we were able—Mike rose to run and grotesquely sprawled never to rise—we fired and grenaded our way forward, a rush at a time, feet at a time, until I could see the slight wisps of smoke, the occasional flashes stabbing from the center of a hillock of bush, and our main target defined. The nest seen clearly, John himself put in the grenades that ended its fire.

I had lost all track of time but it must have been noon before we had "cleared" the lower field—how easily the clichés and terminology fall to hand—and had "silenced," I believed, a dozen nests and a score of holes, so that, at last we were up, those of us who remained, and moving forward, seemingly in disregard of continuing fire. How intricately we were related to one another, like knots in a net joined by invisible threads to the whole, so that as one chose to move, others joined it, so the whole skein or tissue moved. I am not sure what comes over a soldier on a field of battle like that, perhaps the spurious conviction of his immortality, as he has this far miraculously survived, but it is as though on an instant he is no longer "in" fear but rather "in" wonder. Suddenly, on a moment, I looked about me on that field and saw a landscape of tattered soldiers, for me all squad and platoon and even company definitions lost—by now neither John nor Holmes nor Knuth nor any others I knew were to be seen. I passed at one point an officer kneeling and holding his throat, and a Medic beside him trying to hold bandages, cloths against it. And I walked forward, beside others—the spaces between us now large and uneven—at last even firing from the hip assault fire, watching with interest and some curiosity the slow lazy flight of orange tracers, like stunning golden bees, winging about the field in an elaborate cordon or net of lines. This amazing transformation inside oneself, perhaps in part because of a witnessed similar transformation inside others, is the incredible thing. It seems almost now worth "my" war to have discovered it: a space of rest and stillness in chaos and urgency, a place that I can only describe as the "heart of amazement" inside which there was an infinite place from which to observe and function and know. How long had I fought before I seemed to have come to this still place inside myself, so that all fear and sense of terror and urgency were gone, and the truly amazing thing was myself standing on that field filled with arcing burning rivets and burning bees, with my eyes very quiet and only a great sense of amazement and ease. But this well being was fatal.

A dozen or so of us had made the upper ridge above a long slow ascending slope of field, and it was over this that we saw the withdrawing German outpost gunners disappearing. I had deceived myself into believing that to "take" that ridge, to possess it, was to attain our "objective," and I remember in the last several hundred yards before rushing towards it, finally finding myself in advance of the others who had been around me and turning to wave them to their feet, crying out, "Come on! Come On! Let's get it over with! Let's get it over with!", knowing, even as I heard my voice, that surprised me, that my earlier "quiet" had been a cap over vast pain, for I heard the deep sob in my voice, the utter inner weeping beneath, that my seemingly solid cry concealed. I now know that my sense of wanting to get "it" over with—"it" being the seemingly little left to do to end the battle—was a full misperception, and that having "taken" the ridge, we should have regrouped and considered the best way forward, if forward was truly the wise direction. But a zealous and eager dozen or so of us—avid in our exhaustion and pain and sense of achievement and desire to end it—were suckered into believing the flight of the German gunners from the crest down the field to a further far distant crest was retreat and that their withdrawal meant our advancing, when in actuality it was the carefully prepared for falling back of the primary guns to let the "enemy" advance into the utterly open and entrapping plain landscape of doom, where the secondary and dug-in machine guns could have a field day indeed. So that when they at last opened up on us, it was after our vanity had lured us well and irretrievably into the field, from which really there was no exit, only, to our left and down a slight slope, as though the whole field were slightly tilted at 5 degrees, where there was the far edge of a wood and the appearance of safety. And that image, too, was a "prepared" image, meant to win our decision, for along the edge of that wood, between the field and it, were laid down the killing zones into which they undoubtedly hoped we would go. What rat in a trap like that has an alternative choice? And so we went.

How many of us made their run and were chopped down well on their way towards the wood but certainly as they neared it, I do not know. But then, for me, there was no longer any other choice, for the guns were searching the earth that gave no cover all around me; it was merely a matter of seconds before they "found" me. And I was up and running, running as I had never run, dodging, crouching, dipping and weaving, racing, so that just as I believed I would, I might make the wood, my legs were chopped out from under me, exactly as though a baseball bat swung by an immense and celestial batter had struck them sheer and away. I can remember going up and going up—my God, but I must have been running!—and I suppose it was that speed that saved me, for I made a gigantic leap at heaven, carried by the velocity of my run, up and up and on. So that when I finally landed, fell flat and long on my face, like coming down, pancaking on a runway out of the skies, I was yards beyond where I had been hit and within a few feet of the edge of the woods. As I landed, my helmet sailed off into nowhere, as did my rifle, and I must have lain there like one who, dropped from a tall building, resembles nothing so much as a bundle of rags. Even as I lay there, their machine guns searched down to me and neatly and exactly tore into my pack on my back, those copper and steel jacketed bullets as burningly near as the cloth of my shirt. Their guns' cyclic rate had always appalled me: while we stuttered and pattered along with our 30's at 350, they were throwing 550 at us with the sound of a ripping sail, a giant canvas sail tearing itself across in the wind; and even with the decreased accuracy, enough lead must have flown across my back to have sewn an intricate seam. To hear their guns was immensely impressive, immensely frightening: it seemed like sheer overwhelming power, and it conferred an enormous psychological advantage without a bullet finding a mark. But as I lay there at last "under the guns," I found on an instant lost and atavistic senses that had been numb since my birth: every minute centimeter of my body, my flesh, was alert, apprehensive, waiting for the impact of its bullet; each pore totally sensitive to and sensing the flight of those bullets towards me, into me. It was only gradually that the mind apprehended that the mounted guns, fixed for their killing zones, undoubtedly could depress no further in their mounts, and that it was to the almost invisible, indistinguishable contours of that land that I owed my momentarily saved life.

But this is to make a long story long, when the salient fact is that I was not hit again, that I lay there as though dead for what seemed time without time, while the guns ceased, chattered again, sought other targets of opportunity, conversing with each other amidst the moans and cries from my wounded but not yet dead buddies elsewhere on that field. And then infinitely slowly, with infinitesimal movements, I began to move myself, slithering forward towards the edge of the brush and woods that lay a few feet beyond me. My movements must have been remarked, for suddenly the guns were there again and what remained of my pack seemed to be blasted on and from my back. After they left, I have no sense of how long it took me to move finally into the wood's edge and to, with a great rush of relief, pitch myself face forward into a shell hole depression within a tangle of brush and fallen boughs a few yards beyond the edge of wood where the fallen leaves began. I was, to my then limited knowledge, the only one to have made it, however unsuccessfully, yet alive, off that field. And there at last I turned myself over onto my back and considered the damage.

My right leg was certainly shattered, broken, pierced by a bullet that had entered on the right side and, as I later learned, neatly drilled out almost the entire interior of the tibia and emerged from my leg on the other side. Had it not been an extremely high velocity armor piercing bullet, it might, after passing through the bone, have carried away most of my leg. I quickly pulled the elastic edge of my Long John's over the wound, that the blood might clot into the material and the elastic bind it as it could. There was little bleeding, just dark bruise-like discolorings and distensions near the holes. And there must have been burn marks on my back and on one arm from bullets, and I remembered a scrotal burn that a bullet had given me as I had earlier been advancing up the lower field. Feeling its impact and sear, I had gotten down there on that instant and noted that I was lucky indeed, the slight holes in my trousers there between my legs and the dark purple-brown burn-crease almost signs of divine intervention. But there I was, without helmet or rifle, out of commission but inside the "action."

Some may ask just why it has taken me until now, my 62nd year, to begin to tell this tale? I suppose because I have had to go first through a series of disillusioning awarenesses and beyond a cynicism fostered inevitably by the vast gulf between tales of truth and truth. However urgently a tale seeks to be true, it necessarily at last resorts to the imprecision of the imperfect vehicles of words, and whereas words in or-

dinary interchange are remote enough and abstract enough
to help our usual fastidious desires to be remote while talking,
and hidden while revealed, and deceiving while confessing,
they are too rude and imperfect a means for the most important communications. That's why the most important things
we have to say find their way into poetry, which usually must
"do" something to language, as it uses it carefully and spar-
ingly, to get it to be "true." I suppose one might define poetry
as supremely important communications hovering on the
limits of language's imperfect means. And therefore I have
been forced over many years to admit that what I had to say
about my war could not be confided to language, yet. Now, I
see, as I look back over a paragraph or two of what I have
written, that it has been written only because I at last am willing to accept the compromises my youth and earlier years
could not. I seem to be easily using terms like "action," "advanced," "pierced by," "cries from my wounded . . . buddies,"
"my movements," the "next wave," "I considered." They are
all false, false, false. They are totally untrue—NOT because
they intentionally distort truth but because they inevitably
distort truth. Nothing, nothing is sensed so simplistically,
monistically, in such isolation from other apprehensions, sensations, or recognitions. Nothing is done so or perceived so.
And my experience in my war has been too valuable to me to
be translated into lies, to become what it was not. I suppose,
always, our realest truths are never spoken or written, and
the love poem received is really an ominous sign that the love
can look at itself in its linguistic surrogate and find satisfaction there. Usually, we confide dying or dead values to words,
or use words to slay them, while waiting for the writer who
presses at the edge of his unwilling compromise to force feeling back towards its sources, which it will only know in an
escape from its medium. Living values are lived, and when
the values are thus true, they seem like my war experience,
untranslatable, too true for language. That's what the poet
is trying really to say as he stammers over and over about
the insufficiency of stars to compare to his mistress' eyes. It is
true: to write something is to be rid of it. I think that the one
thing of which I never wished to be rid was my war, my
battle, myself on that field, myself as I was and became, there.
Then why have we, over these many centuries settled for, as

we seemingly have, this imperfect means of transmission of what is most vital? Because, I suspect, the business of life must always remind us that it is business, and sensibility must be kept in its place, back where it belongs, inside the sensibility. And the bluntness of language itself as vehicle is one means of keeping us human and ungodlike, or of keeping us within importantly insensitive human dimensions. Sensitivity is not a primary desideratum but rather sensitivity in a functioning human being, and functioning implies a certain callous disregard of most things. The millwheel does not ask how many fish it crushes, nor the hot water heater, who died of silicosis young to hack coal from damp and dark corridors in slagheaped mines in Pennsylvania. "IF we move," says D. H. Lawrence, "the blood rises in our footsteps." How utterly right he is, but most people, or "mostpeople," as e. e. cummings would choose to say, couldn't care less or refuse the recognition: "What in the world are you talking about?" they say, wiping their bloody hands off on the bloody sheets. Our sentimentalities are outrageous. That's why I would much rather have a General look after our peace than any politician, who has small consciousness if any of his culpability and bloodletting.

So there, in that shell-hole at the edge of the shattered wood, on the hills beyond Metz, in mid November of 1944, I lay. By twilight of the first day, the 14th, the day of our battle and my wounding, I had seen (but mostly heard) from my vantage point at the edge of the field at the edge of the wood, our battalion's attack falter, stall, become again pinned down and finally be apparently defeated. That gradual dying out of our guns was like listening to a death, witnessing health become sickness become erratic breathing become a gasping and final stillness: the diminishment, the movement from sustained fire to occasional bursts amidst the sound of larger guns and grenades, and from erratic fire to firecracker cracklings (as the sound of their guns began to intrude and mount, like one music contesting another in a cacaphonic contest of noise), and then our guns dropping down to only occasional bursts and then to only a shot and then again a shot or two, against the mounting crescendo of their burp guns, machine pistols, and machine guns. Finally, in the extending ensuing silences, there was a terrible feeling of the withdrawal of the sense of the safety of our army and of those others on whom I had once relied. I listened to the moans and cries of other wounded gradually still but never subside, the occasional weeping or cry of "Medic! For God's sake, Medic!" uselessly called. I also heard what I thought were the sounds of ambulances on the lower fields, which created a momentary hope that was never to be fulfilled. When I tried to throw up a parapet of mud and dirt between myself and the field, my movements immediately drew heavy fire that smashed and tore into the edges of my shellhole, so that I knew that I was now a fact that "they" had to deal with. And as the day wore on towards twilight, I could hear German voices crying out to one another from upon the field and around me far in the wood. The skies greyed hard, and a small icy drizzle began that, gradually, towards nightfall, turned into a slight steady rain, so that under the small of my back a puddle of water began to accumulate and fill. I had only my field jacket, into which I had sewn some extra wool lining, but I felt I was freezing, lying there, my legs awkwardly, numbly rising before me, my hands only able to hug myself close, my eyes widely open and staring up into grey and darkening sky and the small rain that fell upon my face. As imperceptibly as I could, I reached out for the tips of branches and for twigs and brush on the borders of the depression in which I lay and drew them over and upon me, for concealment and the illusion of protection and warmth, but they were few and I could move only with great difficulty. And there I lay, hearing increasingly no more of our guns but increasingly more and more of theirs, erratically coming to life. From somewhere not too far up the field someone cried out "Medic!" and I answered him. For a brief while we, unknown to one another, unseen by one another, exchanged what useless information we could—he was too badly wounded to crawl to join me, even when darkness might make it possible, and I reassured him as I could that surely Medics or ambulances would at last come and find us. Finally, our shouts brought on me (and on him?) sustained and terrible fire, that seemed to eat away from me what defensive parapet I had, and I dug frantically and madly, as I was able, to build again that wall between myself and the guns: "Hey Mack! Where are you? Can you make the wood?" "Hell no. I'm hit." "Are you hit bad?" "I don't think so, but I can't move." "I can't help. I'm hit too. Do you have cover?" "Some." "Could you crawl over here after dark?" "I don't think so. I told you. I can't move." "What's your squad?" "I heard ambulances." "Where?" "The lower field." "You think so?" "They'll make it up in the morning."

Then, just before dark, as I was again working to strengthen and conceal my shellhole, a rustling in the woods revealed a GI about 30 yards from me crouching at the base of a shattered tree. I called to him, and he confessed himself lost from his outfit, unable to help me, terrified, unwilling to move:

"Hey, Joe. Can you help me?" "Where the hell are you?" "Here, in a hole near the field." "What's the story?" "I'm wounded, broken leg I think." "Well, I'm shit lost." "What's your outfit?" "Goddamn. I don't know where the hell my outfit is. Or anyone. I don't think there is anyone."

Even as he talked, I heard the far pop of artillery and the gradually increasing rush whoosh approaching-freightcar-in-the-air note of an incoming shell. The shell landed in the woods beyond us both, lifting an immense shower of rock and dirt, the cone and shrapnel whirring through the air in a long whirling arc. And even as the shrapnel hit with a thunk, there had been another pop, and another freightcar was falling through the air, this time to land on the field where I had come from, where the other wounded and dead lay. I had shrunk into myself, pulling myself over myself. Another pop, and now there was no mistake, this one was on me, on me, on me On Me ON ME!!! And it came screaming down like a whole train with blastoven doors wide open falling from high heaven. It struck just beyond me, lifting me in the air like a wild rag, waving and throwing me back down under a wall of earth that had come up and hit me and lifted over me and came down on me. I thrashed myself clear, and already there was another pop and another freight train was hurtling through the air, this time to land, like the first one, beyond me, where the "stranger" had been crouching by the tree. I called to him, called, but there was no answer and already the arriving shell was coming in, and I was winding back into myself, shaking, shaking. And another "pop," another shell on its way onto the near field's edge—that was the pattern, one long, one short, one on top of me—and on it went, and again and again mainly the third shells were coming precisely, directly, exactly upon me, like steel houses and entire freight trains simply free falling on top of me. And again and again, miraculously alive after the next hit, I dug myself clear, and flailed away the rocks and dirt and tree boughs to breathe clear, to breathe again. How long this went on I cannot say. I only know that I was finally shaking involuntarily, being shaken by each incoming shell, the way giant hands might hold a short carpet by two edges and fiercely shake it in the air. And finally, my nerves were buzzing and shaking and jumping and spasming under the impact and just the sense of arrival of the impact. At last, there were no more, and I was then aware that shrapnel had cut my knee, shin, and side, and my hands were cut and bleeding, and I had partially torn the nails from two fingers of my right hand.

I never heard from or saw again the GI who had been crouching by the tree. I tried to understand it, but I couldn't. The only scenario that made sense was that the guns were our guns, and their fire had been directed at that stretch of woods, the field edge, because they believed the German army was holed up in there where I was. Later, I believed, as I today believe, that an observer had seen what he took to be my "digging in" at the field's edge and interpreted it as pinpointing a new German defensive line being established to meet our next assault—the next morning as it turned out. A whole battery of our guns sidetracked by me to "knock me out."

Actually, our own guns often seemed more malevolent and destructive than theirs. The night of the 12th, two days before our attack, the whole company had gone on patrol to blow up a pill box some several hundred yards in front of E. Company. I, being one of the replacements, not yet comprehending the situation, felt that I had alone been left to guard the whole company front perimeter while everyone else was "out" on patrol. It was a cold, sleety, rainy night, when the wind was icy and every gust among the late autumn leaves seemed German infiltration, which was always expected, and which I had been warned to anticipate. Out in front, I understand it was Captain Carter who called back for two rounds of 105 on the bunker, to tag it for the assault team, but one round fell short, killing D'Gerolimo and Copeland and blowing Hill's legs off. The very next day, one of our own TD's dropped a short round in the midst of one of our squads, killing Haymore and Haynes and cutting up the rest badly with shrapnel. The irony of our own guns doing more damage than the enemy was bitter. And here again it was apparently our own guns searching to find and destroy me.

The night of my own wounding a wind came up, the rain stopped, and there were occasional spaces of cleared sky between low masses of cloud cover. He could see the stars far and full scattered above him and feel the real earth beneath him. His leg had passed through aching into an almost total numbness. He drew as much brush and, now that the shelling had thrown and dropped additional boughs and branches near and over him, as much stuff as he could find onto himself and over and into his shellhole. Earlier freezing, while the rain had continued and then after the shelling had stopped, he now pulled dirt and mud over much of himself for warmth, and he lay there, only his awkwardly angled feet and his hands and face exposed, staring up with naked eyes against the small raindrops, against the blank black sky and, later, the stars.

Suddenly, in the darkness he heard an outcry on the field and burp guns simultaneously erupting. He lay, clutched back into himself, shrinking into the earth under him, convulsing back into and under it and the network of branches over him. He lay in unbreathing silence and then heard slow rushing movements on the field near him. There was another series of cries and a sustained firing: he lay rigid and shocked with horror. They were sending out squads to locate those they could find hiding or wounded on the field. They were shooting the wounded! For a long while there was no further sound, then the rushing movement sounds further up the field and then a sustained shouting and crying and shouting and then the guns again, the guns. He was as though slapped, stricken with horror. It wasn't that it struck him as a violation, just as a fact, a fact. He and his buddies were, after all, "enemy" soldiers, he and the others now lying within German lines, and more dangerous for being concealed and wounded, unable to do anything but strike at anything that came near them—if they had weapons. He felt this because he knew his own dangerousness had he a gun should any German come near him. It was just the sudden recognition that they were searching for him, looking for him, probing for him in the darkness—that was the terror. He smeared black mud and dirt on his hands, over his face and neck. For a long while there was silence and then he heard slow, furtive new sounds, now in the wood where he was, but far. And as he listened, his scalp as though capped with a numbing hand, he could make out the slow, scattered, occasional but continuing and nearing sounds of some who were edging their way in the almost total darkness towards his end and fringe of woods. Suddenly, a stick snapped, hard, sharp, clear, not twenty yards away. He did not breathe, only desperately trying to press back his exposed hands into and under the earth and branches. It was as though his ears were points, that the silence was a great complete weight and space and that he was focused like the point of a steel probe to quiver to life with the minutest scratch, touch, breath in the world: the whole universe come down to that focused space. And then, the sounds. He no longer heard those further off—oh, they were there—but really heard only the slow sliding brushing movement of something, someone angling towards him through the night. How many hours in how many seconds— long, long silences with only an occasional wind or a far outcry, occasional gunfire far up the field, and then the slow sliding, occasional crinkling heaviness near him, approaching him in the darkness. He was as though one dead, his eyes straining, pushing against darkness. And then it was seemingly just at his feet, a sense of a mass in the darkness, a sensed presence of something huge and looming and coming over him. And then he saw, just near his feet, not moving, a new outline of darkness discernible now as it had moved up to be able to blot out a rash of stars that had suddenly by cloud movement been revealed, a black mass of darkness. His eyes were hard squinted down to the barest line of sight, lest they might be seen looking up as he lay on his back in the hole and under the brush and mud, but he saw carefully and slowly the unmoving outline of a man just standing there. And then that darkness moved, the soldier moved forward and upon him. He was prepared to cry out and kick, thrust up and out at his death, to cry out, to scream out, in German, but the man, sliding stepping a foot forward, stepped down noisily into the shellhole edge through the branches. The foot was drawn back and up in a flash, the man instantly freezing in his movement, stifling his own muttered in-cry. And there he stood, directly over the wounded man beneath him now, dark and silhouetted against the nightstars, neither of them breathing now, neither moving. Nothing. After a long while, the soldier leaned, crouched, and probed down and into the shellhole—he was searching for his feet!—turning, reaching towards his knees, missing his uncovered but branch-concealed feet, probing, touching the mud, the rocks, the dirt above him where he lay. Probing, probing. Then he stood back up, neither of them breathing or having breathed. Carefully, a foot moved forward, delicately, like a living night creature, and it came down directly on his hand, on his hand where it lay under the mud and dirt. A huge crushing, enormous breaking weight of a steel shoe on the back of his right hand. And there the man stood, rearing like an obelisk in the night, his entire weight bearing down into the earth upon that broken hand.

For how long, for how long did he stare up at this now very clear black shape of a German soldier, a machine pistol cradled in his right arm, his helmet against the stars, standing there like some outgrowth of his own body mirrored up and against the skies. For how long—it was as if someone had driven a spike through the back of his hand!—the unchanged breaking weight on the back of his hand, the man above him trying to peer down, stare down into his eyes, he staring up and against the eternal night? He would forever after be lying there staring up at this darkness against darkness, at this death against living stars. In how many dreams through how many years would he confront this ambivalent shadow of himself rearing up and as though from his own body and placed like a shadow against blackness upon the night? And then the man moved, moved, as slowly as he had come, on, away, joining other faint sounds like his own that were moving off to his right further in the woods, joining the sounds, faint but able to be interpreted, of others like himself slithering, drifting, probing through the woods. At last "they" were down in the far woods beyond his head, and he took his first breath.

Well before morning a quick wind came up, a heavy black greyness and then, just before dawnlight, a shifting towards icy drizzling rain that began to fall, lightly but steadily. There had finally been much heavy firing (in these bleak towards morning hours) on the lower field and down towards the ridge over which they had come on the day of battle—was it only yesterday?—into the upper field. It was only from the future that interpretation of that firing and what had been happening would come. Our two attacking companies of the Second Battalion, had "reached their first objective and had captured a number of pillboxes" by 0850 (so we were told), after having "jumped off" at 0545. By 1100, so we now learn, we were "on the final objective." We withstood three German counterattacks, all being "successfully repulsed." The breached German lines, however, closed again after our attack, leaving us essentially cut-off and surrounded. When Company G "attempted to move forward to join the cut-off companies, it was turned back by tremendous concentrations of artillery and mortar fire and by deadly small arms fire coming from the complex system of bunkers surrounding the great forts." By nightfall of the day of our attack, "the position of the First and Second battalions was critical" and our two assaulting companies were "cut off from the remainder of the regiment." It was on the 15th that Company G made "repeated efforts to open a route to the remainder of the Second Battalion." These were "unsuccessful . . . because of concentrated fire." It was undoubtedly the first of these several "relief" operations attempted by Company G that I had heard, and its defeat. But at last this was over. Then, again, the terror of the German soldiers drifting back up through his woods through which they had gone, moving more overtly now, less carefully, not searching, just returning. But he was terrified as before and unable to breathe, almost dead in his fright, and his whole body seemed to hum and buzz and shake inside as he had shaken when the shells fell. But when the sounds of the returning German soldiers neared him, he was again as one dead, and they passed, now murmuring to one another, walking together, off to his left some fifteen yards, seemingly unbelieving that anyone could be with them in that wood.

He realized that, having come carefully through the wood, they now undoubtedly felt that whoever had been there, who had been seen "digging in," had drifted on beyond, or had not been able to survive the shelling late in the day. Or was it that, having again fought successfully towards the lower field, they felt careless and secure in themselves, they didn't give a damn. Whatever. They passed him where he lay, unperceived, he now alert and sure that with this day he would be exposed as he had not been before and that they now seemed confident in their ability to come freely into his wood.

In the middle of the freezing rain of the morning, an American attack could be heard being mounted on the lower field to the left of where his battalion had attacked. There was intense and sustained shelling, and then the vast gunfire, the clumping whump of grenades, the hard high roar of either bangalore torpedoes or bazookas, a variety of machine guns speaking. Almost immediately, with the sound of the first attacking and resisting guns, the Germans returned through the wood: first, moving quickly along the edge of the field beside him, and then angling through the woods from that direction. They were coming back again! He had now covered himself so that not even his face might show, only his eyes able to see, his nostrils to breathe. And they passed him by seemingly without any sense that any enemy or wounded remained on the upper field or in the wood. They were talking to one another, occasionally laughing, joking, smoking, all moving down through and past his stretch of wood to reach its lower edge where they were setting up another upper line of defense against the attack.

And that morning and until noon, he learned how to listen to a battle and to understand a battle only from the sounds it made: another attack that had failed, even as the first one. Long afterward he was told that one of his regimental battalions that had been supposed to go into attack with him had never received the notice to jump off, had never come up into line, for whatever reason; and in shame, to make some gesture of restitution to the other battalions shot up, pinned down, cut off, isolated, to the wounded who still lay here and there on the field—perhaps because of their earlier failure of support that these had relied on that they had not received—was now, in daylight of the next day, frontally assaulting "the hill" in a useless and unsupported gesture. The truth of G Company's inability to move out of reserve and into support and then of its attempt to "open a route" to our surrounded two companies would be at last the regimental explanation. But alone on the field that morning once again he heard the established fire lose its authority, lose its purchase and place—and be overwhelmed. From where he lay he could turn himself just enough to see the Germans firing at those few of this American battalion who made it up towards the wood; and he, with no gun, no power to influence anything, watched his enemies killing his friends. If he cried out, they would simply shoot him and go on with their scarcely interrupted success.

When the battle was over and was reduced to the sounds of occasional popping single rifle shots or a rare grenade, the Germans, seemingly genial and relaxed, strolled back up through the woods once again and past him. One small group walked along the field edge just a few yards from where he lay under the underbrush and dirt—they, like the victors they were, joking, laughing—and he thought of others, like himself, who now lay freshly wounded, bleeding to death on those lower fields.

The day shut down, ominously, grimly darkening: a steady icy light rain began that turned before long into an icy sleet-like drizzle and, then, into small but sharp snow. He was grateful for the water, for he was horribly thirsty, and he licked the water from his hands and field jacket sleeves as he could; then with the snow, he was able to open his mouth to it, to let it gather in creases of his muddy jacket as white siftings that he drank with his tongue. His hands were frozen; he could feel nothing below his waist. At first the water in his ditch had seemed to be freezing to his back, but then, he supposed, it warmed from his body, and he was oblivious to it. But the shellings and then the subsequent drizzling rains had created a new small world for him in which the problems were born again. The afternoon brought a renewed series of shellings—when he heard the first distant "pop" from the battery of guns, his whole body seemed to convulse and tremble—and this time he felt sure that he would die, that he would be blown to bits with not a fragment left to suggest that he had ever been there. The shells came down, and came and came and came and came, and he could not think, only hang on, and dig himself clear after the near hits. One shell this time must have actually dug into the reverse slope of his shell hole before bursting, for he was lifted into the air as though the whole earth under him was rising, hurtling up, and then slammed back into it as though he had been dropped in the freight train itself that collapsed upon him. For a moment he wasn't sure that he was alive, and where his breath was or if he had breath or could find it again. And he was bleeding from scratches and shrapnel bits and, he felt, barely alive. When it finally ended, his nerves were shot, and he was sporadically and involuntarily trembling and shaking as though some circuitry inside him was suddenly shorted. He could not control his shaking.

After it had all gone away, he lay there as though in a narcotic haze, knowing now that he would probably not survive this time: he was wounded, had lost blood, was frozen, had no feeling below his waist, his hands were by now almost useless, his chest had been searingly aching—perhaps he had pneumonia?—and if he was not to be found and killed in the dark by German night patrols or by day patrols—nobody, he was sure, was in a position, given the attacks being mounted, to take prisoners—he would be blown up by his own guns. He took from a special pocket he had sewn in his field jacket, where he kept special things—how useless they all seemed!—a short stub of pencil and some paper. Throughout the grey afternoon he composed a sort of letter to whoever might find him, but really to his girl and his brother and parents. It didn't say much; it didn't seem to have very much to say. He put it back into the lining pocket. He ate an occasional orange Lifesaver, the only "food" he had. He urinated where he was. He tried, after the shelling, to restore his camouflage and protective "cover" as completely as he could.

Once, in the later afternoon two men sauntered by exactly at the field edge leading a team of horses. The day before he had heard the bridles of the horses and the sound of the 88's they drew, which seemed to be firing mostly from further up the far rising field or from the edge of the woods far beyond his feet. Perhaps it was the mistaken American assumption that the 88's were hidden in "his" woods that was bringing the fire on him? The men seemed casual, even carefree, talking lightly and seemingly unconcernedly together. For a moment he considered calling out in German, saying "I am wounded here, I have no gun," but he could not, after the night of the shooting of the wounded on the field, truly believe that they would take prisoners. And they passed beyond him. Later they returned the same way. Throughout the later afternoon he listened to what he took to be the sounds of ambulances groaning and lurching about the lower fields, but none of these sounds approached the hill where he lay. There were only the occasional Germans, shouting to one another, talking, passing by through the woods or along the field edge. Towards twilight, he was feeling dizzy and almost lapsing away, and almost out of his head. He woke from what seemed a sleep—or had he passed out?—to believe that he had been singing, actually singing. Had he?

The subsequent night was terrible. The temperature dropped sharply, and he was freezing to death; he was sure that he was dying. He lay in the mud and debris and thought carefully of everything he had done in his life, of everyone he had known and loved. He carefully went over each thing in his mind. He was buried in the mud and earth and branches and, he supposed, if he were to die there, it would not be necessary to bury him. Nobody would find him until, some year, someone tripped over his feet. He could not escape the cold, the sleet, the terrible cold and freezing in the night. The day that followed was, equally, too much to be borne: it was numbing, icy cold, and the skies seemed empty of everything but an enormous pressure of bleakness and drabness. He lived through it like a dream. It seemed hard for him to breathe, the pain in his chest was constant. He finished his Lifesavers. He drank the ditch water as it lay in occasionally more pure puddles. He waited, he supposed, for the battle to resolve itself so that the Americans might attack through and find him, for a "good" German to come upon him, when his plea in German might be accepted, for ambulances and Medics that never would come—they must by now have long given up the sense of anyone alive on the upper fields of his earlier battle. He was terribly hungry.

There was one more shelling before nightfall and before it was over he felt that he would never be able to live through it again. There was no longer any predictability to the third round, for any round now could be "on" him, and each and every far "pop" in the distance started his nerves and then his body to dance like some mad thing. The smell of cordite, the singing off of the fragments, the earsplitting shrieks of the shells coming in, the long slow approach—he was sure that the approach was the terrible thing. Had they been like the German 88's he would not have had time to be shell shocked. With a flat-trajectory fire and muzzle velocity like the 88's, you were zong-zapped, the shell hitting before it had gone off, so it seemed. Meanwhile, he had time to hear the pop, to follow the shush and sizzle and then the fluhfluhfluh-fluh frohfroh whuhwhu ascending now screaming incoming about-to-be-impacting blam of the shells, each one. He supposed it was the fact of being alive, afterwards, after each burst, which gave him the careful and immensely precise and selective way he listened to the whir-whir-whir of the cone and shrapnel bits of casing as they sailed, sometimes like exploring huge bees and birds, off into the trees, or whunked into the earth around him. He was quite sure he would not be able to hold himself together through another night; he seemed to be dissolving inside, to be hurting, shaking, trembling, aching. And the hunger, thirst.

But the next day's morning came with a lightening, a brightening in the air, a relaxing of the cold. He was now too numb to feel most of his body, but the light on his eyes was wonderful after the grey, the dark. Later, he was quite sure that he had been quite out of his head, whether from his wound, his hunger, sickness, or shattered nerves, and when in the late morning he heard a group of Germans walking along the upper field edge as though they would pass by him, he began to sing, he thought loudly, "Die Lorelei," all of whose words he knew in German. And he sang and went on singing while they went past the edge of woods where he lay, amazingly, incredibly seeming not to hear him, paying no heed, as though he did not exist. He could not understand. He sang "Änchen von Thaurau," he sang "O Tannenbaum," he sang all the German songs he knew. And then he sang "Ave Maria" and "Home On the Range." His chest hurt, but he sang. No one seemed to hear him, or they pretended not to hear him. Later, three Germans walked past him on the field and did not even glance in his direction. But when he finally rose in his hole the better to survey the field to his right, a machine pistol opened up from somewhere on the field and his parapet was slammed with the bullets. NOW they couldn't ignore him; they knew he was there, in their midst. Perhaps they knew, had known he was there, and harmless, but no one wanted either the trouble he would mean or the shame of shooting him. Had it not been for the bullets, it was as though he was not there.

In the later afternoon, there was a soft golden light in the air, and in it, he was certain that he was going to die. The day was beautiful, the air fresh and, now, even warm, but he had no feeling in his hands or in his lower body, and he could not see any way in which he might be able to survive. If he did not die by the shells or the Germans, he would die of hunger, thirst, cold, sickness, the breaking down of his nerves and his strength. He wanted desperately to live, and he cast through his mind to find the terms on which life would be possible, to see himself in any fashion possibly returned to life. When he had written his last note, he had made a list on the back of the page, which placed him in history: it began with his identity, name and address, military outfit, his age, 19, the year, and day, and placed this time of his life in his galaxy in the universe and descended down to his world, the earth, and to Europe, and France, and to a field outside Metz near Gravelotte and to the hill of Forts Driant and Jeanne d'Arc and to this field and wood's edge and this shellhole.

Now he similarly ranged through all those he knew and all the experiences he had known and had. He realized that his legs could not be saved, one was shattered, but both were long ago frozen and without feeling, probably in unarrestable gangrene, but he well knew that life without his legs was a question of amputations and adjustment. He accepted that—if only he could live. He had also largely lost feeling in his torn and frozen hands, and he wondered if, indeed, it was a sentimentality to believe that he would be willing to live life as a quadruple paraplegic. He considered that question soberly and long and knew that, yes, he could accept that—if only he could live. But he knew that life was more impossible than that, that after this long time of freezing he probably had pneumonia and, to judge by his chest pain and his occasional lapsing away towards unconsciousness, he probably was ill and shattered in some way beyond reparation, and he wondered if he was willing to accept his quadriplegic life if he were not surrounded by the love of those he loved. So one by one, he thought of those he loved: of Lee, who was his girl, who was the center of his life—and he knew that he would be willing to live, if he lost her, without her, for could he, after all, wish upon her what he would be if he survived? And, similarly, he thought long and carefully about his brother and mother and father, and slowly, reluctantly, let each fall from his hands, fall from his consciousness, knowing that life, to be had at all, had to be had at that severe a cost, the loss of all and every one of them. It was not as though he were falling into death so much as though he was releasing them, one by one, to a great darkness, letting them fall like irreplaceable jeweled stones of solid weight irretrievably through space and away into an impenetrable darkness. They were the sacrifices and the cost. Not he. At last then, seeing himself alone, in an empty room in a ward somewhere, and without a soul about him, near him, caring for or aware of his existence, he asked, BUT WHAT IF you were not only a quadruple amputee but also blind? Could you accept life on those conditions? Yes, yes, said his heart. Yes. But what if you were not only a quadriplegic blindman but also deaf and dumb? You know what I am saying, you hear what I am saying? And he, inside himself, shouted yes, yes. Even then, Yes! All right, You, You Nameless, you Trunk of Body, you Flesh, you Thing, what if you were only Torso, to be propped by day against the rotting doorway of a shitted mud hut in the wastes of Siberia, and deaf and dumb and blind? Would you truly settle for life on those terms? And he felt the soft wind of evening go across his cheek, and he said yes, yes, if only to feel the warmth of sunlight in the morning move across the side of my face, to be able to feel the coolness coming on of evening; if only to feel the wind touch my hair, touch my cheek, if only that. Yes! And at that moment he knew he began to live.

As he lay there now, in what seemed a space beyond the battlefield, a place he had found somewhere inside himself, beyond any further worry, beyond fear, for all worry and fear had been had, he heard a scurrying and crackling in the brush near his feet and saw a giant hare sitting there just beyond his awkwardly angling shoes, there by the tree branches but looking at him. He sat there wrinkling his soft furry nose at him. He could see his whiskers, his large liquid eyes. And then the hare—he knew it was a hare and not a rabbit, like Belgian hares he had once seen, because it was so large, larger than any he actually had seen—raised himself and put a paw on his shoe, placed one paw and then shifted his weight to place the other there, raising himself to look at him. And for long they looked at one another, and then the hare dropped down and hopped to where his knees were, now exposed above the dirt and branches, looked carefully at him and hopped off into the woods. He marveled that to the hare he was like a tree, like a piece of earth, like a part of nature. They had no fear of one another, none. While he was yet wondering about the hare, suddenly a shadow fell on him and he convulsed back, staring up. There, above him in the air, large, so large that it took from him light of the sky, was a huge white bird hovering over him where he lay. It was inconceivable, unimaginable, too large for any seagull or tern or large white bird he had ever seen, and it held there a moment, hovered there a moment, then veered off and came back and held there above him again, its wingspread some four or five feet, its feathers a gleaming white. Albatross? Man of War bird? What was it? And as he stared, in wonder and bewilderment, it leaned away on the air, circled and came back, hovering still above him as though examining him with care but having no fear of him. And circled slowly again and came to be above him, beyond his reach but above him. And then it went away.

With its going I knew that I was going to live, certainly now I knew this. Not because of the bird, or my insistence on life, or because of the hare or the golden evening, but just because somewhere inside myself something lyrical and alive had made that decision. Within minutes I was redaubing my hands and face blackly with mud, and then, almost without fear of consequence but with care, I had slithered over the paradose of my shell hole, dragging my inert hips and legs behind me like sacks attached to my numb arms. There were no shots. I had not been noticed. Once out of the shell hole— Oh God! What happiness!—I lay still for a long still while, and then, inch by inch, lying on my back, I began to pole myself backwards through the woods and away from the field on my elbows. This escape from the shell hole was the beginning of my several adventures behind German lines. Before night fell I was some thousands of yards away, lying covered with boards, woodshavings, and sawdust under a table in a shattered and abandoned woodworking factory there in that forest while German soldiers sat about the table drinking, talking, kicking me with their feet. But that is another part of this life that is emerging from death.

I am aware that you, reader, will discount the white bird as hysteria, hallucination, or as willed religious aberration, my own needed descent of The Holy Ghost. But I had never been a religious person, or, rather, I had never been formally religious if perhaps authentically so. I think that probably by the time real religious apprehension has disengaged itself from its iconography and fled into a terminology of sanctity, when the Paraclete and the Virgin have become ideas— so that Immaculate Conception has less to do with warm-blooded hands that hold the distressing weight and dilemma of the child in chosen hands than with an idea of a way to by-pass the earth—religion has itself taken flight and lost the bough it shoved against to loft it in the air. Even as Christianity yearns backwards towards the lost feet and presence of its redeemer, it exhibits the need for those feet upon those roads and rocks, those hands blessing in their healing touch, the revivification that is immanent in and stems from the incarnation and embodiment of God. The most important thing is that He was. Without that base, the cathedrals would totter at last, having insufficient base for their ecstasy. I can remember being asked in St. Paul's in London for a donation for the reconstruction of the cathedral, St. Paul's being an example, so I was told, of the "victory of man's spirit over inadequate and insufficient subsoil." And so, we might assume, is all religion, but the fact of the matter is that without a true hard core of authentic reality to hold the nucleus of the mystery, the mind is insufficiently enchanted to care to rear its castles in Spain, its immaculate beauty. A thousand galleries witness the intensity and vitality of the dream, spiraling from myriad believers' heads and hands, beginning in each instance with the weight of a child upon a forearm, a mother and babe on an ass's back, the sense of the depending stress upon the brutal nails that hold. It all comes down to a real bull at the center of a labyrinth, poetry does, religion does, and it does not rest on spells and dreams of exorbitant dreamers.

I, a skeptic, looked long and carefully at that long and carefully hovering bird, for whom I may have seemed a possible morsel—I am willing to intrude the irreligious suggestion that the stench of my possibly rotting gangrenous flesh had drawn his hunger—and saw the careful layering of the feathers, the almost hidden clutched claws, the beak, the inquiring eyes. It was a bird, but I suppose, to the truly religious, a god may be a bird, a beast, a cow, a shower of gold. Perhaps he must be so before he becomes more. And a bird may be a God. The heart is moved by a cloud, by a radiance in the air, by a burning bush. Hemingway tells of how his heart is moved by seeing a sail on a canal move across a landscape, by seeing slow oxen. As the heart is moved, the coordinates of belief are laid down. And a white bird above my head, almost seemingly attached to a brown hare whose paws rest on my feet, is as good an emblem for my coat of arms as any, as good a basis for rebirth, like that of Moses out of the bullrushes, as the arms of any Pharaoh's daughter. Before the advent of the bird, it was all a long slow descent, deeper and deeper towards and then into a darkness, a series of incremental but steady reductions, a cutting and paring away—of everything. And then, at the point beyond which, below which I could not go and live, I was lifted up into the air, released from the dark but fertile hole. Like any child crawling towards birth, I left behind me the blood-soaked place of my long entrapment and outsetting, dragging behind me as I crawled the trailing roots of my caul of bondage that had kept me there.

Account of Another GI Who Fought beside Me

John Loomis

Company F assembled several hours before daylight near the top end of the Mance Ravine. The day was 14 November, 1944. We were told that we were to breach the German line between Leipzig and Moscow Farms, that we would encounter a large bunker there which we would put out of action, and that we would proceed to the crest of the plateau, where we would get further orders to swing south to high ground just east of Fort Jeanne d'Arc. I was an ammunition bearer in a mortar squad.

We moved eastward in the dark. Company F was spearheading the battalion, Company E was on our left flank and Company G was in reserve. Our first platoon was to be on the left, the second on the right and the third was to bring up the rear. The second platoon failed to arrive, so we moved out without it.

We reached the bunker just as daylight was beginning to break. All hell broke loose. Flares. Then machine gun fire. Tracers flashing by. Rifle fire. A machine gun opened up directly in front of me. In one fraction of a second I saw the flare of the shot, the tracers going by my head as I hugged the ground, and heard and felt the bullets go by and crunch into my buddy, Jim Northrop, immediately behind me. I called to him. No reply. Then Santi, Knuth and I shifted left into a slight depression to get out of the line of fire.

My only thought at this time was to get that machine gun before it got me. I couldn't move ahead because of the stalled traffic in front of me. Then to my right, the voice of Sergeant Ray Brown: "Let's get home by Christmas, men! Let's go!" At this point, men all around me were getting to their feet and rushing forward. I joined the rush forward—scrambling, crawling, running—tossing grenades in the direction of at least two machine gun emplacements and shooting bursts from my grease gun toward the German line during the next hour or so, and finally reaching the crest of the plateau.

I was at the first objective, about mid-way between Moscow and Leipzig Farms. Morning light was increasing, and I could see the tree line some 60 or 70 yards to the east where the plateau dropped off sharply. Opposing fire had dwindled—it was mostly off to my right. I started for the tree line with some 20 other GIs. We were firing into the trees as we moved forward.

I then noticed a white flag waving over a bunker to my left. I turned to it. A German officer and 6 or 7 soldiers scrambled out and came running towards me, hands in the air. I remembered Patton's admonition that we were to take no prisoners. I was unable to comply. I gestured to them to move westwards towards our rear. They turned and started walking in that direction. After they had gone 50 or 60 yards, they turned southerly and ran in the direction of St. Hubert's Farm and Fort Jeanne d'Arc. I wondered if we would have to contend with them again.

I moved eastwards again. The GIs who had been to my left had disappeared. There was firing to the left in the woods. I felt reluctant to enter the woods at that point without knowing the situation there. Knowing that our objective was to the south just east of Fort Jeanne d'Arc, I turned southeasterly, and walked quickly down the field. There were perhaps 6 or 8 GIs moving parallel to me on my right, and one on my left. We were all moving in the general direction of the final objective, firing towards the woods and down the field as we went. I heard sporadic gun fire in all directions.

The tree line turned in westerly in front of me, and as I approached it, I noted that it swung back to the east, and a new field was in front of me. I moved southerly into the field. A German machine gun opened up in my direction from the other end of the field—about 150 yards to the south. I hit the ground, as did the GI to my left. A few more bursts came from the machine gun as we lay there. I carefully squeezed off a couple short bursts at him with my machine pistol. All was quiet. I wondered if I could have been so fortunate as to put him out of commission. Obviously the Germans had set up that machine gun so that the field could be swept clear of anyone trying to cross to the woods.

The GIs to my right were still slogging south. There was a fence line between them and the machine gun. I decided I should shift to the right and join them to move on the machine gun from the cover of the fence line. I looked to my left, and saw that the GI I had previously observed was lying on the ground about 15 feet behind and somewhat closer to the woods than I. As I contemplated the situation, I heard a voice. I looked towards the woods from whence the voice came, and saw Lieutenant Crabbe from Company E standing just inside the trees and beckoning to us to join him.

I gathered myself together, sprang to my feet and dashed as fast as I could for the woods some 20 yards away. The GI to my left was also up and running just a few feet ahead of me. Machine gun bullets were rattling past us as we ran. My companion was hit and cart-wheeled through the air just as we were reaching the tree line.

I dived into the woods. I crawled forward down the slope a couple of yards, then I stood up, and looked back for my companion. He was not to be seen. I concluded that he must have been killed by that machine gun burst, and that I was once again spared. Lieutenant Crabbe called me again, and I turned and joined him and some other officers and GIs gathered around a radio operator who was trying to contact our command to the rear.

Orders came for us to proceed to the objective. An officer turned to me, and said, "Lead out!" I took off at the head of the column and led it most of the remaining 1000 yards or so to our objective where we, some 60 men of the Second Battalion, were then cut off from our rear for the next three days.

About six weeks later I was a patient in DeWitt Hospital near Auburn, California. There I met Robin Gajdusek, for the second time, as I found out. As we compared our experiences, it was clear that he was the GI who had been hit by the machine gun fire and had cart-wheeled next to me on the dash across the killing field on that bleak November day.

John E. Loomis, PFC, F Co.,
379th Infantry Regiment, 95th Division

"Honors Due":
A Short Story

To reach this place in this Chronicle is, however natural it may seem, a species of achievement for me. It marks a distinct plateau, as though whatever happens afterwards is really the tale of a new life, of a new life form bizarrely emerged from the mud of that mountain, out of that hole on that ravaged hill.

And therefore I rest awhile, and take a deep breath before proceeding forward—into and towards whatever may await.

I suddenly realize that what can best fill and establish this interval is the first telling of this shell hole tale, a look back at the first time I ever put into words the chronicle of events you have just read. It was 25 years ago when I and my wife and infant son went to live in Southern France, in the small town of Soubès high in the mountainous Causse du Larzac region well north of Montpellier and not far from Lodève. While living there, in a medieval apartment built on several levels between the stone and arrowslit windowed outer fortification walls of the ancient town, I wrote a book of short stories. I called the collection TRAVELING. It was in one of these, aptly entitled "Honors Due," that I first explored the events of my wounding and three days in the shell hole—in a story that attempted to understand premonitions of death and therefore perhaps necessarily retrieved it from my interior darkness.

79

Since this Chronicle is first of all to please myself, and second, to give an accurate sense not only of the war events but also of the way I dealt with them and was affected by them, I think it perhaps important to place here the first version of my war experience, however entwined within a fictional frame. In any event, it will allow us a rest on our journey in time and across this mountainside, in which we can relax, get our bearings, and learn how best to proceed, when we buckle up and fall in for the march—albeit now somewhat of a crawl— forward.

———————⇒➣●⋖⇐———————

Ah! Phoebus Apollo! Why are you here,
Still haunting this house,
To infringe, usurp, annul
The honours due to the Powers below?

Euripides

It was in the night that he suddenly knew that he was going to die. His son had come into their bed, as he often did—waking from fitful sleep, slightly chilled, and asking to be taken in with them. Of course, this meant bringing Lion and Bear along as well, and his father turned so as to accommodate the boy closely in the curve of his body, bringing with his hands the animals then close against the boy, fitting them snugly into the curve of his son's arms, belly, and thighs. And so they had slept, closely, tightly, his wife pressing firmly against his back, so that they were like a family in a cave, sheltering from the cold and dark in one another's warmth. It must have been an hour later that the first stab of sickening pain struck him, like a knife between his ribs, but coursing with an almost flaming intensity inside his ribcage and down his left side. He had cried out suddenly, and his son, waking, having heard his father's cry, having felt the involuntary tightening of his arms, said, What's wrong, darling?" There was concern in the boy's question now, and Stephen had simply said, "Nothing. I just had a pain; it's gone. Go to sleep." And the boy, quickly again, slept.

But his father lay awake, acquainted with a knowledge he had not before permitted himself. It had all been suddenly summed by the quick pain: it added together and phrased for him a truth that sporadic and episodic physical events had avoided—his death, not as something eventually to be faced, but as something imminent, hovering, certain. This was what was spelled out in the incremental waves of nausea, the dull aches, the sudden flashes of pain, gone before they could be studied; this was the meaning ultimately of the neck pain that had begun some two years ago, which several doctors on several occasions had laughed away, but which dug in and gradually gained a certain hold on him until it remained like someone's finger pressing upon a vital vein. His blood lately had felt like lead, like some dark, heavy viscous fluid, unable to push itself through his body; the area around his heart ached with the effort to pump the weight it moved. So now, with little fear but with a new knowledge, to which he had to adjust, he lay, trying to understand how his world had changed.

His son turned in his sleep so that his head rested upon his father's head, his cheek against his father's cheek; they were breathing together, a doubled face. In his sleep the boy said, "It's a monster, Daddy." "What is?" "There's a monster here." But he went on sleeping, despite his recognition, and Stephen wondered if they were so close that his son instinctively knew and could sense the presence in the room. The weight of his son's head was the pride of Atlas; but he felt himself bearing it like a world that blossomed out of his own body, he beneath becoming the world to its rising. That was how it was, and how it would be: his son succeeding him, rising above him, out of him, as that son in turn would support the sons that would go forth from him. There was pain in the thought that origins would not be remembered: there would be no authentic memory of all their closeness, their life together, not even an image other than the false and bad ones that cameras recorded—not life but its frozen image; himself, always more absurd than he could recognize.

At three, Karl was too young to keep later this intense and full time; all this would simply become, he supposed, temperament, what he met the world with: his ready laughter, his resilience, his organic wholeness. He would carry the gifts imprinted upon him by his father's love, but his father would be sloughed into an oblivion, as forgotten as the earth beneath passing feet, as the air that was breathed into ardent lungs. He remembered his own youth, how fully he had lived, how joyously he had sung in the face of pain his way across a brimming world, and without attribution, without a sense that his gift of gaiety and resilience, his ability to laugh deeply, to sing loudly, to climb high and exultantly over the highroads of the earth was special, or unusual. All right, be sentimental! Be proud! Be vain! Lose the quality of earned joy in forgetting the battles, in under-rating the suffering. Well, then, the suffering, too, the whole of it. What was special was to have been able to lose the sense of the suffering, to have no regrets, no animosities or remembered hatreds, to have no scores to settle, only praise to give. This, after pain. It was a certain undismayed spirit, not indomitable—who had borne the ulti-

mate testing—Job?—and had remained pliable after rigor, objective after cause for hatred. That's a good self-praising thing
to say, he thought; a way to make compromise wholesome.
You have to make it good in the face of everything, don't
you? Under how many rugs have you swept the refuse, the
evidence? You've seen to it that there are no victims, no ac-
cusers, not even in your own absent conscience.

But spirit was not inherited, or if in part inherited, it could
be muted by unmasterable sorrow, by the pressures of a con-
suming world. What inheritance needed was the two or three
years they had had together of scarcely qualified love,

[Before me as I write, the yellow leaves of the poplar are
dancing in a strong wind against a blue sky.] No, they are
not dancing; that is crap, he said. They are being moved; they
are being tossed, hard, against the purchase, the grip of their
stems, they are being forced back on the conditions they have
inherited, which they would change if they could—and to
one uninvolved, it is beautiful, but it is not "dancing." They
are being driven further and further towards letting go, their
muscles being incrementally tired, the way a bull is worn
down, any man's grip is loosened, until holding on becomes
impossible, or absurd. The blue sky is blue. *That* you cannot
take from it. Nor the yellow of the leaves. In any leaf is always
its possible yellow, in any sky its possible blue; the times of
the creature are in the creature, are awaiting their fatal blossoming. It is all beauty, it is all beauty, he said; all the seasons.
Any stance on any moment.

For a moment, just for a moment he felt blossoming
in him the redolent and exotic flowers of his special fatal ill-
ness. For one second he held it, his death, sufficient unto itself, within him. Before the terms and conditions of combat
make my adversary ugly, he thought, watching steal over him
the fear. He had adventured—no, he had gone, he had gone
too close to the physical face; he had almost imagined, and
by imagining taken away the possibility of reprieve from the
source of the death whose reality he conjured. It was this time
of conviction without certainty that made his fear manage-
able. He wondered about the faith of the Apostles: could he
have acted with only conviction without certainty.

Also in the Musée de Lyon he had seen a painting by Felix
Vallotton that had arrested him, that he could not forget. At
first glance it was a modern, almost campy study of a reclining

nude; she was just lying there, bedclothes barely covering her lower hips, one hand upon a book she had been reading and had put aside; her right arm was bent at the elbow and flatly turned back so that its wrist against the bed supported the girl's head; her eyes stared straight out at the viewer. He could not forget it; it haunted him.

At first he thought it might be the glib sense of entrapment given by the contrast between the very realistic richness of the girl's attractive body and the book that she held: a message conveyed about the loss of possible personal life, the loss of the woman, caught as she was in lonely isolated reading, given to abstractions of real life, real as she was. He wished he could make out the title of the book that so held her but that she had nevertheless gently put aside. Her fingers of her left hand rested upon it so carefully, caressingly.

No, it was not that simple contrast that held the power. It had more to do with the naked quality of the girl's gaze. Her hair was bobbed in a fluff-cut fashionable in the 20's, her lips were full but together and unsmiling; there was a line beside her mouth. It was a used face, a face that had loved much, that had given exorbitantly and without demands, that rested without regret in its achieved personality, but personality not as a possession, simply as where she was. He knew she was not conscious of, did not care that one breast was pressed flat towards the bed beneath her, that the other, not too full, gently swagged downwards; it would never occur to her that she could be judged for her . . . humanity. It was these eyes that observed quietly, that were wide, liquid, silently assenting to being seen but making no judgment of the viewer, expecting none, that stayed him, that made him weak with wonder before what he knew must be considered a trivial painting. She was not aware, would have thought it remarkable that one could have been aware of the mortality expressed in the pelvic couch, the hollow between her upper left hip and her falling belly, suggesting so faintly yet inevitably the skeletal armature to which her beauty was held. The flesh of her neck was firm and yet but gently creased in a slightly falling fold; her arms were straight, failing to enunciate the curves considered beautiful; her hands and somewhat blunted fingers suggested the use and abrasion of life. Perhaps it was that her used beauty in her early thirties—he would guess— was made slightly poignant by the unringed fingers of her left hand: or was it just that the direct honesty of her wide gaze made one feel the enormous world—O brave new world!—and not enough in it to give any lover adequate rewards. Those were satin bedclothes that but barely covered her lower abdomen, her lower thighs: were they too rich, too suggestive of the luxuriousness that placed its demands upon her; and did the quietness of her eyes, the book so carefully touched suggest another world that luxury could not possess? Was it that the painting set forth a struggle between not two possibilities, but two actualities, a struggle which could not be resolved, which remained faintly tragic, if heroically accepted? Wasn't this what religion at its best was all about, that recognized tension?

Years, many years ago, in his carelessness, in his desuetude, he had had many affairs and a few mistresses; and each girl, he supposed—he knew—had taught him something about the possibilities of loving, the range of human communion. But there had been one girl whose loving mystified him, who had given a new respect for the possibilities of love. When he would call her, whenever he would call her, she was there—there was nothing that would interfere ever with their being together if he were free. She was a wild, wonderful lover, utterly, utterly accepting and giving; her touch immediately led him to know that no demand was different from any other demand, that there were no demands. And the slightest wavering in his whim, in his desire, in his will was as though upon the instant known and accepted, so that should he suddenly, abruptly leave, should he stay away and not call again for a long while, or should he press himself upon her again and again, impetuously and daily, she was happily open to what needed to be. While he was with her there was no iota of herself withheld from him—her joy, her laughter, her happiness for the trivial details of her own life, her full passion—but when he needed to leave, she offered no flicker of judgment, no impediment of mood, no question. Her eyes were like the girl's eyes in the painting; you could live in them. What she gave she totally abundantly gave; somehow, somewhere she accepted as her own problem, as her own human and lonely encounter what was hers when alone.

Probably a man with a greater conscience, greater kindness, would have been cursed by such a mistress—the weight of the responsibility, the unseen but unavoidable cost. But at the time he had been too depraved to recognize her sumptuous giving, although he had often wondered why it was that his own passionate desire for her remained so perfect. What had he given to her one bit as valuable as her total acceptance—accepting whatever rain, whatever hail, whatever seed, or rough or careless ploughing, answering them all with her abundance . . . of everything but harvest. Wasn't that the long delayed indictment? Of him? Of her? Everything but harvest. What did he know of her? Then? Or now? Where was she now? Would they die together? Had they ever lived together? What was it they had had? Say her name. Say it over and over again, or you will lose it. My losing and soon-to-be-silent lips will lose it. The girl, or the name, he asked himself, smiling wryly, like a death's head, against the darkness. All right. All right. It is your name I keep, I extricate, I separate from our oblivion. We are death. We made death together, in our tender keeping. That is our child, child of our unwed unloving. She was like a forgotten spring, the way a childhood's seasons, whatever they were, gave only abundance to childhood. The disregarded earth, his first lover. But had I not held you as you held me, I would not be able to hold you now, name I hold against our darkness, he said. It was Valéry who wrote:

> Il dépend de celui qui passe
> que je sois une tombe ou un trésor
> que je parle ou me taise
> ceci ne tient qu'a toi
> ainsi n'entre pas sans désire

He held closely against himself one of his wife's arms that held him; his other arm brought the boy in tightly against his own body, bringing also his animals. Lion had been their attempt to assuage Karl's loss, his fear when he had had to remain in the Montpellier Children's Hospital alone, far from them, and among alien strangers. Karl had become seriously ill the very night that his mother had returned home from hospital after an operation for a dangerous ectopic pregnancy, but it had seemed more than a reaction to the sustained deprivation and the shock of her return: for weeks his stomach had hurt him daily, he had been unable to eat; he had become incrementally more tired and listless, until finally he woke to throw up and to remain afterwards almost comatose, hardly responding. Leaving his wife, who was bedridden, in Soubès, Stephen had numbly driven the road to Montpellier with his son.

At the hospital the doctors all agreed the boy must be immediately hospitalized for close observation and emergency tests. But when his father had left him with a nurse on the ward, he had rushed out into the hall, clinging to his coat, placing his back against the wall, screaming at the group of nurses, interns, and doctors who gathered with amazement about him: "Don't you touch me; don't you dare touch me! I am going to wait here for my father, until he comes to get me; he told me that he would come back, and I will wait for my daddy here; don't you touch me!" And the group of confused, amused, bewildered Frenchmen, who never had to cope with such responses in their own disciplined children, simply stared, uselessly. The chief on the ward told Stephen that if he entered the ward now to pacify his child, they would wash their hands of the whole matter—"We can't deal with children if their parents emotionally disturb them; leave him, and in ten minutes he will be all right, he will accept it." No, he would not accept it; the man did not know his son. But Stephen had been forced to leave him—there was no place else to take him—and return alone to his waiting wife. Had it been anything but a question of the boy's life, he would never have abandoned him so, permitted him to seem abandoned.

For several days Karl had *not* accepted it, giving the hospital staff hell. When they both came to see him the next day, they had brought Lion along, as a friend, to be with him when they could not. The boy had been unable to focus upon anything but his fear of abandonment—"Don't leave me, please don't leave me; please don't leave me; take me home with you; I'll be good; I love our house, really I do; please take me home!"—his parents aching with grief. He had clung to his daddy until the boy's mother and a nurse had been forced to break his hold, and Stephen had had to leave the ward. His wife joined him in a minute, but with Lion. Karl had thrown Lion after her, refusing cheap pacifications, tawdry substitutes, screaming "Take him away!" But while Karl was still briefly absent from his room with the nurse—she had taken him to the roof garden to try to console him—Stephen had gone back to leave Lion for him. He knew that the boy's rage was legitimate and beautiful, and he also knew the profundity of suffering that lay for him ahead. He had to leave something with the boy in their absence that connected him to them, that would give him the sense of the reality of their visit and the probability of their return, something he had received at their hands. The next day the nurses described how their son had refused to eat, to sleep, to go to the bathroom without Lion firmly clasped to him; he would rage when anyone went near the mute beast. "Rage, rage, against the dying of the light!" A patrimony of beasts. His father had named him simply Lion.

So now the father held the animal in against his son, knowing that this, too, would warm him, was not pacification merely, was a legitimate friend. Holding and being held. "Christ, that my love were in my arms and I in my bed again!" It was a beautiful charm once, and it would apply for tomorrow, but for now, what did he want? He had it all, he had it all there with him. He wondered whether it was truly better to die in fullness or to die in want. There was Emily Dickinson's poem about the defeated warrior who waited for death. That, too. Perhaps the best were the moments of reductions: was any second in any man's life richer than the moment, stripped of everything, he walked empty out into a new strange world, the only stranger to be met, the unchanged self restored to him again? Well, he would find out about that soon enough: the longest journey to answer the short, short journey of authentic love. It made him feel good to know that the small rain had fallen as it always would so many centuries ago.

He knew where he had learned about reductions. Once before he had had to prepare for a death, but that time there had been reprieve. In an insane, in a madman's full regimental attack on the entrenched forts and the multiple rings of bunkers surrounding Metz, in a daring assault, he had been wounded. The attack was the utter failure they all knew it had to be—they had written their last letters, given away what was worth giving, and some had even disabled themselves with wounds during the night—and when he had finally been cut down by an armor-piercing machine-gun bullet that smashed his legs out from under him, it had been as he had tried to run through the obvious "killing zone." The only chance for safety for any of them caught in the open on that clear field lay on the other side of it. And he had been the only one, the last one to get off the field. The gun that had caught him, cut his pack from his back and slashed his jacket to ribbons as he lay there, but it could obviously depress no further in its mount, and he was spared. When he was hit, his helmet and his rifle had sailed from him, describing a greater arc preceding his lesser one. Protection and power—divested of both: so stripped, he lay, every pore of his body awaiting the steel. Later, as the battle swung elsewhere, he had dragged himself from the edge of the field where the killing lane had been established and into the shattered ghost of the wood that bordered it. Here he poled himself backwards into a shallow shell hole, dragging his legs after him like some encumbrance, pulling in over him what dried brush he could grasp.

With the attack a failure, it was behind enemy lines that he lay wounded through the sub-freezing cold, the rain, the mists of the next three days. Early, he had tried to build a parapet by pushing mud up higher about the edges of his hole, but a German had seen the motion and bursts of fire hurled down what he had built. An American artillery spotter had probably also observed his activity in that small stretch of wood, for soon the shelling began, his own TD's and artillery opening up on him, where he lay; it continued intermittently and frequently for the remaining days. Several times he was almost buried in mud by almost direct hits from his own guns; he tore the nails from his hands, frozen as they were, digging himself clear. On the first day as he lay there weaponless, he had observed the Germans snaking through the brush about him to line the lower edge of the wood, from where they fired down on his pinned-down comrades. On the evening of the first day, he had heard the erratic drone and buzz of ambulances working the lower fields, but they never came near the crest where he and so many others lay wounded.

In the night, he could hear the German killing squads moving about the field he had escaped from; there were occasional bursts or sporadic shots or screams when wounded were found. One huge German, his machine pistol silhouetted with him as darkness against darkness, roamed carefully through his woods and at one point stepped into the edge of brush where he lay, the great boot smashing down on his hand. Without moving on, the man stood there in the night, immense and dark rearing above him, standing on his surely broken hand. It seemed forever before he walked away. As Stephen thought of it now, it was like a Kokoschka in its dark blues, blacks, and silvers, but it was starker, an engraving of a German soldier standing on the edge of a grave at his feet, where a boy lay on his back looking up at him and at the night sky beyond him, a further darkness.

Towards the end of the second day a group of Germans strolled along the edge of the field beside him; he could hear their voices, understand them, see their faces. They were everywhere about him: he could hear their conversations, the plod of hoofs and the jingle of the harness for the horse team that pulled an 88 battery about the hill, bringing in more fire upon him. He thought of surrender, but knowing the conditions under which they were fighting, decided against it, although occasional Germans that day often came near him.

The succeeding days there were no chances. Someone saw a move he made; a burst of fire tore away his wall. He had lost much blood, despite his tourniquet; he was without feeling below his waist; his hands were torn and numb and he could not straighten them; he undoubtedly had pneumonia; he was delirious and weak with hunger. When he had gone into attack, he had had an orange roll of Lifesavers with him; that was all. He drank the bloody ditch water in which he lay; he ate the frost and snow when it fell; he opened his mouth to the rain. He waited to die.

That was the time of reductions, the three days. Sequentially and incrementally, slowly, without haste or, finally, fear, he had rid himself of what he could survive without. Had he to live without ever seeing again his world, his own country—*that* he could endure. Were the terms of survival more strict: were he to survive only on condition that never again would he see his mother, his father, his brother—would he accept life so? That he would accept. He yielded them as sacrifices to the flames. But life only if the girl he loved, he so deeply loved, his only love, were also lost to him, never to be seen again, never to be touched? Ultimately, that, too, was worth the cost of life. He had long ago accepted life without legs, but slowly now he began to dismember himself:

were I to be mute and legless? That, too. But not mute only. Blind, blind also—blind, mute, legless: is life worth living so? Yes, yes, life is worth that. But life without father or mother or brother or beloved or friend or country or sight or legs or voice—all of that: you know what you are doing? Yes, yes, yes—I would give all of that. But then, let it be more—each hour drove him further in the terms—let me be a basket case, a bloody raw torso: no arms, no legs, no sight, no voice, nothing—yes, and let me be placed leaning against a shitted wall in a mud hut on a Siberian waste, let me be propped up there! And I will yet feel the air upon my cheeks, the changing coursing winds of the air; I will sense the changing warmth of the changing sun; I will hear the song and sounds of birds of the earth. The felt sense of air touching my flesh. That fundamental. That far a reduction. Yes, on those terms, asking nothing more. I will settle for life!

And then, at that depth, it had been given back to him. It had taken until the evening of the third day for him to have found the metaphor of exchange—the blind torso in the wind of the Siberian waste—but that evening that he came upon it, an evening of a day he had been delirious, discovering himself suddenly singing aloud, knowing himself close to death, of hunger, of freezing, of sustained shock and exposure, the evening skies had cleared, had become soft and beautiful. As he lay there, a giant hare hopped up to his rising, absurdly detached feet. He placed his paws upon them, reared up, his nose twitching; he hopped nearer, towards the man's chest. He knew he must be near death, the animals seeing him only as earth, unafraid. And then it was, even as he puzzled about the hare, that a giant white bird—he could not remember ever having seen such a large white bird inland, never afterwards would he see such a giant white bird—descended, came down low over him, hovered for a moment, still circling above him, almost within his arm's reach directly above him. Then the bird was gone. Had the hare called down the bird? He could not think. It was before twilight of that day that, by daubing what remained of the unbefouled whiteness of his face and hands and clothing with mud, he escaped from the shell hole in which he had been imprisoned. Reductions.

Who would believe the improbable? And so he never told his story. For two more days he had wandered, crawling, poling himself, staggering on an improvised trellis of crutches behind enemy lines, and when he was finally taken prisoner on the fifth day, it was after miracle after miracle of narrow escapes: spending a night under rubble under a table about which sat a squad of German soldiers, the next morning being confronted but not seen by two machine pistol carrying Germans, and after an old German had forced him to take *him* prisoner.

Prisoner of my own, he thought, imprisoned. It was Admetus who had been jeered at by his father: "You are ingenious; you have hit on a way never to die at all—get each successive wife to die for you." And so Alcestis had died in his place. Euripides had observed that he possessed a memory "that will torment him as long as he lives."

Stephen extricated his arm from Karl, leaving him to his beasts, and reached back to touch his wife's legs. They were unreal, like the ivory legs of a Chinese effigy one brought to the doctor, a surrogate self upon which one might modestly indicate the place of one's pain or ail. His hands blindly explored the alien but attached limbs. It was like a blind torso, a piece of cool mute flesh, lying there propped against him.

Escape from the Shell Hole and Events behind the Lines Preceding Capture and After

———⇒●⇐———

As I went over the paradose of my shell hole, I went on my back, face smeared with mud and facing the sky. I backed myself over the rear edge of the hole, expecting at any moment to be seen and fired upon. It was my elbows that did the work, lifting and moving me away from the field to my left and near my feet—my feet, numb hulks being dragged behind, without feeling or sensation. As I moved up and over, my eyes were striving to see motion on the field, to get a sense of what was there that I was trying to slither from. Once over the higher ridge at the rear of the hole that had been home, I slid backwards fast and down into what I hoped would be a concealing tangle of brush and broken tree limbs, the torn and blasted thicket that once was there. But it wasn't—the shellfire had seen to that—and I lay there feeling almost as exposed and vulnerable as I had on the field after my wounding. Still, there were some branches near, some cover, and I poled myself into it. Once there, I breathed for the first time, waiting, listening, silent and clear. It wasn't much cover, just a veil of dried leaves, not a place to be hidden and hide, but it was away, away from the hole and back into the world.

I lay there unmoving for some while, hardly daring to believe that I had been undetected, unseen. And then, sure it was so, I had to get further, further from the field where *they* were, from where the gunfire had come, and I angled myself away from the field and into an area of still standing brush in those slight woods at whose edge I had been shot, backing, pushing and pulling myself on my back still further into what I took to be shelter. I remember angling towards where the large tree still stood from where one of my buddies had called to me—how many days ago—before he disappeared during the shellfire. Slowly, by small increments I moved, largely impelled by my elbows, until inch by inch I gained the tree and found there nothing to tell of the shellfire and the lost soldier, just fractured branches and scattered tree limbs, the ground hard with upturned broken rocks and frozen earth.

Dragging myself at an angle behind the trunk of the tree, so that I felt I was mostly concealed from observation from the field, I threw back my head and gulped great gulps of air, of cold and frosty and gray and wonderful free air. Not that I was free of danger, or free of anything but the hole in which I had germinated for three days, but I knew I was alive again and coping as I could cope with what was now my new life. All the imperatives were there, to hide again, to conceal myself, to get away from those on the field, to somehow make contact with American troops, wherever they might be—but first, to get somewhere where I could deal with life and death, with where and how I was. I had no direction that told me it was safe, no sure sense of where the lines were drawn, where enemy and where my outfit, and no sense of what kind of aid or help I might find. While in the shellhole, I would have surrendered gladly, if I could have done so safely, but now it was another thing. First, my mind told me that any attempt to surrender was highly dangerous, and that the Germans about me, coming suddenly on a man in my uniform, would hardly be inclined to take me prisoner. Second, I had been given a new lease on life, and I was at the center of my own action, and needing to play out whatever chance I might have to find my buddies, to locate a house, to find a civilian, to find Red Cross or medical personnel, anything but the hard-core German front-line troops, who had, I had judged from sound, been shooting the wounded they had found. And I knew that

I had to try, before nightfall, to find some concealment, some place to again, as in the shellhole, hide.

Behind the Lines

I quickly saw that the woods into whose edge I had crawled when wounded was only a small strip of woods, not more than a few hundred feet wide, if that, and that this narrow strip continued on up a gentle slope of hill in the direction we had been attacking. And it was that way, after I had reached the other side of this brief woods, I went, once I discerned that beyond the woods where I emerged there was only a short strip of grassy open land before it seemed to plunge down towards a ravine, for in the direction where the hill rose slightly, the largely clear and softer grassed area seemed to widen out, becoming a small, very young orchard, recently planted with occasional slender sticks of trees. I, now, cannot understand how I was able to crawl as I did, for there must have been great pain—my elbows having poled me over winter hard-frozen ground and rocks, my hands doing whatever they did. Yes, I was frozen and numb it seemed from my waist down, and my hands were in terrible shape, but I was slowly but methodically and steadily covering this new ground, staying low, almost even with the earth, on my back or on my side, and trying to avoid making any sound. Undoubtedly, I now realize, I was so exhilarated by my "escape" from the shell hole that I would have been unable to feel pain as pain, and had I not been frozen. And so I made my way as I could up towards this widening strip of new orchard.

Within some 80 yards it widened out to include an arc of dirt road that swung back past me and towards the edge of the woods I had passed through and then seemed to loop back—and even as I observed this, I froze with horror at the unmistakable jangle of harness not 30 yards from me, where that loop of dirt road seemed to swing behind near trees. I had long already turned over onto my belly and now my cheek and face were fast against the earth. Immediately with the sound of the harness, there was, near me, just those few yards away, laughter and a joking interchange in German and the sound of horses in traces being backed or moved briefly forward. Lying fixed there, I gradually saw what I took to be a horse-drawn 88 in the edge of the trees, with three men busying themselves with whatever they were doing. They were partially concealed from me, and, for that reason, *deus gratia*, so was I from them. But I lay there like part of the earth I pressed myself against and prayed that they would not move, would not urge the horses ahead on the narrow dirt road, for that would bring them into the open again and nearer to me. And there I lay without cover, out in the open.

It's hard to say how long I waited before I knew that I, without concealment of any kind, had to move again, however dangerous any movement might be, and so I began to ever so slowly inch myself further ahead but angling now into the narrow strip of orchard, and to my left, trying desperately to gain distance and somewhere some place of concealment away from them. Had they looked in my direction, had they moved, I could not but be seen. Now the intensity and the fear and the heightened adrenaline rush of those moments is lost to me. The image of those men moving back and forth behind their horses behind a fringe of trees, talking and occasionally laughing, will be forever with me. I only know that I gradually and ever more quickly slithered forward over frozen grass and ground until I discovered at the left edge of the orchard that very edge of hill falling into ravine that I had earlier abandoned behind me. But now I had no choice. The orchard sticks offered no camouflage or cover, nor did any grass or brush, and I had to commit myself to going over the cliff edge, which was inordinately steep at the edge I came to, descending into what seemed tangled masses of thorn bushes and thicket, a tree-filled hillside with a chaos of dried leaves. I had little command of my body to help me maneuver or go down carefully or with safety, but I let myself go over.

I imagine I believed I could hang onto the soil there, or catch myself immediately and grasp a root, a branch, a rock; I only now remember, however, finding myself in a ditch bordering a road somewhere down that hill, some 200 feet below the upper lip over which I must have sharply fallen, or from where I had obviously come. I do not remember going down the steep slope. I must have immediately lost what little purchase I had and rolled, tumbled, and hurtled down that steepness, perhaps ricocheting from trees and stumps and rocks to finally come to rest like a rag doll in the ditch where I seemed to have awakened. I was probably, by virtue of my frozen and almost unconscious condition, impervious to pain, however my shattered but frozen leg had undoubtedly turned and twisted during my descent—or, was it rather that the pain of my twisting leg had quickly rendered me unconscious, so that I fell or tumbled inert and senseless down that hill. Whatever crashing and breaking and crackling thrashing sounds I must have made must have been absorbed in the consciousness of the Germans as only another German running falling down the mountain, or something they didn't wish or choose to investigate, and perhaps even had themselves hidden from. In any event, here in this ditch I was unable to be seen from the top through the intervening brush and trees except as a mud-mass part of the earth of which I had grown ever more closely part.

I was surprised to find a road beside me, as I had been surprised to find the farm dirt roads above, for whatever information we had been given before battle, it had not prepared me for this network of them here, in what I had been led to believe were to be fields and forests surrounding the forts and bunkers, with an occasional isolated farm. Even as I lay there, regaining the world about me, I was amazed to see directly across the road, the shattered remains of a large and extended broken wooden building, which seemed to be almost like an extended thin barracks. The whole side of it that faced me was, directly across from me, opened up to the outside, with bits of wall and beams and flooring and roof scattered about as though a tornado had ripped it apart. It looked like the aftermath of an exploded woodworking factory that had probably been but recently built, for the wood was unpainted and fresh. Even as I lay there, on my back in the ditch, I felt the probably freezing water beneath me in which I partly lay, and I looked up into tree branches and sky, and assessed the silence about me. I could not tell what of me might be further damaged or broken, but I felt intact. Surely I ached and stung, from new bruises and abrasions—there was fresh blood on my hands from the scraping and scratching gained in my descent, and I had received a hard blow to my side. Wounded in my hands and feet and side, I still really didn't "feel" any of that, largely, I suppose, because I remained

under the pressure of fear and anxiety, still unrelieved, however miraculously still free I seemed. Also, I was distinctly
within an extraordinary "high" of exhilaration at actively
moving, my destiny to some extent in my own hands, and
free from my shell hole of death and rebirth. I was probably
living on adrenaline. Extraordinarily thirsty, I rolled over to
drink deeply from the very medium of my entrapment: wonderfully icy and delicious ditch water.

And then, suddenly, it was all upon me again. From along
the road well beyond the direction of my feet, there were
again voices, someone shouting to someone else, briefly, and
the sound of something being moved or dragged, and then—
and this terrified me—from the other direction on the road as
well, as though approaching along it, sounds of feet striking,
hitting, and voices talking. I, lying in that ditch, had to somehow get away from the road. The ditch and the hill down
which I had fallen gave me no suggestion of safety, but across
the road from me was the opened up disemboweled building,
too destroyed to be occupied, undoubtedly a shellfire casualty
and abandoned. In a moment I had hauled myself up onto the
road by my arms and elbows and, seeing nothing yet in either
direction along it, I quickly slithered across it and down into a
ditch on the other side and up and through and into a tangle
of broken boards and shattered laths and roof and wall fragments. There was the suggestion of where a door had been,
the door itself shattered, and I made my way, hauling my useless legs like a body I dragged behind me, through that destroyed entranceway, and back and further into what was
once the inside of that building. Once partially concealed behind masses of board and broken beams and what had been
crude furniture in what I felt had been a kitchen or dining
area—for there was a large table still standing—I stopped to
intently listen, to know what might be approaching, where
my danger might lie. But now there was no sound, and so,
carefully, very carefully, I hauled myself into an entryway area
beyond that dining area room, a small entryway just long
enough to allow me to lie with my back against a concealing wall that kept me from being seem from the road, and allowed me to extend my legs before me so that my feet rested
braced against an intact door that opened to the back of that
building. And once there, where I felt I was unseen and could

not readily be seen, and in momentary safety, I seem to remember my nerves going crazy, my whole body shuddering
uncontrollably, myself being shaken wildly by an electricity
that controlled me. For how long I shuddered and spasmed
beneath that inner storm I cannot say.

After awhile and in that position I either lapsed from consciousness or fell asleep, for I startled awake—awakened by
what?—only to immediately know myself safer than I had
been but also in total danger of being at any second discovered. It was already dusk, darkening everywhere, and what
would I do for the approaching night, and how would I negotiate my eventual surrender, for surrender I had to—I saw
no alternative to that. I was badly wounded, frozen, perhaps
internally injured beyond my knowing—perhaps I had pneumonia from the days lying in freezing water and mud, for
my chest now ached when I breathed, and there was little or
no feeling in my hands or feet. From my waist down I was a
leaden block. I was, it seemed, in enemy territory, behind
their lines and surrounded on all sides by "them," and there
was really no alternative. Yet I lived in terror within the memory of what I had some days ago now taken for the shooting
of the wounded upon the field, and of what I knew, logically
and certainly, would be the instantaneous reaction of any
German soldier who came upon me. In his position, terrified
of seeing me there deep in their midst, if I were he, I would
fire first and ask questions afterwards.

Now, in time, alive after the events, I see the utterly privileged position I was in: essentially that of a noncombatant,
an unarmed observer "behind their lines." But an observer
in military battledress? Of course, my position was of one
hampered by wounds and attrition, by all the psychological
impedimenta I carried—shell shock and fear, terror and un-
maneuverability. Still, it was privileged. No, I never thought
such thoughts then, and now, I write too glibly. Seeing how
readily the detached perspective gained by these intervening
years can intrude, I here try to bear down, to discipline myself
to remain only within what I felt, what I knew, as I try to picture myself there then. I carefully don't want to falsify now
what were my real emotions then. But how do I, fifty years
after that day, recover "real" emotions, remember anything
accurately enough? As I continue with my tale, I find myself

writing, "Springing my eyes awake, lying there in that entryway, I was undoubtedly in terror of what came next." No. That's false. I really don't know that. I instantly arrest myself in the writing. Is that truly true? I can't say that I lay there in terror, for I cannot, I absolutely cannot remember that it was so. Was I a victim of my fear? I can't remember it as such then, only the earlier very real reality of my fear when under shellfire, the terror of being searched for in the night darkness, the shock of hearing German voices near me when out in the open near the 88. I may have lain there in that entryway in a keen joy of happiness, for being still alive and hidden and away from the shellhole—for having come alive out of death.

We are more animal than we know, and we defend ourselves in intense adversity with diversionary tactics within us that work to guard us from too great fear when there is nothing to be done to allay it. We use sleep as a narcotic, use shock as a painkiller, and we hibernate or retreat as we must—to endure, to stay alive, to continue to function. I remember shortly after I had come up to the line when I slept like a babe deep in my foxhole under a sustained night barrage, so that when I woke in the morning and emerged, it was to a strange and changed landscape about me, branches and trees scattered everywhere or no longer where they had been. This shutting out of the world—when nothing more can be done to further defend oneself—is what the nervous system does to survive; it is also an increment of almost deadly tiredness, nervous exhaustion so deep that, the sentries fixed and nothing to be done but make it through to morning, one dives into sleep as into a cave. And so, to tell the whole truth, I am not sure I can disentangle my relief at escape from the shellhole from my fear of what time was to bring me.

A man running, running, seemingly uphill through dry leaves and branches, and running directly towards the house where I lay, towards the door behind which I had propped myself! In a second, the panic crashing down upon me again. I only had time to brace my back against the wall, to brace my insensate blocks of feet where they were, against the door before me, and "he" was there, rapidly running up what must have been three or four steps leading to the door behind which I lay like some already assumed victim watching a metal mass falling down upon him from the sky. And, his hand on the handle, the door was opening against me. It butted against my rigid boots. It butted and pressed, and butted again—and I watched the knob turning and being turned. There was nothing I could do—I couldn't move my feet if I wished: they were propped and buttressed against the striking weight of the shoulder that I now heard and felt being thrown against the door. It was open, unlocked, but it was blocked. The man on the other side shouted something in German and something again, again tried to throw his weight against the door to force it open, and then he was off, down the steps and running to his left behind the building. He was gone. I was in a terror lest he merely went to circle the building and enter it from the front where I had entered, or elsewhere. But his sounds were gone; he was gone. I don't think I reflected then that it had been my legs and my feet, by means of which I had first been wounded and brought down, that I now was momentarily saved. I listened, I waited, but he had given up finding what he wished to readily find where I was. My terror, however, was real and remaining, for I saw that the building was not abandoned despite its state, and that he, whoever he was, had expected to enter or to find someone there, or to pass through.

But where to go, where to hide? I could no more risk crawling out into the open. It was already late and towards nightfall, and it was freezing, and he or "they" might appear at any time. I had to find someplace to hide, anywhere, anyhow, until morning. But where, in that building? Remembering the great pile of boards and timber in the first room, I dragged myself quickly there. No, the noise I would make moving and arranging and building a cave of fractured and broken pieces of wood could not be risked. And then I saw that the large table there against the back wall of that room was almost completely stocked and blocked beneath by litter, by a great mass of what I saw were wood shavings and small odds and ends of wood, as though someone in a woodworking factory had swept up the refuse of the lathes and saws and, like a lazy housekeeper, simply pushed it beneath the table. It was almost solid and tabletop high beneath with this detritus. I had no recourse. He might be back at any moment, or others might come. Quietly as I could, I pulled and dragged clear some common chairs that were inexplicably still standing against and under the table and dragged the "stuff" away to reveal, entangled in it beneath, a table length reinforcing strut that ran from end to end. I pulled out all the refuse I could that had been shoved against the wall, and keeping within reach all this mass of sticks and pieces, of sawdust and shavings, of small boards—a garbage pail mass of thrown away remnants of wood—I crawled beneath the fortunately long table. Pressing myself beneath the crossbar so that, lifting and constricting myself, I was able to get to its other side and against the wall, I from there reached back and drew in upon me and over me, carefully covering myself and mounting up a great mass of stuff over my feet, the majority of what I had originally displaced, and then I reached back and out to draw nearer in the chairs. In all my fear of detection, as I moved and unavoidably made sounds, I remember noting that it was freezing and I was suffering at least as much from cold as from fear.

How assiduously, how carefully and systematically and hastily I worked, and how quietly, to hide the sounds of rustling and scraping—which must have been undoubtedly as from some burrowing animal—as I drew my cave in and upon me. I am sure I recognized that I was almost replicating the work I had done when I had drawn in over me the branches and brush I could gather to hide myself in my shellhole. Now, the sawdust and woodshavings were my first and best concealment, but were simultaneously becoming almost immediately an encasing covering to keep me warm. And upon this mat, made as thick as I could with what I had and could reach, I had dragged the laths and boards and sticks and pieces of sawed and broken wood, building these up high as a defensible wall against the exposed outer side of the table.

Having been able to do all this without further incident, I now sophisticated what I had, arranging a head and neck pillow of stuff, and a specially carefully contrived mask of refusewood for my head. And there, at last, exhausted, I lay, more warm, more concealed, than I had been since being wounded, to try to survive till morning, when, with another and new day, I would be able to see what could be done. It was already night when I finished, and I slept.

My eyes flashed open, for there they were again—voices, Germans coming down the road in the night and towards the building. They were casually talking, though with guarded tones; I could hear them but not understand, and they came down and—horror!—at the broken opening of my building through which I had initially dragged myself, they turned and began to mount and haul themselves through that same tangled mass of wood: and into the hall—Now! Now!—and into the room where I lay! I was frozen, shocked, rigid with the shock of fear. I could not breathe.

They came directly to my table—as though they knew I was there, they knew!—and threw on it what they must have been carrying, their guns, heavy guns, and packs, talking meanwhile quietly to one another. Their tones told me of their security—for they talked low but steadily in the ordinary rhythms of a natural and unalarmed conversation, guarded but subdued. As I could tell, there were two of them, and they had come deliberately and without hesitation apparently straight to that table—my table!—as though they knew where they were going, familiar with what they would find there. And I lay frozen in terror, unbreathing, my entire body one rigid length of shock. One of them pulled out one of my defensive chairs—it seemed my whole body must have jerked back at this rupture of my concealing outer wall—and then the other dragged the other chair away from its place where it sealed me in and towards the far end near my feet. And they sat down, their feet in heavy boots striking and pressing in my remaining wall upon me and against me. This was especially true of the one who sat at the broad side of the table near the center of my body. They must know! They would know! In any second they would surely know! The resistance of the wood pieces and shavings and my body behind them against their pressure would tell them! I could not cry out, I could not cry "Pity!" and "I surrender!" and "Help me!" "Spare me!"— for I knew that my slightest movement would throw them into a panic of terrified and violent response. To be heard, to move, would mean my death.

And, sustained now, my shock went into a locked tension and tautness of my whole body, so that I did not—could not!—breathe, could not afford to breathe. A movement, the slightest movement, would undo me. Any slightest vibration was unthinkable. I lay as one dead, and I learned in that darkness that one did not need to breathe, that one could suspend oneself as though encased in glass, locked in iron, that breathing itself could be suspended.

They didn't know I was there! Their boots butted against me—or rather, the wall of stuff between me and them—and occasionally they seemed to strike the strut that divided where I lay from them—but they were unalarmed, and their conversation went on, sporadic and occasional, or sustained, with soft banter and light joking, interspersed with a lighting of a cigarette, the drinking from a canteen they took out and drank from and set back on the table between them. So I read the sounds above me and upon me. The one sitting nearest me seemed to take out some bread and unwrap some cheese, cut from it with a clasp knife, and then share it with his companion. So my imagination read sounds and words.

I could get fragments only of conversation—it was only high school German I had to hear with—and I got only words here and there, for they seemed to talk in a heavy dialect I could not follow. But words leapt out, this one and that, and they seemed to have settled back into a waiting, lingering relaxation. But what did they wait for? Were they merely passing the night? Were they on guard duty along the road? Did they come here each night now? But the battle lines had changed, yet this was their territory, their building. Maybe that explained why the table was standing and the chairs— they had come here before—it was they who had swept the refuse of the room where I found it, they who had given me this very armor in which I was so vulnerably encased; and they had come as though to an assignation, directly to it, and knew they could sit here and pass the time. The one nearest me, crossing his feet, slammed into me, or rather into my still unpenetrated wall, and then withdrew. Surely, had he been there before, he might know the difference between what his feet now struck and what had been there! I lay as one already dead.

Time passed, and they fell into silences, and even seemed to lean forward upon the table above me and doze. But they were ever quickly then shifting and stirring—rummaging in a pack?—exchanging a phrase or two, and then subsiding. I lay as one dead. They murmured this or that, and then, again, seemed to sit back up, and at one moment the more verbal one, the one seemingly in more charge, pushed back his chair, stood up—I was instantly in a panic of hysterical tension! but

I lay as one dead—and walked back towards and to the entry-way through which he had come, seemingly to just stand there and listen. And after a while, he returned and resumed his seat, with commentary on someone else, and "they," and being late—"spät"—that I could make out. Then, there would be others, they were truly waiting for someone or others!

I lay as one dead.

After what seemed another hour, during which I was sev-erally kicked and pushed and butted with their feet, there were sounds along the road where they had come, and some-one came down the road and, at the building, turned and en-tered as though coming home. I thought he called out "Kurt" and the one who had listened for this arriveé grunted an ac-knowledgment. The newcomer entered the room and spoke and the three exchanged queries and answers and informa-tion which I could not follow—this time the speech brought the two who had companioned me through part of the night back and up from their chairs, shouldering packs, to packing up, scraping their guns and whatever from the table. I felt as though my very skin was being torn away and exposed, I felt seen and vulnerable as I had not before, now with the chairs back and all three now standing near in the dark room. But then, they were gone, apparently in file moving back out and into the street and down the road in the direction they had been going.

I lay as one dead.

And then it was, again, as before, after the essential and real danger had passed, that my whole body became un-controllable, and shook and shuddered and spasmed. I was unable to either discipline or stop the electrical surges of cur-rent that coursed through my nervous system: I simply was shaken and shaken, again and again and again and again and sustainedly, by my nerves no longer under my control. I cannot tell how long it was before this mastery of me by a short-circuit in my nerves began to subside, and then lessened to allow intervals and spaces of rest between the extreme shocks, which left me exhausted. And how long before I again slept, dark in that nightcave, slept deep and darkly and pro-foundly.

Then, it was morning. How late into the morning I could not say, but when I awoke, there was the light seeping and slashing through my cover, and when I slowly moved away this or that to be able to see, there was a blaze of sunlight in the opened sky of that roof-blasted room and out in the area of the street that I could observe from where I lay, and for a while I reclined unmoving, thinking, trying to acknowledge my survival through to this new and other day, and preparing to understand what I must do and what could now be done. All right. This would be it. This day would see me through to escape or imprisonment. I was filled with a strangely luxurious and wonderful energy, one that was not in any way accompanied by fear but rather by anticipation. And I was hungry. I was starved! I was ravenous, dying of hunger. Almost literally, this must have been true, because from the moment of my wounding until this moment I had had only one package of orange Lifesavers to eat. Lifesavers! Indeed. (I would never pass them in a store or on a stand again without a feeling of complicity and intimacy towards them.) But now I had to eat. I HAD to eat. But what? Where? How? I had to drink, I had to find food, and these imperatives seemed to have wiped away whatever fear I had of whatever enemy. Perhaps my several miraculous survivals had at last gifted me with a sense of invulnerability, of immortality, of strength, however weak and ravaged and injured I really was. To have survived the night under the conditions in which I passed it must have argued in me somewhere for my ability to meet whatever emergency, to confront whatever situation. And to confront it without fear! Without fear! That's how I felt. Totally unafraid and anxious to get going into this final day—for I knew it could not go on: this day would see the end of it all, one way or another. And I didn't worry! I really knew "it would be all right."

God, what a glorious day! As I threw back my blanket of wood, as I pushed open an opening back out and into the world and crawled like a grub emerging from a chrysalis out into life, it was with exultation and even—now!—a feeling that I did not need to be careful. I was no longer attentive to sounds, concealing as I might my every move. I simply emerged and pulled myself up to a chair there in that damaged destroyed room, meeting the shining day with joy! It was a glorious day. Sunlight poured down outside. It seemed warm, like a spring day. I felt I could walk if I had to, I felt I could sing if I dared. I wanted FOOD.

Where? I studied the room or remnant of a room in which I found myself. The table beneath which I had successfully concealed myself seemed now, by day, so ineffectual, so vulnerable, so improbable. I was sitting where one of them had sat and it seemed a place of power, a vantage that loomed over that insignificant space beneath in which I had lain. With my winding sheet and its wrappings scattered now, with the walls pushed back and rolled away, I found myself feeling more like a victor than a victim, and, disarmed, more like one armed for combat. But the hunger! The thirst! And I studied the room and the building it was part of. What I had not considered when I entered was that the building extended well beyond the room and along the road along which my night's visitors had come. When I crawled into it the night before, I had needed rest, reprieve, and concealment so badly that I had grasped at whatever presented itself: the tabled room I first entered and the entryway. Now, by daylight and sitting up, I could see that the room was indeed attached to and part of an extending building, that to the right of the main entryway through which I had crawled—to the left as I now viewed it— but also beyond a great clutter of boards and timbers reaching down from the ceiling to almost mask it, there was a destroyed but maneuverable hall which led down the building. It would take me deeper into the building, and somewhere in it I might find something. It might also hide me better than the opened room in which I sat. I lowered myself to the floor and slithered to the large mass of boards and broken wood that almost masked the now revealed hallway.

Could I stand? Could I prop myself up? I wanted to be on my feet, however insensate and numb and unfunctional they were. Quickly searching among the boards, I found several about armpit high, and a few of these were broken or cut at an angle to be wider at one end than the other. I took one of these latter in hand and then hauled myself up, and up some more, and still up again by grasping boards radiating down from the shattered ceiling. I was standing. What an immense rush of giddiness and vertigo, what a reeling and then finally stabilizing of sensations. And what an exultant rush of joy and delight, to be standing erect in the image of a resurrected man, functional. Or almost. At least myself standing, and observing from my own level a world that was confrontable, meetable, engagable. Quickly now, I placed the straight wider edge of the crutch I had selected under my armpit and, grasping parts of wall and jutting boards, explored the possibilities of my feet. They—my whole legs—were like blocks of stone attached to my hips, but I could alternately move my feet, swing my feet, forward. If my leg was badly broken, there was no pain in it, for there was no feeling. I moved, however, slowly forward, hopping and propping myself as I went, through what had been a doorway into what was another hall beyond it, one with intact roof and ceiling, a verifiably intact part of the structure.

What a rat's nest! As I came to a small side room and then another, I saw that the whole was a building where the insides had been tumbled out and strewn about as though by a cyclonic ravaging force. Nowhere in its extent, however, was it smashed and broken as it had been in the part I had entered the night before. I could see that the first two rooms I came to had been lived in but old bureaus and small tables and metal bed frames were tumbled upon one another, with the paper and cloth contents of drawers lying helter skelter everywhere. I was, however, intent upon food, and my one thought was that there might be some sort of kitchen or pantry or cooking area in the ravaged building. Therefore, I did not explore these disastrous contents of rooms off the main hall that I came to but rather made my way as I was able, replacing boards I used as crutches for others whenever I came across any that suggested an improvement on the last. Finally, a plank of door with an attached handle at just the right advantageous height gave me a crutch-hold for my hand, and I could move my strut about with ease and swing myself upon it. Explored, the building offered no kitchen or pantry and there was no food of any kind.

I retraced my hops and swings, to look with greater care at what I had bypassed. Again rooms littered and hastily abandoned. With an extraordinary leisure I picked up great numbers of letters, opened an unopened highboy drawer, and found more letters, as well as stamps, and I was shocked to see they were mostly in Russian. I never did determine what the building had been for but my first impression was that it had housed Russian workers, perhaps prisoners from Russia who had been forced to work in the forts or on the roads. I

now let myself wonder if, rather, it had housed a Russian outfit that had fought with the Germans on the Russian front. In
any event, whatever ravaged parts of clothing or uniforms
were there, I could draw no conclusions, nor was my concern
one that would let me explore such arcane questions.

Then, while rummaging on a bureau, there it was—black
gold. An almost totally black frozen remnant of an age-old
potato lay there in the litter. It was smaller than a baseball
in size and unmistakable. I tore at its outside blackened coat.
There was only further blackness flaking beneath, and I broke
inwards, looking for something edible, anything there. As it
opened, at its very center was a small area, about as big as a
penny, of whiteness, whiteness that quickly darkened down
to the blackness that had taken over. I remember devouring
that cent of food and trying to eat outwards as far as I could,
until it was just like eating pure ash. But how wonderful that
first act of eating, that potato, divine potato, which I ate until
I revolted my stomach. The world would provide!

Feeling luxurious in freedom and without any of the con-
straining fear of the days before—perhaps because so far that
morning I had heard, despite my own activity, no sounds of
Germans in the vicinity—I hopped over towards a door that
seemed, at this end of the building, to open upon the same
street that it fronted. I threw back the door and the bright
wash of all the wonderful alive world poured in over me. It
was a blessed and glorious world! And I stood there drinking
in great gulps of temperate, fresh clean air, standing in the
doorway with the street just a step down before me. It was as
though I had thrown off my cerements and grave clothes and
now stood alive and revealed in the outer wild air.

And suddenly it happened. There, not ten yards to my
left was a German soldier striding down the street towards
me. I instantly saw the machine pistol cradled in his arm, and
around his neck the shield of the Waffen SS—I saw everything with total clarity. I had no time to move, to say anything, to lurch back. He was THERE! UPON ME! and I simply
stood in that doorway, frozen and immobile. And he strode
right up to me—and BY ME!! I could have reached out with
my hand and touched his shoulder! I was there, now erect,
life-size, totally revealed to the street and his world—and
he MOVED STEADILY RIGHT BY ME!!!! How? How could it

happen? I stood there watching him go on past and down the road beyond me. He MUST have seen me. He could not *not* have seen me! But it was as though I had been utterly invisible, unseeable. He had walked towards me, up to me and by me, and I had stood exactly beside him and widely visible in the opened doorway. I was certainly as shocked by the circumstance of his NOT seeing me as by my sudden fear upon seeing him. He was there, and then—NOW!—he was gone, on down the road.

I had no way of explaining it. I thought of the hare that had placed his feet upon my knee, not distinguishing me from the earth in which I lay. Was I now so mud-smeared, so totally no longer a living human thing, that I had become part of nature, unnoticed and indistinguishable within my surroundings? The events of the night before undoubtedly also worked to make me feel unnoticeable, not there! How could this have happened? Was it all dream life in which I moved, no more real to others than the air I breathed and addressed? I was shocked vividly more than awake.

I somehow knew now what I would do. I would swing myself down that road towards where he had come from, the direction of Metz, and walk down it until I came to others like him or whatever. I could no longer hide in ditches or shellholes, lie under tables and starve and freeze further. I would declare myself in the open, and there—what better place than in the middle of a road, defined and fully seen?—be available for discovery and capture. I had no doubt that had he seen me as he should have, as he certainly could not but see me, but there standing in a doorway in an American uniform, his startled reaction with that machine pistol in his hand, would be to shoot, an instantaneous defensive response. But, if he had had time to see me distantly, to consider me, to reflect upon my being there, obviously without gun and on crutches, that would be another thing. I was quickly down and into the road and slowly lurching, hopping, swinging down it towards where it was bordered by woods on the ascending hill to its right and by falling off hillside and trees to its left. I abandoned behind me the shell and carapace of the broken frame form from which I had emerged. I carry with me an image of myself, standing tall and distinctly light surrounded, however mud daubed, in that doorway on this eternal bright morning.

And OH! the air was singing! The sunlight was warm on my shoulders and the day was wonderful! I was—strangely! incredibly!—alive and well and behind German lines and without fear, able to move and reflect and consider and, in the midst of what should have been ongoing tension and terror, be aware of the wonder and glory of life. Everything about me was radiant and wonderful. There was a relaxation within me that I had not felt since well before we had gone into attack, since behind our own lines, and I attributed it to the multiple escapes, which must have provided me with a sense of invulnerability. Now, looking at it more soberly, I imagine I was lulled by these "miracles" into a false sense of security, which realistically could have been smashed at any instant with a bullet or grenade. Surely the very alertness and tension which had been partially responsible for the "miracles" was now off guard, and I was as a result probably more vulnerable now than I had ever been—for, despite the appearance of the German in the road that morning, I was not, I know, as concerned to listen, to hear every scrape of wind, every far rip of gunfire, every distant echo. I was appreciating and glorying in every alive sense, in every drawn breath, in every movement of my body, in every beautiful surface and texture of tree or road or hill. But I was less attentive to my enemy.

Moving along the road, I came to where the open spaces and the ditch ended and where the trees began to edge the way, and I immediately noted how these were wired and prepared to be dropped at any moment across that road. Around the girth of almost every second one here at the beginning of the bordering trees were tape-attached explosive charges. Most of these were unfamiliar to me, but among them were occasional rings of grenades, with a lead wire leading to each ropepull, as in the case of the German stick grenades, and to each ringpull attached to cotter pin, as in the case of the American fragmentation grenades I also saw about some trees. These last undoubtedly had been captured and liberated from us and were now being used against us. I was intrigued, wondering just to where and how far the lead wires led that were reaching back up the hill and into the woods. Alternative lead wires, that could have had their free ends attached by night, were now, in open day simply lying in coils by their trees and probably meant to be by night strung across the road where they might be anchored to what trees were there. It looked as though this whole arrangement was rigged to drop the trees across the road should a vehicle or anything try to advance up or descend that road in darkness. My weather and ordeal injured hands were mute paws, and could not untie the wires, and I was too dizzily unsteady on my rigged crutches to balance myself to dismantle the armed trees, and I ineffectually tried to pry loose grenades from beneath their taped ties. There was, however, a species of joy in my attempts to arm myself and to disarm their trap.

I continued on down the narrow dirt road that, after the trees, began to slowly descend the hill, the trees on the right giving way to a steep and steeper bank leading up an increasingly steep forested slope. On the left the road also more steeply fell off. I was slowly and awkwardly, on my improvised crutches and my frozen legs, descending the mountain in a very gentle curve that swung around its flank to the right. A small culvert ditch began again on the right, the trees thickened. I listened to the occasional and never-ending battle elsewhere, I listened to the wind and for what might be near. I sang in my heart.

I am not sure just how far I had gone—certainly not half a mile—when suddenly, out in front of me, rearing up like a dark shadow from the culvert-ditch, was a man before me. He simply was there, rising like a silent utterly dark apparition before me, his hands, one holding a rifle, thrown above his head in the air. "Bitte! . . . Bitte! . . . Bitte!" he was saying. "Bitte!" while waving the gun above him, his other hand now wildly shaking in silhouette. I also had thrown my hands to either side, instinctively leaning my weight onto my crutches. I so placed my weight while extending my hands as I could to either side, gesturing their emptiness and harmlessness. And there we stood, like two absurd and phantom icons confronting each other, trying to emblematize our helplessness and our farewell to arms. He lowered his gun horizontally across his body and stiffly held it out in front of him towards me. "Bitte!" He kept saying. He was giving me his gun, offering me his gun. It was fantastic. It was hard for me to understand, hard to accept. It was too hysterically absurd. Here was I, wounded and propped up on makeshift crutches, barely able to stand erect, and here was this tall German in uniform trying to surrender to me. Again, he pleaded, "Bitte!"

and practically placed his gun in my hands. I reached instead for my crutch handle to take the weight off my arms, and his hands were instantly again waving wildly above his head.

I could see that he was old, surely too old for combat duty, an old ragged German in heavy coat and looking the worse for wear, desperately asking to be taken prisoner. I lowered my hands towards my sides and, as I did so, he sprang back, throwing his hands and gun again over his head. No! No! I again showed him my extended-to-my-sides empty hands, and he once more lowered his hands, but now shoved his gun out before him and this time actually placed it in my hands. "Bitte!" he said. He was insisting that I, wounded as I was and on my improvised crutches, should take him prisoner. For a moment, leaning my weight on my crutches, I took his gun in my hands and held it, considering my possibilities, my options, perhaps enjoying momentarily my ironic role as captor, and then, somewhat reluctantly, I gave his gun back to him:

"Nein. Nein. Ich habe kein Gewähr. Ich bin verwundert. Ich kann nichts. Ich bin ein Amerikanische Soldat aber ich bin verwundert und kann nichts mit sie tun. Ich bin hier allein. Ich kann sie nicht eine Gefangene machen." [No. No. I have no gun. I am wounded. I can't do anything. I am an American soldier but I am wounded and can do nothing with you. I am here alone. I can't take you prisoner.]

[Throughout this account I will use the sort of German, the high school German, I still have, as I imagine I used it. I am not concerned for either grammatical or orthographic correctness—for, surely, nothing I said was correct—only with approximating what I must have said, or what (I imagine in my German) I heard the Germans say. It is interesting, at seventy, to still have this remnant German, really untutored since I then used it in 1944.]

I could immediately see I had failed him. A great sadness and weariness overcame him, now the danger of the moment seemed over, and I was proven to be helpless, but worse, useless to him. He had undoubtedly dreamed, his every reluctant and compelled absurd moment at the front, of a chance he might have to somehow surrender. He had, even as I, feared and desperately hoped for that possibility, and when it came, when he finally met his "American captor," his rescuer, it was a useless broken-legged wounded "enemy." I was no use to him.

I tried to console him with a steady patter of reassuring sounds. I was not in the least dangerous, I could do nothing to him, or for myself, really. I had been wounded on the hill some days before and now I needed food and medical attention. Could he help me, help me!

He was undoubtedly supremely startled by my German. [Thank God for Frau Scott, my wonderful German teacher! Had it been anyone but she I would never have gained anything like a serviceable high school use of a foreign language.] And he made the usual mistake: assuming that I spoke perfect German because of the few words I knew that I had carefully moved into simple patterns, he relaxed in a voluble outburst, from which I gained just about nothing. But he guided me on my crutches back to the ditch culvert where he had been sitting and where he had his pack. It was his outpost, and he led me to know that he could do nothing for me now, could not really take me prisoner, but that others, several others—this for his protection?—would be along soon, soon, and I would be all right. He helped me down to sit beside him in his ditch. Food? Food? Did he have something, anything to eat? He opened his canteen—my God, he had coffee, hot coffee. He had also black bread. I drank what must have been vile and raw coffee as though it was life itself; I finished his canteen; I tore at his bread and wolfed it down: ravenous maw and ravenous claws. My God! My God! How good!

After a while, during which I ate and he sadly stared at me in bewilderment as though I were some Martian come to earth, he offered me a cigarette. "Danke vielmals." And I drew the smoke deeply into my lungs, drinking it, too, like the air, like the water that had returned me to life. "They" would be along soon, he repeated. Then, groping in his pocket, he drew out a much worn wallet and, rooting in it, extracted pictures: this was his wife; and these, his children. I admired. When he tried to gain from me from where I had come, and I explained, back along the road, and that I had been wounded in the battle some days before, he could not comprehend. He gestured towards the hill above us and into the woods, assuring me that I was mistaken, that I had come from there. I assured him no, but he kept gesturing there, to tell me I was from the Amerikaner who were there! There? This was my first inkling that my American buddies, those who had made it through the first day's battle without being killed or wounded or captured, had somehow made it to this mountain/hill and had here joined up, linked up, and were actually there now and on this hill above me and had been there surrounded as a unit from the first day on. But I did not understand this then and what he was implying and let him say what he might say.

It was a great relief, an enormous weight lifted, to be a prisoner, but I still looked forward apprehensively to the arrival of "the others" he promised. This was partly because he made himself so negligible, of so little account, as though it was not up to him to be able to take me prisoner—my problem was not yet fully solved!—that he could not do such things, that the "others" would. Or wouldn't? Despite his reassuring presence, there was still a worry, an apprehension as I waited with him. And, with a brief preceding announcement of their presence, "they" were there, coming up to the road from the slope below, hoisting themselves onto the road and gaping at the two of us together there, like two irreconcilable figures of speech locked in an ungrammatical bond. I use the simile to best express our gutter garbled language and the Mutt and Jeff figure we presented: he an old ragged grizzled captor, I a young wounded prisoner or pseudo prisoner. I saw that he instantly had prepared a face to meet them, gesturing and almost swaggering to show off his "prisoner" he had "taken prisoner"—should I tell them how he had surrendered to me? They, five of them, were grim, and remarkably uncommunicative. They simply listened and watched, with suspicion and distrust. They undoubtedly distrusted his story, and couldn't see how it had happened, how he had got hold of me. And then, seeing my "crutches" and learning of my wound, they were more skeptical. How had I gotten there, gotten, so wounded, so far? My being wounded also reduced his bravado and made everything seem less plausible.

I was becoming more worried by the moment. They were younger, two of them only boys, another an obviously reluctant conscript, but the two others the sort of hardened line soldier I distrusted instantly—and they distrusted me. His assurance of my German didn't help at all, even seemingly made them more uneasy. All right, I was there, but what did that mean? What should they do with me? The discussion that went on was one to keep me on trigger edge, intently observing, watching every expression and response with genuine apprehension. The one in charge, surely a battle-seasoned veteran, a sergeant, led the discussion and planning for what was to be done with me. All right, they wouldn't take me back up the road, but down, down to somewhere. Even as they were talking to me, they were again and again glancing anxiously up the hill and into the woods above them, as though alert for something. They were anxious to get away from there and, I could see, contemptuous of my captor and his genial attempt to get them to see that I was a prize, a something to have captured. I was grateful for his attempt to assure them that I was harmless and a good boy, but they didn't especially see it that way.

At the sergeant's signal, I was helped out of the ditch, in which I had, crutch assisted, stood as they arrived, and back up and onto the road. Now, the two younger ones, the boys, assisted me as they could, as we slowly made our way downwards along the road towards its next bend. My un-happy captor, who had undoubtedly hoped to be relieved of his guard duty, was left in place where they had found us, and with hardly an acknowledging farewell. I, however, had genuinely and warmly thanked him—for his kindness, for his food and drink, for having attentively overseen my first hour as prisoner. The others had perhaps with disgust or ap-prehension looked on. The sergeant indicated to me that we were going to go down—here!—over the left lip of the road and down a steep slope through scattered trees and towards a cleared field that I could see lying on the hillside below. And over we went, with three of them lifting me to make the descent possible, to protect my leg, to help me. My "crutches" would be of no more use—they were thrown aside and left there at the road's edge. I reluctantly glanced farewell to those lovely boards that had helped bring me back into the world.

They were good at carrying and aiding me—whether propped between two with my arms over their shoulders, or lifted by one or another, and we went down the hill through the diminishing trees. At the edge of the field we briefly halted while they discussed the best way; then we started, angling down and across, I being swung between two of them. On an instant there was a crackling rip of gunfire and the thunk of bullets around us, and all six of us were face down in the dirt. We were being fired on and bullets were striking about us. And they were coming from above, from back up the hill we had just left, where I had left my captor. It was crazy. The Germans were firing on the Germans and on me! The sergeant ordered the others to go fast across and we all, made equals under this fire, hugged the ground, groping for cover in an impossible situation where there was no cover—not being fired on as we were from above. Four of my five, one after another, and in short and longer rushes, took off for safety on the other side, one of them additionally carrying the sergeant's rifle. The sergeant remained with me. "Those are yours"— "Deiner" or "Ihrer"—he said. "Yours!" Mine? How could that be possible? Not where we were, and not from up there. "Yours!" he assured me, to establish the responsibility and blame, to let me know how I was implicated in their danger. "Then go!" I said. "Go. Go on across . . . Sie wollen mir nicht schiessen. They won't shoot me. I'll follow. I can get across after you. Go! Go!" "I can crawl. I can make it. . . . Ich kann es machen."

"Was denkst du? Das wir sind Tieren? Niemals, niemals sollen wir ein Verwundete oder eine Gefangene so lassen. Niemals! " It was something like this that he said, in contempt and in pride—there, there under still occasional fire: a wonderful speech under fire!—". . . So, they tell you we are animals, are barbarians. But we never leave a wounded man or a prisoner alone under fire on a field of battle." That was the gist of it. All of that pouring out of him in an almost insane burst of self justification and pride and anger. And he quickly rolled me onto my side and in one movement into a sitting position from which he slung me onto his back, and he was off across the field, running heavily. We were down and then up twice more before we were across, each time he swinging me expertly and easily onto his back for the run. We were finally across it with the others and all safe, and now probably out of range. The only way I can account for the bad shooting—it must have been like shooting at fish in a barrel— is to suppose, if they were my buddies shooting, they were trying to avoid hitting me and trying to scare off the Germans, scare them into abandoning me, one of their own being taken prisoner. I was still bewildered about their whereabouts and how they conceivably could have been shooting at us from what I had taken to be German positions.

On the other side of the field the others were waiting, and although we were undoubtedly "safe" now, they were crouched among sheltering stumps of trees bordering a large ditch and a hedgerow. At the sergeant's orders three of them flung themselves over the hedgerow, and then he and the other, without a word to me, hoisted me and passed me to the hands of the others on the other side. Then, we were all there on the other side, sitting in the dirt road, that must surely have been the one I had been on above, it having now by a circuitous route circled the waist of the mountain and dropped down to where I now saw I was, on a relatively flat and easily descending hillside of young orchards and vineyards sloping towards a road and a river at its foot. We sat on the sun-warmed earth and leaned back against the solid mass of earth and roots at the foot of the hedgerow. They took out cigarettes and lit up, offering me one, which I took. "Lucky for you your comrades are such bad shots," one said. I tried to thank the sergeant, "Danke!" but he refused my word with contempt. Everyone smoked silently, while we listened to the far thumping and whumping and ripping tearing sounds of battle in the direction of Metz, with its interspersed sporadic points of rifle fire. It was for us a moment out of war—sunlight, soft air with blue skies above, the plowed fields and tended orchards and vineyards of peace around us, the pungent acrid tobacco in our throats, the smoke drifting up.

"Nahh?" The sergeant stood up, they all stood up, hauling me to my feet, and began to buckle up. One asked their leader "Wo?" and he gestured with his head towards a field and young orchard hard on the other side of the road. I was slung again between two of them, and we, in a straggled group went on down the road to where an opening appeared in the matted tall hedgerow on the other side of the lane. Into this we turned, where the indentations of car and wagon tracks had made a primitive orchard road, and we moved on it and along it to the right towards what I saw was again a young, relatively new orchard. As we entered this, suddenly ahead were large numbers of soldiers, lying about—at least a company on break. But we continued forward, angling towards what I saw must be a field set-up, with table and chairs and a field telephone—what must have been the C.P.—near which stood two tall well uniformed men, undoubtedly officers, smoking. As we had made our obvious way through the orchard, groups of soldiers had attached themselves to us, exchanging some words with my captors, or joining us as we advanced. Here was an American, captured and being brought in. As we neared the heart of the matter, one of the officers broke off and advanced on us, and as he did so, my captors no longer half carried me but stopped and, half supporting me where I stood, awaited his command.

"Warum haben sie Ihn nicht geschiessen?!" [Why didn't you shoot him?] The words cut through like a knife, and I was chilled to the bone. Without waiting for my captors to irresolutely or indecisively reply, perhaps sensing that this officer was different stuff and was not to be trifled with, I myself took my fate into my own hands. Reaching back into whatever high school German I had, desperately reaching for articulateness in the midst of my ignorance, I blurted out, directly to him, "Denn si können das night tun. Es gibt die Genevische Conventionen, und ich bin ein Kreigsgefangene und verwundet, and ich habe kein Gewähr. Ich benutze Hilfe, Medezin, und, bitte, etwas zu essen. " [Because you can't do that. There are the Geneva Conventions, and I am a prisoner of war, and wounded, and I have no gun. I need help, medical help, and, please, something to eat.] All this improbable speech poured out. Undoubtedly, there was method in my madness—for I wanted to impress him with my value, as a person, as a human being, as someone who could communicate and arbitrate the conditions of my capture, as someone who understood the situation and could discuss it. After what he had said, I simply wanted, I suppose, to immediately seize the moment, to direct it away from the fate he had suggested. Perhaps I somewhere understood that in verbalizing this in this way before the crowd of my captors and the others, I could win support and create sympathy and embarrassment, and in some way cease to be unnecessary baggage and be a person. "Warum haben sie Ihn nicht geschiessen?" It still rang in my ears, like the death it told of.

He studied me, while the other officer came up and joined the group, and in that moment I studied him. I could see that for the first time in my life I was confronting an SS officer—I read the dual red lightning bolts upon his lapel. He was everything powerful that the "Why We Fight" films had warned me of, and he met the image I had been given. He was in his thirties, meticulously dressed for someone "at the front," and manicured and polished in his manner, icy in his rigor. And yet I had, I saw, impressed him, intrigued him. "So . . . you speak German?" "Ja, ich habe ein bischen in Hoch-Schule studiert. Nur das." [Yes. I have studied it a little in high school. Only that.] "Nur das?" he echoed, and then, cajoling me, "aber es ist *parfait!* Sie sprechen gut Deutsch." I wasn't going to let this become an "after you Alphonse" exchange of pleasantries masking malice, so I refused the denial and instead continued, "Ich habe ein bischen in Universität auch studiert, und dafür kann ich mit sie etwas sagen." I lied. I hadn't studied German at Princeton, where I had gone for one semester before being drafted, but I was reaching for all the straws I could grasp to draw him away from his first idea. I was shamelessly appealing to his snobbery, to that sense in him I might stimulate that indeed we could talk together. I was trying to snare his curiosity and his interest.

And it worked. By God, it worked. I watched the exchange of a glance and a smile he gave the other officer. The group of soldiers about us was thick but I think he and I now never took our eyes off one another. Slowly he articulated, mocking me, "Die Ge-ne-vi-sche Conventionen! Aber es gibt keine hier! Hier ist Krieg. Wir sind ins Mitte des Kreigs. Verstehst??" [But there are none here! Here there is war. We are in the middle of a war. Do you understand?] I had to continue where I had begun. To lapse now and leave the initiative to him might be fatal. "Nein. Hier sind wir ins Mitte eine Feld an die Grenze, und ich bin sicher deine Kriegsgefangene." [No. Here we are in the middle of a field on the border of a war and I am certainly your prisoner of war.] He was back at me, "Es gibt keine Grenze in Krieg." [There are no borders in war.] And I was back at him: "Wir können unser Grenze selbst machen. Hier." [We can make our own borders. Here.] And his repart was immediate, "Und hier können wir unser Krieg selbst machen. Auch!" [And here we can ourselves make our own war. Also.] Perhaps trying to shift the basis of our exchange and give me greater leeway, I sidestepped, "Aber sie können

Englisch vieleicht sprechen, besser als ich Deutsch?" Nein,"
he demurred, "Ihrer Deutsch is gut genug." [But perhaps you
can speak English, better than I can speak German? No. Your
German is good enough.] From the way he was enjoying our
exchange, I knew that I was, I would be, probably, finally safe
from him.

With his last remark, he turned from me, took his fellow
officer by the arm and stood there, facing away and talking to
him. They were discussing my fate, and I knew it. Meanwhile,
the crowd of German soldiers about us was curious and
amused, having been royally entertained by our exchange.
My captors, I could see, were also enjoying their role immensely and some were discussing the history of "my capture" with the others, while my sergeant, called over by the
officers, was talking now with them. When they were finished questioning him, he returned to where we stood, stoic
and silent, obviously concerned, worried. He kept his eyes
on the officers, who went on talking. I had read him wrong.
From my first glance at him on the upper road, I had taken
him for the brutal and experience-calloused line non com, but
I gradually learned that it was his understanding of me and
sympathy with me that had worked to save me and was arguing ever in my favor. But I was probably in a sweat of fear.

At last the officers turned back to us. My SS man called
the sergeant back to him and a corporal from his own men
and spoke briefly. Then, the officer turned to me, "Sie haben
Gluck! Wir sollen sie weiter schicken." He smiled, mockingly
said, "Gute Reise!" and was off, walking back to where he
had been before my advent had disturbed him. [You're lucky!
We are going to send you further on . . . Happy journey!] My
sergeant was happy. "Gut!" he said. "Wir müssen weiter.
Diesen soll nun mit du gehen," [We have to go on, but these
now will go with you.] and he indicated the corporal and
two others, into whose hands I was being given. Reassuringly,
he said to me, "Alles ist gut. Es gibt jetzt Medicin, Etwas zu
Essen, Vielleicht 'Conversazionen'!" [Everything's OK. There
will be medical attenion. Something to eat, perhaps "conversations!"] As he said the last—obviously a reference to future interrogation but a joyful reference to my "conversations" with the officer—he smiled. He was complimenting me
on the exchange! "Wiedersehen!" he waved—I returned the

expression and added, "Und Danke"—and he was walking off, gathering his other men with him. One or two also briefly nodded, and one shouted back a mockery of the SS man: "Gute Reise!"

The corporal's two men took me under my shoulders, as had the others before them, and with the corporal leading, we made our way back along the wheel-marked track through the orchard to the original road. There we turned to the right, where the sergeant's group had before us turned to the left to reascend the hill—they were already small in the distance against the hillside, black marks against the white road—and we steadily and slowly advanced down our widening and improving road towards the artery it descended to meet, obviously a main highway bordering a river and running towards Metz. There was no speaking, just silence as we made our way. At the junction, where a line of houses now were on our left shoulder, we turned towards Metz and, within a dozen yards or so, stopped at an open garage where half a dozen German soldiers were busily engaged with others. They startled, seeing me; there was an exchange of information with the corporal, and his interlocutor went into a backroom closing the door behind him. I was eased into a chair near the door, and those who had accompanied me departed, returning to their outfit in the orchard. We had never said one word to one another.

Given my mud-smeared, unarmed, and derelict state, I must have seemed immensely pathetic rather than ominous, and those in the outer room who were at work, though intrigued indeed, turned their attention to their business. I could see the garage had been pressed into service as a primitive forward aid station for minor wounds: several of those there being leisurely attended to were being bandaged, but mostly for apparently minor shrapnel wounds, and facial cuts. There was no officer in sight. The back room, however, seemed to hold more important matters, and soldiers went in and out regularly, always carefully closing the door behind them. The Germans being treated were curious indeed about my presence. It had undoubtedly been carefully explained by the corporal, but not to them. Finally, one of the aid men broke off and came to me: "Ja? Was ist's? Ich verstehe das du sprichst etwas Deutsch. Ja?" I explained that my legs were both completely frozen, I showed him the alarming condition of my hands, and that my right leg was undoubtedly badly broken where a bullet has smashed the bone, but that there was little or no pain now. He was far more concerned about the freezing than the break. He had someone else give me pills to swallow and then, calling others to help him, they removed my pants to my long johns, and then sat me down with my feet propped up to remove my boots and my stockings. My feet were an alarming dark-grey color where they were not icy white. They were utterly without feeling in them. His hands expertly went over my toes and ankles, exploring and questioning to know if at any time I felt anything. As he addressed himself to the break, we all saw that the elastic of my long johns had been locked by clotting to my leg over the wound. That was as I had designed it, for knowing I was bleeding and the leg was broken, I had, once in my shell hole, pulled the elastic part over the wound, that blood might in just this way clot there and the pressure might hold everything steady. It had worked as I had hoped. But now they cut away to get to the wounds on either side. They were amazingly small but ugly looking, opposing on either side to reveal the direct line of passage of the bullet through the leg. My aid man swabbed and cleaned the wounds, put on a sort of iodine and bandage, and then he and the others improvised a leg splint, which they stabilized in place and then wrapped fully with a sort of ace bandage. My foot they covered with three successive pairs of heavy socks. They replaced my left stocking, added another, and then replaced my boot. Throughout this process, which was efficiently and quickly done, we had only exchanged necessary information about the wound, how it hurt or did not, how long ago incurred, etc. Finished, my aid man stood up. I thanked him, and he just said, "Machst nichts. We can not do more for you here now, but when you are in hospital, they will take care of everything. Now, wait here. They will call you."

I sat there and waited, continuing to draw the curiosity of many, and finally a field soldier, probably a tech sergeant, came out of the inner room and gestured to two orderlies. He preceded them as they awkwardly lifted me and swung me with them, and went back inside. Here I was placed carefully in the chair that faced a desk, and he sat across from me and the orderlies left. "Nun? Was kannst du uns sagen? Du wisst dass du unser Gefangene bist, und dass bald du sollst mit deinen Comeraden zusammen in einem Kreigslager sollst. Das ist bald, aber nun müssen wir alles wissen." [Now. What can you tell us? You know you are our prisoner. And that soon you will be together with your comrades in a prisoner of war camp. That is soon, but now we need to know everything.] When I began to stammer back in my German that I could tell him my name, rank, and serial number, but that was all, he held up his hand, and in instant excellent English continued, loudly: "No. You see, we are not playing games here. We are in a serious mood, in a serious war—this is no abstract theory you are in—it isn't some sort of intellectual drama. People die here. They are dying around you, and all because you so self righteously come here to make war against us. NO more of that nonsense about name, rank and serial number. I am asking for facts, some few and simple facts, easy to remember and no betrayal of anything. Begin with name rank serial number, and then go on. "I told him the three possible facts, and stopped, silent. "Yes?" And with greater irritation and exasperation, he went on:

"And what outfit were you with, when were you wounded, where, how many men were in your company, how many were killed and wounded, and what was your objective when you came here?"

"I can't tell you that."

"And why not? Why not? These are simple facts, easy to verify. Begin somewhere. When did you come up to the line? What kind of casualties have you had?"

"These are the very things I cannot tell you."

"And why not? Why not? That part of the war, your war, is over. This is history. It has nothing to do with what is there now."

"I am forbidden to tell you these very things, and I, as your prisoner, cannot be compelled to answer." I don't know where I got the foolishness or stupidity or bravado to say that.

"Cannot be compelled? Cannot be compelled?" He raged. "Just who do you think you are and where do you think you are? And more, who do you think we are, that you threaten me, you threaten us with your statutes and laws and conventions? You are an almost nothing, an insignificant part of an army, a broken thing and, but for us, thrown away. I can, however, send you on to be with your comrades in camp, I can forward you on to hospital and the care you need"— he gestured at my legs—"I can send you along to food, and drink and comfort till the war is over, or I can keep you here until you tell me the few and simple things we would like to know."

Quickly, he shifted his manner. "Where did you learn your German? How many others in your outfit also speak German?" He waited after each question now.

When I was silent, he offered another. "What is your outfit and who is or was your commanding officer?" And this time, when I was silent, he burst out: "For Heaven's sake, we know all this. We just want your verification, for our records. You are from F Company of the 379th Infantry Regiment of the 95th Infantry Division. Your immediate commander is Captain Carter. You went into attack four days ago; you lost two of your battalions."

He was exactly and precisely right. I was stunned. I could not understand how he could know any of this. And he had known I would be stunned. He was watching me as carefully as I was watching him—to see my reaction, to see me flinch, or startle. I don't know how I didn't. How in God's name did they know all that? It was all precise, exact. He knew!

But he went on without hesitation. "You see, we know all this. We already know it all. All we need is your verification, so that we can pin down our records and send you on. You want to be sent on? You want to be with your comrades?"

The phone on his desk rang. He answered. "Moment! . . . Moment." Then he listened. "Wann? . . . warum? Vieviel?" He listened, said "Ja" and hung up, then turned to me.

"All right. You are silent—now. But you will tell us what we want to know. I am sending you on to Metz, where you will be interrogated by someone else, someone who needs answers and more answers than I do. And before you will be allowed to join your comrades or go into hospital, you will speak." He hesitated, rose, and, before going out to the outer room, turned again to me:

"'Cannot be compelled!' You schoolboys and your schoolboy war. You in your innocence lay waste a country and a culture. We all die because of your naiveté! You are lucky to be alive. You should know that!"

Oh, I knew that all right. I knew that.

I ventured, almost throwing my remark at his back, "But if you know all these things you tell me, why do you need to ask me?"

He threw up his hands and left. I sat there, awaiting further developments.

Within a minute the door opened again and there were my two orderlies who pulled me to one foot, lifted me, now dexterously, and maneuvered me back out and into the front room of the aid station garage, now largely cleared of those who had been there. Where had they gone? My bearers brought me to the open doorway where a tall young man in a blue uniform waited, holding a bicycle. I saw that he was a sergeant also, in an air force uniform. If air force, what was he doing here? My interrogator was beside him and spoke to me. "This man will take you on his bicycle into Metz. Whatever happens further is not my business. You will be taken care of there." With this ominously ambiguous phrase ringing in my ears, I turned to meet the air force man. He smiled at me reassuringly: "Ich kann nicht Englisch," he shrugged apologetically. The two orderlies lifted me to the bar so that my right, now splint-braced leg stuck out at a wide angle, and the sergeant, standing on the bicycle's other side and reaching across, began to push us by the handlebars out of the entryway and into the empty street. We were moving. On to Metz.

November 17, 1944. American artillery and infantrymen (2nd Battalion, 377th Regiment, 95th Infantry Division) move in as American forces enter Metz, the last big German stronghold in France.

La Porte des Allemands, part of the old walled city, Metz, France.

November 19, 1944. Four infantrymen of the 5th and 95th Infantry Divisions, the two patrols that closed the gap east of Metz and cut off the escape of the encircled Germans in the town, shake hands after their mission has been accomplished.

November 22, 1944. Men of the 377th Regiment, 95th Division, cautiously move a 30-caliber machine gun through the streets of Metz in search of enemy snipers still lurking in the city.

December 13, 1944. Beneath a flag of surrender, German officers walk toward Fort Jeanne D'Arc in Metz, France, followed by Americans who took over the fort, the last to fall in the area. With their ammunition exhausted, the German soliders in the fort capitulated after heavy bombardment.

December 13, 1944. Food and ammunitions stores used up, Germans surrender Fort Jeanne D'Arc, Metz, France. Here the commanding officer of the fort reads the surrender terms proffered by the 26th Division, 101st Infantry Regiment.

An Early Attempt
to Revisit Metz and to
Re-enter the Cellar
Room: The Battle Within

―――⟫●⟪―――

Introduction

After the war, I felt I would soon write the prose narrative of my war adventures. I had, even while in the
hospital recovering from my wounding, written some
88 sonnets of the war, but despite the fact some of
these were published, in two short sonnet cycles, I well
knew how inadequate they were *to me*. They found for
themselves a language not my own and controlled by clichés of the genre. I vowed never to try that again. Still,
somehow I felt it was just a matter of time, opportunity,
and will before I would be compelled to come to terms
with the great part of my life that was sealed within my
war experience. I was wise enough to know that writing
about those events was a very complicated matter, that
the whole process was implicated in and determined by
emotions that lay too deep to be readily discerned or
mastered, that reluctances to begin were also controlled
by a number of moral considerations. It was not simply a
question of ambition or determination. First, I had to determine whether this experience *should* be "touched"?

Wasn't it too private, too special, too personal, and too much part of my uniquely created being? I had felt that way immediately after I was "liberated" by the Fifth Division and afterwards in the Army hospitals, for no matter how probing was a questioning, I kept from any interlocutor, even my relatives, the vast and importantly personal parts of my experience: I felt that "to put my mouth on them" would be to lose them, and myself. Would I truly injure myself in some unpredictable way by exposing these holy relics to the variety of compromises a prose account would force upon me?

The truth of what had happened to me was entirely—I knew!—too complicated for the simplifications of prose. Anything said was not the truth of the matter. It was always more, always more ambiguous, more intricate, more multi-faceted than I could say. Even as I might be describing one thing, I knew I would be simplifying or neglecting or distorting something else. I had early learned to recognize the deep wells and profound sources from which we draw, and I was always asking myself if I had really the right to touch or tamper with those events that were, I well knew, at the center of my identity?

These were but the initial questionings. Somehow I knew—by virtue of the white bird—that this "information," this "tale," was of a magic that I possessed, and that to tell it all would be at some level to betray it, or myself. I may have lied to myself that I did not yet have the tools, the techniques, the ability to tell of it. I may have persuaded myself that I needed first to have more information or that it yet needed to simmer and season and ferment inside me for awhile. I felt that surely in time the season would come when to tell it would be "right." And so I put it off, waited, or simply dismissed the imperative sense of this material, my own fallow mine and mother lode, when the truth of the matter always was that I was emotionally and psychologically still unable to deal with it, that I was still incapable of bringing it all to light.

Not that it didn't bedevil me. Again and again in dreams I was caught crawling up a gully or ravine under fire, an endless ravine in which I was exposed, vulnerable, and about to receive the bullets that would end everything. Or I was hiding, fleeing and hiding, and trying to be undetected, unbreathing, under the feet of those who pursued me. And when I woke to breathe deeply, to sense the clarity of new air and life available and there, supremely there, I would rejoice in my heart. My entire spirit and delight in every moment and nuance of my life sent its roots deeply down into the darkness of my war experience, which I blessed.

It was in the early Seventies that I wrote the book of short stories called *Travelling*. Among the stories were two, "Honors Due" and "Evening at Abendberg," where I found the contemporary tales, based in my travel experience in Europe, compulsively reaching back and into my war years. I readily saw how the character in my everyday stories in the present, a projection of myself, was so conditioned and created by a yet unmastered and unrevealed war experience that the tales could not honestly reveal their meaning but by a return to this deeper and more authentic source. I saw clearly my "art" had to be "rescued" from or to its implication in that past if I was ever to advance in the present. And so it was shortly after *Travelling* was written that I tried for the first time to confront my war experience "head on."

And so I began to write, but after I had written what I then could, which almost flowed automatically, as though another hand than my own, another mind, brought the tale to its pages, I recognized that the story was more complex than I had realized. I had always conceived of it as my "shell hole" story, the tale of my wounding and my resurrection from that death—it was to be my restoration, after a descent into the depths back to life once again.

However, what I found myself writing, then, in this first direct treatment of my war, was NOT the shell hole story, but an attempt to bring myself back into The Cellar Room that I might there confront *that* imagery so that I could go on from *there*. What continually gnawed at my unconscious mind was imagery from "The Cellar Room," and from my descent into a species of death there, where I had been taken after my capture. I knew that the first tale was vitally important for me in terms of my identity, but I also knew that I could not be free until I had equally dealt with the material of the second, and, apparently, that material, that was second in time, urged to be dealt with first.

The fragment I wrote then in the Seventies rested incomplete and as an exploratory fragment. I put it aside, forgetting about it, and nothing more happened until, as I have said, I finally wrote at length of my shell hole experience in 1987. That is the part that I have now, on this year of the 50th anniversary of those events, rewritten or rephrased in part, impelled by the anniversary celebrations, and by Johnnie Loomis and his kind gift to me of some official now published accounts of "our" battle.

But, I have now, in January and February of 1995, chosen to go on, to take myself finally out of that shell hole and across that landscape outside Metz through the variety of my experiences and towards and to The Cellar Room where the other confrontation awaits. This is what you have been reading. It is because I now advance towards that room that I must now reach back to revive that Seventies attempt, which also tried to get me to that room, to get something said. And I therefore present it here, where it I truly feel belongs in the account, for that first attempt to deal with my war experiences head on began with my sitting on the bicycle bar as my Luftwaffe sergeant began to push me on the road to Metz—and here I am, in my newly told tale, at *that* point in my narrative: the sergeant is waiting. [As I write that, my mind whirls instantly to Shakespeare: "Fell Sergeant Death is strict in his arrests."] I present this early attempt here not for its details or its information and certainly not for its accuracy but rather for its documentation of my state of mind, the depth of psychic reluctance then to proceed, the variety of mental inhibitions that opposed that writing *at that time.*

What I reveal here is a mind fighting with itself in an internal almost schizophrenic dialogue, as it tries to bring itself to a confrontation of THE CELLAR ROOM. As I look back on it now, I see how accurately it has dealt with my unwillingness to arrive at its intended conclusion and also how inaccurately it has dealt with the real history, and I wonder why. Later, after it has its say, I will need to bring this material to bay and proceed to where we must go. "Bring this material to bay"—even as I say it, I wince back from the arrogance. How did I ever have the temerity to write those words? The truth of the matter is that it brings *me* to bay, and I only pursue the tale that is pursuing me.

The Cellar Room: The Battle Within

January 9: I shall have to begin the story tomorrow. Unattended, it no longer will leave me sufficient freedom for other projects—I am too troubled by my inability to put it aside or behind me and by its refusal to leave me in peace. If I could simply (simply!) say, "All right: it won't be written; it will have to be put aside," but I refuse to abandon it and it refuses to be so selected for abandonment. Interesting, how it becomes, as I speak of it, the other person, the second term in a dialogue, the alter ego. It's a question of "it" or me. I don't suppose I ever expected to grant it this much liberty, that it should have the independence and agency that it seems to have taken for its own. After all, it only exists because I let it, because I consider it. It owes me that gratitude, that amount of humility and dependence.

For several days now my dreams have returned me there, to the cellar room where we waited for the battle to end, and each time that I return, I come more filled with pain, with dismay, with a desire not to leave, not to be recaptured, repatriated, returned to "our side." I want, in my dreams, I want to go back into that darkness to stay there. It is only as a collaborator, as a criminal, that I continue to be forcibly rejoined to my own.

So let me go back now, go back with my words, with my pen leading me like an almost blind and staggering dog nosing his uncertain way through unfamiliar corridors in a maze of time, leading me towards I know not what darkness that I seem to need. Trusting those instincts, that bewildered nose, and following the erratic prints he leaves.

There was a time when a writer might have begun his attempted journey to recapture the past, to discover the necessary words for the discovery and revelation of what he sought, with an Invocation to the Muse. He would invoke that he might, with bestowed felicity—bestowed because won, available because received—come closer to the lost history, the elusive story. It is easy to understand the psychology of his appeal and his sense of his need for special power, yet the truth is never those things we understand, the easy (and often glib) way we come to terms with what cannot, truly, be understood. Let it better be said that his prayer at the outset of a journey is real, and in appealing to the spirit, it has really nothing to say to the mind. His journey is a journey hesitant and embarrassed because it quickly moves through time with the speed and advantage of thought, no longer implicated in the veins and the hands, in the tensions and abrasions of time. There is an embarrassment for any abstract rendering of life, and every artist shows it, however skillful his manner, however he is dedicated to his medium. It is most frequently revealed, like the tic of a beggar or the lameness of a banker, in a peculiarity of style; in metaphoric bizarrarie, as though by taking motley unto oneself one acknowledged the clown's abdication of heroism; in the cowardice of wit, which always holds off the imperatives of life with an obvious hand; or it simply comes through in the vengeance or retribution which the author visits upon his characters who metaphorically embody his stance. The greater the height of the abstraction, the more necessary it is for his perverse protagonists, as in Poe, to hand themselves over to the police, to undo themselves. Perhaps the requested blessing of the Muse is no more than the legitimization of an author's search, the agreement between the subject and his conception of it which seems to bestow authenticity, seems to permit him to proceed without the need for the special embarrassment a man might have who spoke of that he did not know, who affected the vanity and the presumption of insight into mystery. It is, then, humility which a writer must have, never knowing enough of any subject to reveal it, only enough, often, to present it with all of its mysteries luminously or obscurely intact and undisturbed. Perhaps the sign of his adequate reverence for his medium is just that sense of refusal to name, refusal to posit, refusal to reduce his subject beyond the point where he, with technique, has been able to bring it to focus. Perhaps the gifts he places at the mouth of the dark cave of his memory and mind are precisely those reorderings of nature, of experience he has known, which, without declaration, simply are an annunciation of a yet-to-be revealed event, for which the experiential journey of the reader is the miraculous birth.

I have come a long way from my Vergilian dog staggering about in an infernal darkness, from a suggestion of bestial tracks and pagan origins, to end with a metaphor of angelic visitation, but perhaps this discursus is necessary, trying as I am to put past history together with the present, to understand just what happened, and who I am as I have assumed this air and this light and these words, knowing as I do how they rest upon and never escape from their source in a great darkness.

And so to the dreams into which I am led again and again now, unable to understand the imperatives that bring me here but able to respect what they urge me to discover. And so past and beyond and before those fantasies to their sources, to whatever retrievements can be made out of that distant night. There was the cellar room. And the way I got there.

January 11: *Very nice. Now that's a real beginning. I'm especially impressed by that business of the good Dogsbody who leads the staggering poet on the end of his leash.*

Dogs and angels, God's beast and Christ's cur leading him a Mary chase. Well, I see he didn't get very far. I'm still waiting to feel a solid wall, a single stone: he'd better be embarrassed for "abstract renderings." No wonder he needs the Old Fat Lady, the heavy-fleshed Rubensdoll of the mind to flesh out the story; he'd better add her, all 300 pounds of her simpering down to his Cellarhell in her high teetering Rhinemaidenstoned shoes. Now, that's an image to keep, the lanky lean Don of an old line of a quickpen dragged by his slavering Cerberus to Erebus, Dame Dowdy his DollMuse all fluttering in her gauze veils as they hit the Sunset trail downwards to darkness. On extended wings? I suppose that's why She's there: a poet's idea of an antidote to God—so he can clear his throat to say Amen. And I always thought "renderings" were what was left over after you'd fried the fat—that you dripped on the toast of the Holy Ghost?

As for that business about luminous mystery: If he really re-spected it, he wouldn't be able to lift the pen. That's what life is. What is? Death is. Life is death and death is life. Thank you, Tom. Down, Boy.

Well, if he needs her, he needs her. Mommy's hand as we go down the dark stairs. It's awfully thin food, though. I'd like to drink one tree, eat one river, have a "rendering." It's DogChrist lonely in a landscape of soulspirits. Maybe, if Tomorrow doesn't run off with the next day and the dogleash tangle and trip the Lushlady, our Intrepid Adventurer (IA) will next tell you the adventures ℰ%+++%ℰ@+ of Schmo, who was there also in the A***W***F***U***L room.

A German Luftwaffe sergeant had brought me there, side-saddle on the crossbar of his bicycle, wheeling me through the increasingly battle-filled streets of Metz. It is only now that I think of him and his responsibility for me—towards me, rather—for it went beyond duty and specified toleration of a captured enemy soldier: it came down finally to what he, as a man, was willing to do for me as a man. Or for me as a "boy," for he was, as I remember, in his late twenties, and I, I was like the other GI's in my rushed-into-the-line outfit, pink-cheeked and "too young" for battle. Maybe it was special Providence that I "drew" him, for the Germans at this point were also throwing their babies into the line. I have recently seen pictures of Lebanese soldiers of twelve and fourteen, holding their machine guns with the insouciance of confirmed killers. It is perhaps this that lets me say "too young for battle," knowing how much maturity and time it takes to teach a man how to arrest his finger on the trigger, how much humanity we have to have suffered into ourselves in order to bestow it. I am only too well aware of the methodical idealism of all Red Guards, all young soldiers of the Khmer Rouge, whose dedications, springing like fountains of bravery from their hot and life-filled breasts, overflow into slaughter. I would like to dedicate this brief history to all tired old soldiers who died be-cause of a decision—made for reasons they could not name—to spare life that had been surrendered into their hands for execution.

Initially, it must have been no problem for him, even relief from danger, to wheel me away from the outpost on the edge of the city, where I had been brought after being cap-tured, and into the center of the city itself for interrogation.

Even though it was a city under siege, with shellfire variously picking its pockets of opportunity, with bombers overhead occasionally sewing a reasonably straight seam of deadly seed down this street or that, or with the sudden exasperation of irate savages knocking down these blocks they no longer chose to ignore, the journey into the city as escort for a wounded disarmed prisoner was preferable to remaining on a line that might at any moment be erased by the capricious cartography of battle.

Because my broken leg and leg-wound could not take the stress or shock of being angled away from his cycling feet, he was forced to be satisfied with wheeling me while walking beside me as I rode. That slowed our progress, but he seemed in no way eager to arrive anywhere, and so with him walking and pushing steadily if leisurely beside me and I gliding rather smoothly over the pavements of suburban Metz, we advanced on the city. The day was cold but bright, the lining plane trees in mid November still bearing many of their leaves, some of them yet green, and we continued like a rather absurd act escaped from a circus, looking for a manager or a ringmaster's control.

January 13: *Too much. You forget, Charley, that the absurdity is of your making, and the Ringmaster is* you. *When you let your circus animals desert the Big Top and wander in the streets, this is less the opportunity to remark on their freedom, than to "round" them up, to make them bloody well get back up on their chairs, like civilized beasts. "Civilized beasts"—get it? Oh, God, words are wasted on one who wastes words. Literature is the* act *(ring-master!) of Psychic Synthesis, where wildness and form, the incidental and the norm, architecture and storm, inter-act—sect. It's sex if you will— and you'd better!: the intersection of the Virgin and the Pornographer. (What, in God's name—in God's name!—is Perdita doing in that brothel!) Man and maid, they make a green shade: forcing the bestial romp into the limited terms of that formal garden that we all know best of all. It's a question of what a tongue can do, a mouth. Fellatio is the heart of it, unnatural as literature: concavities-convexities; the mouth eats the formal embodiment of its own created hunger. You are not going to get any spectator loyalty by letting your creatures—yes, yours, Dr. Frankenstein—loose in the arena, especially when you ask me to stand still to have shellfire pick my "pockets of opportunity." Now, that's sweet, that's what it is: seed sowed, pockets picked, and exasperated savages toppling blocks. I like your bloody distance, your author hauteur, your authorial memorial to battle: why, it's just like, just like Count Ciano from his high flying bomber counting the red roses he causes to blossom below among the desperate Ethiopian masses.*

The long walk into the city. A walk out of time, virginal with reprieve for both of them: the day bright, clear, the trees unusually sharp against the sky; the dappled sunlight on the mottled bark of the poplars; variegated life in all its nuances, its varieties of experience and sensation; the taste of the released morning upon the tongue of day. The slow and almost stately turning of the wheel over which he sat, the two of them, like conspirators escaped from battle, like comrades strolling away from onerous duty—the problem of life solved: he would live. Both of them avoiding thinking beyond the day to the possibilities of tomorrow. Now, the balanced seat on the holding bar over the turning wheels where the light played on the whirling spokes; now, the easy stride on an inexplicable errand away from the line and those casual and almost inadvertent deaths between assaults and battle.

And casually, they talked. Not of war, the forbidden questions, but as though somehow, in a cleared space, both of them had been restored to identities that went beyond and before the day on which they were actually so perilously placed. Homes, towns, regions, brothers, sisters, hopes, and of the incidental facts of the day: the pain in the feet, the distance into Metz they would go, the apologies for failing to see a bump in the road, for making the other walk. Awkward German, but good communication.

The air they breathed, deep, clearly, was sweet and fine, the reprieve, even like the slow leisured journey, seemed infinite—and such a journey, taken out of war in the midst of war, interrupting, bracketing orders of execution and witnessed sudden death, was as endless as any moments in life can be, taken from the whole of life, what one had and could cling to—the discovered raft in the otherwise drowning sea.

Aside: The morning after the St. Bartholomew Day's massacre, Charles IX is reputed to have awakened to a beau-

tiful summer morning, refreshed, and to have gone to
the windows in the Louvre exhilarated to see the fresh
new day, looking out beyond and over the uncleared
piles of bodies in the courtyard and along the quays to
where the sun played warmly on the impartial if corpse-
filled waters of the Seine. One might cynically accuse
man's sensibility of indifferent monstrosity, or super-
naturally posit that the vast bloodletting, as of that of
a surgeon, had somehow cleared the blood, the air,
of malice, rage having had its day, been given its expression, its damnable fires burned out and gentler humanity able to discover itself healthily once more (the
promise and lie of all revolutions). But better to think of
restoration: after the end of horror and the threat of
death, the perpetual repossession of the possibility for
everything, once again offered, as by spring in its season
to a revisited earth. The new day, the new breath of life:
the old bawd touched with unexpected and overwhelming love.

About them as they walked/rode the long way into Metz,
between the alert and lovely files of the poplar trees, the air
crackled crisply with the gunfire on the near hills. They could
see the smoke appear here and there and drift up almost
unmoving in the cold crisp air; they could hear the whump
of grenades and the sudden accelerated crackling of a firefight, the ripping tearing sound of the German high velocity
guns, the slower pop-pop-popping of the American machine-
guns, the slam of the 88's—the battle sporadically about them
on the hills. On both sides of them, near and far, the fight was
joined, and they walked on in sunlight in a delight of weather
in a slow and gentle rubber-tired shock-absorbed advance
upon the city in an air as young and deeply sweet in their
mouths as the thighs of their first loves.

January 15: *Listen, Thighlicker, Humphrey Humbug Thighlicker,
an interlude is an interlude, but it's brought this whole sermon to a
screeching halt. I see your fastidious soul has backed off into third
person impersonality—he did it, Moms; he did it!—changing guilt
for gilt? Leaving the blood on the leaves. Who ever told you that mon-*

sters didn't often enjoy monstrosity? Nobody told Charles or the
dragon they were anomalous; if they had, they wouldn't have been
around to appreciate their objective point of view—which, by the
way, you have not got.

The battle lines had rapidly shifted during the day and
a salient had been made by the Fifth American Division that
brought the front down from the mountains to the North
onto the slopes and into the very gardens and fields and
the narrow espaliered vineyards of the suburbs. A school—
"the" building to which I was to be brought?—lay closely
against the foot of these sloping hills, totally exposed to the
guns above, so that it seemed any soldier on the line could
fire down into the black mass of the buildings below him as
he might choose.

There was little wisdom to bringing me there, only perhaps economy and kindness, for it was a foregone conclusion
that the "hospital" would before long be taken, and when
it was, I could be recaptured—and they would have one
less wounded soldier to treat, one less mouth to feed. It is
only now that I wonder if there was also policy in placing me,
perhaps one of a few (?) American captives they had at that
point in the city who spoke some German, where I might in-
tercede, might be used to plead for them for conditional surrender.

We see so little of those forces that use us, by which we
are used. I have the narrow perspective of the wounded
American POW, who was taken to be given succor. I have the
speculation of the historian who sees the soldier as a pawn, as
a statistic in a larger game. And yet, soldier and statistic—
caught in the imperatives of the forces that use them—exist,
demeaning the reality about them. What can the soldier see,
frantic for safety, so aware of firelanes and defilade, of parapet
and paradose, that his landscape is only exposure or cover?
And that soldier, historically named, has moved so far beyond the gloveless, cold, reddened hands of the sergeant who
reached about him to hold the handlegrips to push (so that he
embraced him in his arms), that neither of them can be seen
except as they may be resurrected by the subversion of art,
ally and enemy locked in a cold moment in a courtyard where
real shells were actually falling.

There was another factor that complicated the sergeant's mission. Not the shells that exploded erratically in the courtyard of the building, and not the machinegun fire that could be heard spattering the outer walls and smashing the windows above us, but rather the reality of soldiers, his own comrades under fire and dying. What sympathy could the sergeant assume he would meet, the nearer he came to the front line, that would accord with his own? Neither side was interested in taking prisoners, and to move a prisoner back towards the front and not behind it was a dangerous maneuver. Any German soldier they met now would be more survivor than soldier, surviving only by virtue of killing those, like me, in the American uniform. I was, in that uniform, the closer I moved to the German front line, an impertinence, an insult, a provocation. And insofar as the Germans had been forced to retreat and in defeat lose more men than they could afford to remember, insofar as the recent battle stored each man with loss and grief and suppressed hysteria and rage without adequate outlet, why should either I or the sergeant expect compassionate mercy and rules of war? It would be like expecting stasis in flow, or diplomacy in an angry hive.

I remark all this that I may the better let you understand the man who, with jest and gentleness, concern for my comfort, dismay at my pain, and careful anticipation of the danger of meeting his own comrades, balanced the cycle, led me, and held me upright as we traversed the bald and empty streets of Metz to approach that exploding courtyard. There are gifts we take at the hands of circumstance without wonder, accept and absorb without adequate gratitude. But towards whom are we to show adequate gratitude? We give our prayers for deliverance to God not in appreciation of his gifts, but rather to him as surrogate, He receiving a gratitude for the mercies of life for which He is less responsible than the overseer. Peasants bring a part of their abundance to the manager of an estate, a tithe of their produce owed actually to a remote lord who owns the earth they work, metaphor of God beyond God, closer to the earth itself, the earth and rain and sun towards which their gratitude is real. And I who thanked God and prayed for providential deliverance, probably never well enough acknowledged how that providence spread from hands at the ends of sleeves bearing a German Luftwaffe sergeant's stripes. It was incongruous that he should have been so dressed at a battlefield, but war is incongruity, and what about this history suggests that life is decorous or predictable?

Note to the Critic of the Journal from the Writer

I don't know why, why you are getting so snotty. I'm having my problems with this history (because it's history, *his* story) and you move off (immediately!) away from me, apart from me, cold, hostile, and simply bitchy. You don't try to understand, you merely sit back there, detached, and sneer and bitch. And it's you who compound the problem; the attitude you take is the attitude I'm obviously exemplifying—the more detached your sympathy, the more remote part of me is from my subject. I'm holding the whole thing out at the end of a long stick, not letting it get in close, not even letting you get a whiff of its own smell, only what I tell you it smells like. It would have been kind of me, but beyond me—beyond me, get it?—to let the sergeant say a few words, but I simply could not, not as long as I had to drag in those Lebanese monsters and grow misty-eyed over the generosity of a character's gestures. That bit about the narrow perspective of the soldier, the historian's point of view, is only another way of saying I'm at the other end of the stick, I'm out of it, well out of it, out of the well of it, and unable to enter. I keep circling a room I'm beginning to feel I will never see. Another fact to you, O critic!: my toes began to ache last night, with all the shooting sharp pains and jabbing needles I felt there in that room when sensation first began to return to my frostbitten and frozen feet. It's strange that I begin to be physically sensitized, restored to life in a place of death, when I seem to be becoming mentally narcotized, further and further immunized against the pain of the subject I am trying to explore, as though I unconsciously put on gloves and gas mask and deep-diving costume as I recognize the nature of the descent that is called for.

January 15: *It's one thing to be apologetic; it's another to be boring. Nobody wants the acrobat to descend and approach the microphone to explain in detail why he couldn't make the called for twists and* *twirls. Get another acrobat! It's that simple. That's what the wonder-ful hook of Amateur Nite (days of Major Rain Bows) was all about: just as the sweet young thing who muffed her high note was about to launch into an explanation of how her mother had just had a—the hook, thank God! By the way, did She? I mean did Sally of our Alley, your mint-flavored Lillipop, expire beneath my badinage? I mean she might, she just might consider us closely enough related to believe the bad taste ridicule of an Unfashionable Dame a bit too much in the family, revealing another side of the "real" you she never suspected. And without Her—H**E**R—are you able to get one foot in front of the other? I'm sorry to be flippant about death—but as you can see, I'm really not. What better to be flippant about? Life?*

But when you come staggering back up for air and grab the mi-crophone from me and try to tell me how you haven't been able to reach the entrapped child in the sewer, the miner in the cave, the sol-dier in the cellar, and explain just why you have failed—it's just BAD TV! That's all it is! You're not supposed to fail, Buster. That's why we sent you . . . Did we send you? Who's we? Jesus H. Christ, don't tell me you're a self-appointed savior? I know, I know, I know. You're the only one who knows the way to the room, to this precise and only room. O God. We'll have to endure it. What an agony! Waiting for A.C. Doyle to find his way back to the Mummy's Tomb, the scene of the crime, so we can get on with the solution. Turn here? No. Not there. Here? Oops, wrong again. O God. Tedium.

Only let us get across this bit of ground, this interval and space. I recognize how words will at last transgress and bridge, how time—the time of your reading—will be the physical-mental act that permits the crossing to be again made. I know now, at this side of the rectangular yard, knowing the history I must relate, that we will move from here to there, from the memory in me to the surrogate experience in you, from the conception of the event to its consummation, and that, in a pseudo-physical world, we will reenact actual history. Time I play with now, yours and mine—we live!; I feel the heart beating in my pen, the intervals between systole and diastole no less real than those between that year and now, no less real than the crossing of a 't,' the encircling of an 'o'—is the substance of life searching for shape. The space I manipu-late—you glide from word to word (hop here, slide there, and jump across periodic arrests)—is the present's ability to put itself into metaphoric relation with those leaps, crawls, slides, and falls that once, that day in November, slowly advanced us across the hard, abrasive surface of that dangerous open space. I close an open space after first opening our focus on it; that act of physical closure directs my pen.

They lay for a while on the ground beside the wall that at the near gate opened upon the large school yard. A grey concrete and plastered wall—plaster over stone, fallen away, broken, cracked, stained in innumerable storms—rose beside them, a safety they would have to leave to cross to the center of the building opposite where a set of stairs descended. But now they hesitated, waiting for the erratic shelling to stop. Where they lay, behind the wall, they were relatively safe, for the guns had accurately zeroed in, for whatever absurd reason, on the empty yard—as though they knew that it was their (his and the sergeant's) specific and important mission to cross it, a mission that had to be frustrated at whatever cost—as though the war had suddenly focused upon them, the way a microscope searching a slide might search across and suddenly stop, seize upon and focus hard down upon the one responsible micro-organism to be isolated. It was at once a stupidity and an alarming fact: all that gunpower, all that steel and technology operating to cover an empty and reasonably insignificant space with deadly power, that they might be deterred. A warning not to cross, not to enter, not to bother with the completion of a scarcely carefully defined mission. But the sergeant had been instructed to bring me there, and out in the open city I was probably more anachronistic and absurd as a loose fact than I would be under the cover of the hospital facilities reputed to be in the cellar of the building to which I was to be transported. And there I *was* to go.

The sergeant described how this crossing was to be made. I, balanced on one leg behind him, was to throw my arms about his neck and grasp one wrist with the other hand. He, standing and bending, could so throw my weight on his back and swing my legs from the earth. Like a gross sack pendulum, I would be thus carried as he, crouched, would run across the yard.

And therefore, when there was a reasonably prolonged lull in the shell fire, we started out. It was as though our departure was the signal for the gunners: we had gone about twenty yards into the yard when we heard the far whump and thunk of the guns and the sudden nearing scream of the shells. Flat, hurled down, shriveling ourselves into ourselves and against the earth, we felt the shock of the air from the bursts beyond us slap across us, listening to the whine and spatter and then the whir and thunk in their wake, only to hear a series of knocks in the distance and the overlapping accelerating rising screams of following shells. The earth struck us as though a force beneath it kicked it against us, and knocked us about.

"Go on," I shouted. "Go on over. Don't bother about me. I can get across by myself."

He was improbably crazily smiling. "What is it they teach you? To leave a wounded man? We don't leave a wounded man. We aren't who you think we are." There, with his jacket covered with dirt, dust; there, in the acrid smoke, the shrapnel fragments about us; there, with incoming shells.

Then it was image. All for image? I didn't think that then, only later. To vindicate, to redeem an image. How vast a guilt to risk so much for a conventional expression, for a significant gesture. Or how great a pride? (Or had the German High Command, knowing the nearness of the end, and knowing the enormity of their crimes, put out directives to their front line troops to seed the advancing enemy with an humanitarian bias towards "our" enemy?) Even the mad smile—that, in the face of the shells and our exposure; to be able to say words like that which might be one's last words.

Quickly, as he hoisted me and ran, I only felt the gratitude of one not abandoned to helplessness, one cared for in danger.

Again the shells. Again the tumbled pain, the shock, the wave of the blast, the near miss that punctured my knee and tore my jacket; and he was up and bowed under my weight, running across and to the other side and the top of the descending steps, and down, down behind the cover of the stair abutment.

Note: A Dilemma

Let me approach it again, the better to understand it. I tell the story, recounting it for you, carefully, what happened, and as

we—he and I (and you, of course, you together with us)—
reach the stairway that descends towards the cellar of the
building, as we approach that stairway, the incidental begins
to mount, to monumentally grow, to demand recognition dis-
proportionate to its role, its insignificant not even secondary
role. It is a vast hypertrophy of detail, a gigantism of acciden-
tal totally extraneous and impertinent effects. I take myself—
he takes me, I take you—towards the stairs, the point at which
we descend towards the cellar room: it is a simple problem in
narration, it asks for nothing more than going down and getting through, going through that door, and immediately something seizes hold of the story, something directs and sidetracks
attention, something demands an attention of its own to its
own and quite separate, quite radically unrelated existence.

It is not the place to argue philosophically the validity of
the incidental, the significance to a whole event of the simply
(there it is again!) supporting features, but it is precisely as
though that very philosophical observation demands that it
be made, as though what my writer's-teller's-narrator's mind
would discard or disregard calls out to be rescued from such
oblivion, cries out to make itself historically known. It is as
though the stone that fell away from the point of the sculp-
tor's chisel were to cry out its violation, the lost possibility, the
negated chance for life, as though space taken by a musician's
tone were to agonize to be heard in its agony of rejection, as
that silence, obliterated, ceased to exist as a possible place of
rest, of escape, of alternative rhythm or sound; it is as though
space architecturally occupied were to make a demand for the
destruction of the impertinent structure, becoming the haunting ghost crying out for the dissolution of the reigning house,
the usurping owner—each stone cast aside, and not involved
in the mind's journey forward, the creator's concept, and each
word of the existing language not implicated in the teller's
tale pressing with enormous power, insisting, swelling and
urgently trying to gain access to that dream, that idea, that
creative vision. "Take me, take me, take me!" cry out the star-
lets dancing frenziedly towards camera range. "Mira! mira!
mira!" cry the unborn children, standing on their heads and
lifting their skirts that I may the better see and appreciate their
charms. Everything neglected, everything untasted, everything unused, everything unloved, like a vast and monstrous

and urgent horde jamming the perimeters of my vision, so
that the line I am drawing becomes more than an impertinence or folly, it becomes a monstrous usurpation of the available breath in a room, the culpable and totally selfish seizure
of the few life preservers for a favored few while the women
and children stand there, hands out—voices, lips, eyes, bodies
crying out—to be taken, to be saved. O God, it is unbearable
torture to be guilty of everything for any step, any step forward. How is it possible not to bring love to the widow of 80,
the child of 6; how can any living creature endure the cries of
denied life, of emptiness thirsting to be filled, of life waiting to
be born? How can any artist be selective, any man married;
who has the audacity to mark the blank page? I do, says life,
casually easily guiltlessly stepping forward and being born,
conscious of no exclusion in its advent, no displacement in its
presence, no denial in its affirmation. Yet my eyes, resting any
where, anywhere, are guilty, guilty, guilty of what they have
unconsciously chosen not to see. As though sight, my sight,
were redemptive.

As we are about to descend the stair, through my alert
consciousness—I prepared for danger, for exposure to new
terror—comes the utterly meaningless, totally insignificant
sound of our shoes scraping the sand on the stone, of our
clothing brushing against clothing; and my eyes suddenly fix
not on the door below but on the friable concrete, the fraying
edges of broken plaster and bolts extending from the wall, the
rust of iron railings, the patterns of rust, the very grains of it,
and the alternative coloring of its darkbrown, wine brown,
saffronbrown. And as I try to tear my eyes away, new and
other incidental details lay hold of them, reach out to seize
me—like hands of condemned men in boxcars reaching out
to seize, to hang onto, to touch the flesh of a survivor.

I cannot leave the patterns of broken brick, of fragmented
stone, for there are other and other and other patterns of
broken brick and stained concrete and crumbled stone that
wait to stop my eyes should they try to look away. Or should I
try to outwit them, to deceive them and so escape, to look or
pretend to look at the first irregular and chaotic nonpatterns
of stone and brick, so that having done so, I have bought
them off, have won reprieve from the relentless rest of them.
It is as though they contemptuously wait for me to finish my

pathetic act, merely stand aside and wait, only to rush upon me as a more insistent horde, a more demanding and now relentless need. They are not to be so fooled. Even worse. They are not to be satisfied. They are omnivorous in their demand—even like the sounds which refuse to leave me, crying out for recognition, acknowledgment: sounds of the stone, the gravel, the leather or cloth or steel, that keep supplying themselves endlessly—the sound of breathing, the very tick of time. I can't outwit these hands, these frantic desperate fingers that reach up to be acknowledged worthy of being saved—they also, worthy. But why here? Why here, to arrest me on the stair, to refuse to let me descend unless I take them with me, unless I relinquish control to them.

I remember that when I was through with my private war, when my personal battles were all over, and I was ZI'ed to safety, flown to the coveted Zone of the Interior, back to a hospital in the United States, I met the one other soldier from my division in my Army Hospital who had also escaped from the battle I describe. Before stumbling upon him, like a piece of a large house one had believed burned to the ground, I had found that I could never, to anyone, recount the experiences of those days. When I tried, I would freeze somewhere a short ways into the narrative, freeze like a cuckoo clock jammed on one hour, or, like a singer in hell condemned to repeat over and over the one note of his one song. I would say, "And then . . . and then . . . and then . . . and then . . ." until whoever was listening would simply get up and leave me to my blocked stutter, to solve it as I could. And I couldn't. So it was. Until I came upon Johnny in a ward of my hospital, and then the two of us, both almost equally incapable of the recitation of our private horrors, would try to tell out, to write out what we remembered. I never succeeded. Not then. All of it has never been told. There were parts of it that I couldn't tell, for whatever reason, not even to him. Now that I begin to tell *a part*, I find myself not stuttering, not unable to vary the music, but unable to further its melodic line, to follow the intention of its form.

January 17: *Have you ever asked the question of the insult of your sight, the violation of your touch, the poison of your kiss? Have you ever considered if your selection of any were not the ultimate prison, the final removal of life from life, of beauty from access, of vitality from appreciation? Isn't it as readily supposed that your disposition of material, of force, of characters or girls, is a profanation not devoutly to be wished, a manipulation into distortion, a radical limitation of possibility for the terms you use? Forget what escapes you, the blessing of your enclosing regard, and focus instead on what you violate with your choice, what you desecrate with your exclusive concern, what you defile with inclusion and use. The defamations of your naming are more importantly the subject you need to consider. Think instead, of the ragged claws of your mind pursuing whatever morsel they need to feed those omnivorous but despoiling jaws of yours, and look upon what escapes you as life, escaping and free life, that lives only as it goes beyond and is not included in your meal. Beauty is not your digestive tract or the neat turds of your excretive applause; it is rather what evades you, what lies beyond the perimeters of your possible seizure.*

And there you are: the American, modern Western syndrome in action—you and your ego finding fascination in failure, making matter out of dissolution, puddling about in the dissolving mud of your own feces. So it fails again, the center cannot hold. And you stand or sit there like a contented child watching the disaster of a collapsing sandcastle BUT ACCEPTING NO BLAME, refusing responsibility for POOR PLANNING, insufficient vision, "inadequate ardour"—as the court described the passion of the man whose hands could not continue to hold his dangling love twisting over the dark abyss, who let her fall to Dis-aster. Dis-aster is the Disease of our Dissolving world! All because you Set yourself to strew fragments over the landscape to make the reader Osiris.

It is there, below the dangerous level of the courtyard, a few feet down a few stairs, that I begin to be unable to go further. Had he carried me there to my own undoing? I, forever after, from that moment on, in someone else's hands, to be lifted, led, carried, pushed, impelled where I must go? For here it all begins to extend, to go out from me, to get out of effective—was there ever "effective"?—control. For now I cannot keep it out, nor restrain its limits, the limits of—is it?—the will of the world, all that beyond me reaches towards me and almost (not quite, but almost) without consent, asks to be taken? It floods upon me, flows over me, I am helpless to refuse its notice, I am unable, unwilling, to restrict its possible power. Meaning or power? And it is not really a question of

ego merely, of conferring meaning upon it, rather of being vehicle for, choosing to acknowledge or not acknowledge what
is there, THERE!—to be acknowledged. Here my anger rises,
for my story, any story, selectively refuses: I arise and go
through a door I have not the right to enter—rather, have not
the right to depart by—and in leaving, I renounce what I have
not the right to renounce; I forfeit what I have not the right to
forfeit. I deny God his own possible world. It is that extreme. I
know well the childish problem of renunciation, how early
and how fully we are made aware that any affirmation in-
volves us in innumerable unaccountable renunciations. Yet
we learn, we learn early, to accept that loss, we come to terms
with the limitations of being human, the compromise of
living. But why was it just there, just at that position of life, of
near death, that I should have flood upon me the problem,
the as-though-never-before-resolved dilemma of multiple exclusive choices?

So in the midst of shells and mortar bursts I arrest you, as
I was arrested, as I am now arrested upon this page, too en-
amored of the concrete and the steel, of the glass and toppling masonry, of cloth and the smell of cordonite and powder,
of broken and split-and-shattered-and-frayed-and-abraised-
and-torn-and-bloodied-and-blasted whatever—and all of this
against blue sky above, cold air about, and the granules of
fallen and descending powder upon the stairs where I (I suppose) cringed, to go beyond—even (and that is the fascinating
point) the way I went and eventually had gone. That should
have freed me, that should have given me a species of freedom, like a cow's tail for a blind man to hold to lead him
down a lane and out of a maze of muddy and unending meadows. (Whatever happened to my good Dogsbody who was to
lead me into and on? Tailless, does he waggle his butt somewhere beyond my eyesight or hindsight expecting me to, will-
less, follow?) And was this all foreseen? For I remember con-
ceiving that Vergilian hound as a staggering cur whose erratic
prints I was—then!—content to follow. And now, caught in
the actual—is that the ultimate meaning of my Prufrockian
stagger, my halt upon the stair?—I can neither fully descend
nor dare to mount the mount, caught between two species of
death? In imagined unimaginable terror and in actual rend-
ing of the flesh are we then the victim of this actuality, the

usual condition now to be manifested in full chaotic proportions so that I should recognize them: the utterly heterogeneous and whelming flood of impressions in which we, in such temporary safety as one crouched within a narrow cellar stairway under shellfire may have? Am I, have I been, being given the alternative ending in all its qualified advantages of pseudosafety, where what the eye beholds, the senses absorb, are only the limited possibilities to limited access that small temporary and contemptible purchases on life may give; and given it under such conditions—the dangers of retreat, the terrors of advance—that I am able to make advantage of, take advantage of, the otherwise utterly senseless, meaningless walls and waste and clutter of a disregarded stairwell in a derelict courtyard?

And of course, of course, any moment, any attention, can be made as satisfactory, sufficient, and as fascinating as the otherwise bored mind would find it undistinguished. On a desert island, our standards of beauty, and of necessity, undergo rapid change. If perhaps, yesterday you thought we were instead in an Alsatian war, you forget the primary battle which permits the secondary one to be fought or unfought; and it is the double battle that determines the degree of truth, fantasy, falsity or horse manure or cowshit, to which either of them demands you submit, especially if you have joined me there, clinging to the tail of that imaginary—Watch Out! *Real* flops come from fictive beasts!—cow we follow down the lane. Art me no anima, says the animal: anima/enema—it's all a question of what's inside that must at last come out!

For a last moment I take a long look at all relinquished loves, at all impossible possibles; I move back away from the average modern death and towards those medieval and ancient solutions which have left us few dissertations upon the art or materiel of stairwells. And the measure of my nostalgia for this lost post of vague dishonor allows me to acknowledge where I—where we, you and I—have been: an authentic historical moment, a place in time which will sufficiently beguile and hold the fascinations of historians to earn their dedicated studies. And what has been gained? Perhaps the insight that fantastic interior realms, solipsistic universes, and return to nonobjective structural aesthetics are as much the products of fear as of leisure, that we make art of necessity when we are driven to it as surrogate satisfaction, in hiding from deeper or more terrible possibilities—just as readily as we doodle to kill time through inanition and unearned wealth, secure and in our security kept from otherwise meaningful activity, the way a man without desire might kill time in tattooing his mistress' thigh with the fantasies of his embarrassed and therefore erotic imagination.

And so I say no more on the subject. I simply rise from my crouch, as bravely as I (perhaps) have ever stood under fire, and hop like a one-legged rabbit—disdaining even the offered almost-insisted-upon aid of my (in-all-this-verbiage-which-began-with-gratitude-but-has-seemed-to-have-forgotten-that) subject.

And so down, to approach, to awkwardly open a door, and enter, leaving behind the toppling towers and falling masonry of another age unable to recognize the historical necessity of a retreating advance.

Commentary

It must all be told again, because that attempt is really only that—an *attempt* to find a way to gain access to the material, to find a way into the space where the emotional and psychological guards have been stationed, to allow the visit desired. But in that writing, the room is never gained, the visit is denied—and the double-voiced guardians at the gate are the only authentic discovery. The past is still shrouded in a mystery, so shrouded because the death so curtained has not been allowed to emerge, to regain life. There is no resurrection there. It is a little like journeying to Hades to speak with the ghosts of the dead and spending the entire epic time in barking dialogue with Cerberus. Yes, now I understand why it has taken me fifty years to get this far.

As I again prepare to attempt the journey, I am not sure that even now I will be successful. I readily recognize that this early account, which took almost 26 typed pages, to get no further than a bicycle ride into Metz from the outlying fields, seems enormously reluctant to reach that destination, and I also see that when there is the distinct and sustained effort to descend into that very cellar, it is fruitless—the tale breaks off with the door to that room finally not having been opened, the threshold uncrossed.

Will this attempt *now* to finally get there be any better? I feel like Columbus outfitting another ship several years after one failed voyage, readying himself to attempt the voyage again: laying in supplies, testing all sails and equipment, and restudying maps. As I try to ask why the early voyage failed, I see where it radically went off course. There are vast errors in the tale offered, and we have been given a spurious route. But if I try to remedy such, to get "on course" again, will we really reach the Blessed Isles?

That's a good question. I can't, at this point, answer it, largely because, despite or because of the additional years since the first attempt, my memory of what happened and in what sequence is scarcely better (or as good?) as the one I am trying to replace as false. Yes, I again remember the journey there, to the smoking city in the distance ever becoming more real and finally, cobblestone by cobblestone, brick by brick, achieved, but I draw an enormous blank when I try—and I force myself, I force myself, I have over these many days tried to force myself day and night—to retrieve a memory of where we arrived, what we arrived at, who met us, who we may have spoken with, and what happened then. I do know that my early attempt to lead myself directly to The Cellar Room is a fraud. I know that there was first a trip to Saarbrücken for further interrogation before being at last returned to Metz and brought to The Cellar Room. I also know that the memory I included in that first story of my sergeant hauling me courageously across a courtyard under fire did take place but not in Metz, as I there describe it, but rather in Saarbrücken. Why it became necessary for my Seventies mind to refuse that trip or to deny its existence and to transpose elements intrigues me greatly. Was it an almost hysterical need to gain, quickly, without delay, the return to the Cellar Room, or was it a way of sidestepping all of that "other" as unnecessary and a distraction from the real purpose upon which my mind was then intent?

Whatever the reasons, the sequence I now perceive as true is an arrival in Metz, probably at the very building we were eventually to return to, within which was the Cellar Room, where my sergeant must have been informed that it would first be necessary—before I could be further medically attended to, fed, or given a bed and a room wherever—to make the Saarbrücken journey. I try, desperately try to see if there is any trace of memory of where we arrived, of whether we had been admitted to a building, or any memory of anyone with whom we spoke. Was I fed anything, given anything to drink, further medically attended, again interrogated, introduced to any officers or officials? I have no memory of arriving in Metz, and first being there, but only of getting into a species of armored command car, with others, to make the trip to Saarbrücken. This break, which seems a repression, a denial of what may there have taken place, intrigues me more than the remnant memories, for if it is not the only lacuna I confront, it is the area where there is most total erasure.

So? Let me continue then with my account now, of what I remember after arriving in Metz. I will let this narrative go forward, and it will be its remembered or retrieved sequence of pebbles dropped in the forest of my mind which will lead me ultimately towards the place of my imprisonment and my eventual recapture. You may note that the image I found available is one that posits the cannibal child-devouring Witch in the dark forest as well as the Journey Home.

The Saarbrücken Journey

In Metz, I begin with the mystery I have described. I begin
with my arrival in that great city, still sitting on the crossbar
of the Luftwaffe sergeant's bicycle, but with no precise memories now of that event then. By the time I finally entered it,
Metz was already myth in my imagination, for it was this city
that we were selected to take by storm, this city whose impregnable reputation had terrified our imaginations. But all
the other myths and monsters that I confronted—from battle
to attack on the forts and being wounded—have yielded to
the pressure of memory and my attempt to establish facts to
replace mystery. They are my real and solid history. This is not
true of my arrival in Metz.

What *do* I remember of Metz? As we approached it, I
saw tall and gradually more institutional formal and large
buildings, built of stone, concrete, brick; a general grayness of
architecture, and an increasing number of signs of a metro-
politan center—streetcar lines, masses of dangling telephone
lines—thousands of lines festooned from poles and trees and
running on the ground; smoke here and there against blue-
skied haze; mud in the streets and scattered cars and trucks,
many damaged and pushed into ditches; the river running
beside us, a bridge appearing; buildings, buildings.

I would give much to have those moments back again, for
I know that the physical reality of Metz—in its afternoon November colors, in its air and skies and trees and streets—must
have been, as an experience, a vividly sensuous and enthrall-

ing one, laden with the details of a city under siege and elements of the ominous, yet filled for me with adventure and excitement and danger. But these memories do not exist: only the sense—something like odor, something like the inaccessible visual sensations of the blind—of a rich full impact of impression, locked behind a door.

My only genuinely remaining memories of the city itself after we arrived there are of my being made as comfortable as my splinted leg would permit in the back of an open-topped armored command car, in which I was "adjusted." All of this was facilitated by an officer—what rank, what uniform I cannot remember—who then sat in front with the driver, while my sergeant joined me in the back. And whether we were mounting this vehicle in a courtyard—of a school? a hospital?—and after introductions and conversations, with others who must have somehow brought me and the sergeant from our bicycle to this diversion, I cannot say.

The officer in front I cannot see. I only sense his character and nature, which intrigued me, for he was one of those men in uniform who ever remains quite obviously not of any service and his own person. No matter how he might be costumed, his interests were otherwhere. He was not even very interested in me, and if he was accompanying or leading us to Saarbrücken for my further interrogation—and, as I soon saw, running an enormous risk to do so—it was obviously for his own reasons which perhaps did and perhaps did not coincide with those of the army. Normally, I would judge him effete, perhaps homosexual, intellectual, aristocratic, arrogant, self interested, and probably manipulating a dozen realities which had nothing to do with the war except as they served his delight and fancy. He was a man who seemed fearless but not courageous, concerned but without a sense of duty, serving others only insofar as he was receiving delight and joy in the ironies and facts of existence. All of this I sensed immediately and completely about him. He was intrigued with me as a phenomenon, intrigued with the war as a matter for adventurous entertainment, and I expect he would have vanished in an instant into another identity and safety when it might prove more interesting or convenient. Such a temperament and attitude, against the vast bloodletting taking place about us, seemed obscenely opportunistic and self serving. He was a survivor, largely because I doubt that he felt anything, and would not have blinked an eye if either I or the sergeant had been shot or vanished. I only know that I have rarely "seen" a person so completely so incidentally, and this was undoubtedly because I knew that my safety and even life rested in his hands.

It was explained to me by him, in a rather offhand mixture of English and German, more English than German, that this trip was deemed important, for some reason by someone, and that it was really insane, since—"Verstehst du?"—it was very dangerous now to make. We would be lucky to get there. I thought I understood what he referred to, for the nearer the sergeant and I had come to Metz itself, the louder and more alarming was the attack being loosed against it: about us, and beyond us, on the hills to our left were the sounds of sustained gunfire and artillery barrages, of bombs exploding and smoke rising against the far hillsides or within the city and on the perimeters. We could hear the attacks being launched on both sides of the city, though we were far more close now to that coming from the north. As he continued his description of what we were going to do, I became distinctly alarmed: he spoke of what I had not understood.

"The city is ringed by your armies," he told me, "and we have now only a narrow, very narrow connecting link to Saarbrücken that is being held open against the pinchers that are trying to close that lifeline, held open at great great expense, only a road and not much wider than that in some places, and we must 'run' that road to get out of here and to there." I am sure he told me more than he should have, more than was necessary, and he was the perfect person to have so explained, for he had neither rancor nor anger, neither dismay nor concern, really—just an historian's objective interest in the intriguing situation. He spoke to me almost as he would have spoken to anyone who might have shared his interest in the difficulties and ironies, as he might have spoken to his comrades and equals. And why he confided so much to me, his prisoner, I cannot explain. He was, I suspect, a born teacher, whose interest in a subject took precedence over any personal truths. Perhaps he spoke so openly to me because he saw that my knowledge of German was a bond, was a signal to him that I could understand more of his country than others, that

I had, even, a scholar's interest in it. That, and his seeming utter contempt for official means of doing things. "Look, this is our 'escape gap,' and through it we are pulling out everything that we can pull. You, your armies, will take the city. Yes, of course, it cannot be saved, but we need this corridor, this allée"—he smiled at the word—"in order to suck out all that is vital to us before the city falls." He was an amazing man.

The sides of the command car were high and armored, though it was open above our heads to the sky. We eased out of what seems in residual memory to be an otherwise empty enclosed yard in which we had mounted the car, and were back out into the streets of Metz. After some swift maneuvering through outskirts and then through what I took to be an industrial section of the city, during which we were often in a rushing loud traffic of cars, trucks, primitive jeeps, motorcycles and even occasional tanks—we were suddenly on a straight-away, where congestion began to diminish and the buildings began to fall away on either side—and the sounds of battle began to intensify in volume. It seemed as though we, together with a great number of trucks, troop and gun haulers, and every possible kind of vehicle, even strings of Panzer tanks that we were passing and passing, were finally driving straight towards the guns; and as though entering a narrowing funnel, we seemed to be pouring into a cone of gunfire and explosion. Then, the rip of guns was about us and we were driving, as though into hail, into a spatter of bullets that were striking the car. The noise subsided, abated, then intensified as we drove; and there were the striking blaps and pings and whunks of hits we were receiving as the driver floored the accelerator and tore through the broken and smashed vehicles on the road and through the gap. Our heads were lowered most of the time to our knees as we crouched and almost lay there under the hail and what seemed an incoming artillery strike. The officer in the front turned to me and pointed up. I looked up to see a small plane high and almost directly above releasing a string of bombs that, like a torn open nest of insects hoveringly swept in their glittering arc down towards the road we drove. My God!

The bomb-load drifted in a gradually opening nest towards, over and then behind us, to strike massively and greatly where we had been. And there was a moment when, as the bombs were drifting down and the volleys of bullets were striking and the shells were loud—all of that there at once and there, in that landscape, in that command car on that road—when I think I knew it was history, that it was my life in my time and my death in my time, and this was happening, actually happening. That would not have been a normal recognition, certainly not for me, intent as I would be upon survival and in the midst of a battle, but I think what I had gone through in the last several days had brought me to this, this ability to be in an event and also observing. Certainly, my shell hole experience and my under-the-table experience both had made me a separate observer on inactive duty in the midst of war. In some ways, what went on about me then—and NOW!—was not even really my own business. So here I was, seemingly at the very center of a number of forces all striking inwards and towards me—the bombs, the bullets, the shells all converging—and I was not going but rather being taken, as though I, too, was riding an armored bullet in flight, roaring down that road through the open barrel of the gap. I saw it and I, in the luxury of being carried, saw it happening.

And then it was all behind us, it seemed, the firing and the others, and we were racing on but into a greater and greater silence where only the sound of our tires and those of the trucks we passed were whirring on road.

I don't remember our coming into Saarbrücken or Saarbrücken itself, but I remember the command car turning in at a gate into a courtyard of an official-looking building where our officer dismounted, explained that he had other business in the city, and indicated to the sergeant what he was to do with me. He then departed, walking back out the gate and away from where we were. He smiled at me as he left. "A good trip, yes?"

We drove to the far side of the courtyard and there the driver helped the sergeant retrieve me from the back seat. Between them both, I was lifted/carried through a doorway of the building and up two flights of stone stairs to a hallway above. My sergeant made an inquiry, and they then together brought me through the first office doorway on the left to sit me in a chair with its back against huge windows that looked down on the courtyard and the command car where we had left it below. A desk faced me. The driver left us, to return to his car, I assumed, and the sergeant waited with me. Clerks moved in and out of the room and through the hallways behind us.

"Es wird nicht so schlecht," he reassured me, but before he could say more or I reply, briskly, an officer mechanically came into the room. He gestured with his head, his large round head, to the sergeant beside me, calling him into the hall. I was left alone in the room for some minutes while they spoke outside, and then my interlocutor, my inquisitor, entered. He closed the door behind him and sat down facing me, staring.

There before me was everything that was the Nazi Germany I had been led to accept. I now realize what I could only have fully realized after Hollywood had had some years to perfect its stereotypes. *Then*, it was an image bearing every sadistic nuance of Eric von Stroheim at his most sinister, and *now* it is one to which has been added the unpleasantnesses of Donald Pleasance or Rod Steiger, the features of every porcine, bristly-haired thick-lensed Kraut we were meant to hate. He was too perfect—from the SS lapels to the thick short body and his head-lowered, glowering, intimidating withering stare. He was more Hollywood than real. Apart from my anxiety, I felt the dislocation of one who gropes for attachment to reality.

A long long look, during which his eyes swam like oil-floating olives behind his incredible lenses, then he carefully extracted a pencil from his pocket, adjusted its lead and, straightening a page before him, jotted something.

"Nun? Ihr Nahmen. . . . . . Ihr Regiment. . . . . . Ihr Wohnung in die Vereinigen Städten. . . . . . Wie alt. . . ." These preliminary details I gave him without demur. They weren't merely "name, rank and serial number," but they seemed to me incidental and natural parts of my identification.

And then he was off, after these initial questions, surely now testing my ability to comprehend his German and respond in it: "Has the sergeant looked after your needs? How is the leg? When was it last attended to? Are you hungry? In a bit, later, you will eat. How was the trip? and Where did the officer who accompanied you go? Where did you meet him? Had you met him before? [I felt there was special interest in these last questions.] The introduction over, he swung over into an accented but excellent English. "Where did you learn your German?"

Very much like my first questioner, he then quickly recited a number of questions sensitive to the situation I had left behind me on the hill—my outfit, my officers, our casualties, time in the line, my background training, my special training. To all of these I answered as I had been trained to answer. "I am only allowed to give you my name, rank, and serial number." He seemed not to hear me. My reply was just the buzzing of a gnat.

I had been at once alarmed and curious about the necessity of my being brought to Saarbrücken "for questioning." What conceivably could have been important enough to have justified either the trip or this as the pretense for it? My appraisal of our accompanying officer was undoubtedly that he had engineered my interrogation as the justification for *his* trip, a means of getting him out of Metz. [And that may be the truth of the matter.] But here was the interrogation again, occurring as though importantly necessary to them, and what was there conceivably about me, a wounded mud-befouled infantry GI, a replacement at that, to justify the waste of time and personnel of the questioning? First, what in the world did I know that could be of value to them? and second, what in the world did they believe I knew? I could only imagine that my uncharacteristic knowledge of German had seduced them into believing we were salting our lines with infiltrators meant to vanish into the population or to bring patrols through the lines by night. Something of that sort.

He kept rubbing his oily forehead and brushing his hand over his short brush-like hair. Again he repeated many of his questions, more insistently, more loudly, and with a measure of anger. To these he added new ones. Talking as though my outfit was one needing to be relieved, he wanted to know when and by whom. And there it was: "How many in your company speak German? Where did you do your basic training? It must have been nice there in Georgia, in South Carolina"—he was angling for my background, my training. I, however, was either silent or parroting my rote line: name, rank, serial number. It had to exhaust his patience soon.

At that moment he exploded: "Genug! Genug! Enough of this! You think you can not answer. You think you can just go on wasting our time and our energies. Why, Why, Why—

Warum?—Why should we waste energy on you? Oh, you will talk all right. What you have to tell us is so incidental, so little, so insignificant that it is hardly worth our while to waste this time. It is only . . . nothing. But whether you tell us or not is the significant thing. If you remain stubborn and in opposition to us, we are hardly in a position in this war to be concerned to look after you. Why should we go out of our way for you, who will not do the slightest, slightest, thing for us? Why? Tell me why? Ultimately, it is you who determine in this war whether you live or die. It is not our decision but your decision. Hear that clearly and know that clearly. You have chosen to decide not to talk to me. It is your decision then what happens to you. It could be a good choice which would put you safely back at the end of the war with your family and friends. Or it can be your decision not to live to see the end of this war. It is not us. It is you. YOU!" He was leveling his pencil at me, striking the air with it towards me. "You!"

"It is that difference that will make an absolute, absolute difference to you. If you tell us, you will immediately, immediately have food, medical attention, and be sent on to be placed with your own troops and comrades until the war is over. But if you prove to us that you are only intent on frustrating our good efforts towards you, it will go hard, it will be unbelievably hard for you. Es wird furchtbar schlecht für sie!"

He let that sink in. He let me consider what he had said. And then he repeated, "When were you going to get your replacements?" And, as though pursuing the same line, he suddenly shot at me "Where was the officer going who left you here? Where did you first meet him? I mean earlier, when was it you earlier knew him? What was his name?"

I was dazzled by the switch and the severity, his rage. This business of the officer. He could surely get that from the sergeant. When I was silent, he continued:

"Look. It is very simple. Very simple. You tell us what we want to know and you are safe, not just now, but for this war. You will be privileged as I am not, as others are not, to be protected in your prisoner of war camp and among your companions till the war is over, and then you will be with your family. It is adequate, comfortable there. You will have food and medical attention. I do not know, maybe you are going to lose your legs. They tell me they are frozen. But—and here it is your choice, and your choice alone!—remain as you are, stupidly stubborn over this little that you have to tell us, and you force upon us options. We have a variety of camps to which we can choose to send you. The one I have described, where you will be with your comrades, or ones where you will not be with Americans at all, where you will be among foreign soldiers, others, who will not speak your language. And there are yet others, others you cannot imagine or conceive of, where it would be almost impossible for you to survive, where we keep enemies of the State, those undesirables who have proven their worthlessness—Jews and Russians and murderers and traitors. These are like prisons but they are, naturally in wartime, worse than prisons. And there you would not only have none who spoke your language, you would find little medical attention or special concern for you, and no one would understand you. I doubt, I seriously doubt that your family would see you again."

I, who at that place in time had never heard of a death camp, concentration camp, who had neither an imagery or idea of one, who had been raised in a Boy Scout culture to believe in goodwill towards men, albeit caught in the ironies and contradictions of war, hardly knew of what he spoke, hardly heard his thinly veiled threat. And so I found myself protesting, like some absurd cuckoo, that I could only give him name, rank, and serial number, and that it was to me equal—"mir ist egal!—whether I was with Americans or "foreigners,"—I was sure I could get along with most people.

It was as I enunciated this vanity and sentimentality that there was suddenly as I spoke a sense of the whole sky falling past me, beyond me, and the world outside the window exploded in a great and cataclysmic explosion, the window behind me dissolving into fragments that disappeared while pieces of glass and wood sprayed about me. It was a great whoosh and clang and again the experience of a boxcar, several boxcars falling, and I sat there like someone stripped of one world and reordered in another. My questioner had fled as quickly almost as the burst itself, his face cut and bleeding in several places. Even as I felt the back of my head and determined that I had been only perhaps scratched here and there—my ears!—my air force sergeant was racing in. He was amazed to see me still sitting there where he had left me and apparently untouched. He examined me closely.

Just then, my judge and jury in the person of my questioner appeared in the doorway holding handkerchiefs to his cut face. "Take him away!" he cried, and disappeared.

"Let's get out of here!" Quickly, my sergeant had me up and with one arm about me and lifting, he brought me out into the confusion of the hall even as there was another blast somewhere outside. Everything in the hall was chaos. Letting me support myself by the banister on one side, he guided me as I hopped swiftly down and to the foyer and through it to the now smashed doors. Propping me inconspicuously behind a niche inside these, he "commandeered" a passing clerk to stay with me, said "Warten!" and he was out. There was a great crying and rushing about in the foyer around me.

In a minute he was back. He explained. "The driver is over there, outside the gate, in the lane with the car. We have to go across, but it is dangerous. Just let me carry you. I can do it, but we have to be quick." The confusion about us on the first floor of the building was great, soldiers and civilians who had rushed out of offices milling about and trying to do what they needed to do. Again, even as we made our way to the outer shattered doors, another blast struck somewhere in the right courtyard. Was it shellfire? Were they bombs? I had heard none of the scream of arriving shells, no warning for any of these blasts. Were they mortar fire? But if so, from where? I had had the sense that Saarbrücken was sufficiently behind any lines that bombing or shellfire from a great distance made the only sense, or a *maquis* mortar attack, but obviously I was confused, and this was no time for questions.

We were outside, my sergeant had linked my hands over his neck for a crude fireman's carry and he was stooping and running, my weight on his back. And then the sudden terror of more incoming and we were down, sprawled flat in the middle of the courtyard while dust and cement and cordite and shrapnel blasted and whirred past us beyond us. It was then I told him, as I had the other sergeant on another field, to go on alone and that I would get across as I could. He said nothing then, but picked me up again and ran again, and then again until we were across the court and out the gate and into a tree-guarded ditch across the road. It was there, when he had got his breath, that he finally explained that it would have been unthinkable to leave me there. Germans were "not like that! . . . sind nicht so." Deja vu! A pattern. A need to undo a sense of a terribly unjust image, to act to recreate who they were. I was amazed and bewildered by the repetition.

The driver was, sure enough, there down the lane, outside the car and crouching in the ditch, but he emerged as we reached the car and I was maneuvered in, this time the sergeant taking the front. "Let's go!": the sergeant. Me: "Aren't we going to wait for the officer?" He smiled at me, incredulously. "He's not coming. Did you think he would?" The driver turned the car and we were off, heading down the road to the highway once again, and, as I immediately saw, beginning to retrace our route towards Metz.

I had a number of questions in my mind, which we had not the energy then nor I the German to explore: How was it possible that Saarbrücken, so far back, was under fire? Was it Maquis mortar fire or a bombing? What was this attack? Why had it seemed to seek out that building, the one where we were? Was it an important military headquarters? Who was the officer who had accompanied us there? Had this trip been his making, was it his doing? Was I merely a pretext? Why were we going back towards Metz? Now that we are well out of it, shouldn't we stay safely clear of it? Why is it apparently necessary to return?

It was only eventually and in time that I was able to enjoy the joke of my SS interrogator, who had obviously counted heavily on his leverage with me as he threatened me with a death camp. He could not have dreamed that he was dealing with someone too innocent of the world, of his world, and of his imagery to conceive of or comprehend the fate he described for me. Not having, at the time of my wounding, really heard of or at any depth acknowledged the German treatment of Jews, I was ignorant of "The Final Solution," and he had brandished a paper sword.

It is only now, in this 1995 writing of the account, that I have come upon a new and totally fresh reading of the Saarbrücken journey. In the past, for these fifty years for me, it was just part of my experience before I became a hospitalized prisoner in a room in the cellar. It did not loom either large or small in my memory, but it seemed relatively retrievable as a memory of my interrogation in that strangely distant city by the one German I met while captive who seemed to be more a fictional stereotype than a human being. I saw him clearly in my memory and I thought I understood his function and my place in that tale. This attempt, now in 1995, to write about it, has suddenly brought me to a far more cynical and skeptical viewing of the "event," one that questions the very validity I believed was there.

After all, and once again, why was I, who must have been in my captors' minds a very obviously insignificant infantry-man—more a handicap to keep than of value—why was I being so interrogated, and in this distant city? What I was should have been readily apparent, to anyone—a wounded GI, probably wounded shortly after arriving at the front. Now, in this writing, it seems to me that I was then used as the excuse for an elaborate maneuvering for ostensible interro-gation purposes, but the only way I earlier could understand the concern on their part to question me was that I, speaking some German—but a bad German at that—had somehow be-wildered their conception of the troops they were facing. If instead of infantry trained GIs, they were getting linguistically capable troops and perhaps even specially trained geographi-cally and culturally sophisticated troops who were masquer-ading as or salted among simple GIs, then it would have been a good question whether the American high command was planning to infiltrate them, or place them strategically inside Germany. Some such nonsense occurred to me as the only explanation possible for supposing that I knew anything that could be of interest to them. With this sort of explanation lull-ing my further inquiry, I over these fifty years accepted my several interrogations as natural.

But with this writing, I have come again on the inade-quacy of that explanation. Nothing that I conceivably might know would justify my being taken back to what I now begin to see was a major or central government building in the distant city of Saarbrücken, especially when it meant a dan-gerous ride through the narrow escape route under fire. What-ever I might know would mostly be of service only to those still on the line and facing my regiment there at the forts before Metz. As I now evaluate my questioner's questioning of me, I almost immediately see what I did not linger on be-

fore, his skepticism, his bewilderment that his time was so em-
ployed in an interrogation of me that seemed at once unim-
portant and suspect. I now see what I think he must have at
once seen, that someone somewhere in Metz had engineered
the myth of my importance to justify the requisition of an armored command car and driver to make the dangerous and
bizarre drive to Saarbrücken. Suspicion immediately focuses
on my intriguing officer, who maintained the front seat for
the journey and who so quickly and expertly disappeared into
Saarbrücken upon our arrival. My porcine interrogator had
undoubtedly questioned my sergeant about him, but probably received no more satisfaction than he had from me. When
I questioned my sergeant on our return journey as to why
he was not returning with us, I could see by his cynical smile
and his angry answer—that "he obviously had other business
in Saarbrücken"—that he was perhaps aware of having been
used. It is even possible that the sergeant's return to Metz with
me was less due to the reason he gave—that that city was
"going to fall" and that it would be best for me, for quick good
medical attention as well as my future, to be placed as a prisoner somewhere in that city, to be recaptured when it fell—
than his own sense that he had been irretrievably compro-
mised by our "officer's" manipulation of the entire trip and
needed to reestablish his own integrity with his own unit.

I am perhaps being too cynical—was our "officer" only a
coward, finding a way out of a falling city, or was he rather an
OSS implant moving strategically within the chaos of collapsing armies?—and I should instead credit the wonderfully
generous and humane nature of my sergeant, which he had
severally demonstrated to me, as well as his firm sense of duty.
Having been made responsible for me, by God, he would be
responsible.

As I lay back in the command car during our return journey, during which we spoke little, I was thinking hard. It had
been a hell of a day. It was already dark by the time we were
on the open highway, but this day had begun with me high
on the mountain outside Metz and under the woodshavings
and the table in the destroyed building. And then it had accelerated. After my stroll down the road, I had briefly been
"recipient" of a prisoner, then taken prisoner, been taken down
the mountain, been fired on by my buddies, been almost shot

in an orchard, been attended to and interrogated in a garage, enjoyed the wonderful trip by bicycle into Metz with my sergeant, gone somewhere to meet an officer and command car, raced through the escape gap under heavy fire to Saarbrücken, been interrogated there, been there almost decapitated by shellfire, and now, here I was, whirling back up the road to Metz once again. Yes, it had been a hell of a day.

With the night all around me and the cold night air pressing down, I prepared myself for the "running of the gap" once again. It was unnecessary. This time, it was relatively quiet as we roared down the road and into Metz. There was some firing near us but apparently less at us than related to situations I could not imagine. Inside Metz, we wandered a maze of dark back streets and arrived at what I now believe was our starting point, the courtyard of the building we had initially come to inside the city. It was a large, now darkened official building that reminded me somewhat of the Public Grammar school I had attended as a child—perhaps three upper stories with many classrooms and offices. Everything, with the exception of a light bulb over a far doorway, was dark, but here there was much activity, of soldiers into and out of that doorway on the far side, and groups of them, line soldiers apparently, standing about in small groups in the courtyard talking. They were black knots and clots of men, or men seen as darkness against darkness or in silhouette, except where the doorway light fell upon them to dramatically heighten their severity.

The command car slowly eased its way towards the door, and there stopped while the sergeant and the driver helped me out. The sergeant briefly spoke with someone inside the door, while I waited with the driver, German infantrymen, nearby with their weapons, falling silent, silently watching. Then the sergeant was back, "Nun, sollen wir gehen? You will be all right here. They will take care of you." With him on one side and the driver on the other they brought me to the door.

At last I approach that door to at last enter it, the door that I tried so enormously to enter somewhere back in the Seventies.

"Evening at Abendberg": A Short Story

Even as my several attempts to "get at" my past war history have ever moved me incrementally towards a closer approximation to a lost or unknown truth, so I have been brought to a recognition of forgotten or lost "documents." As I, writing my 1995 revision of my "shell hole" story, was brought to remember my Seventies account of my approach to The Cellar Room, I have also been brought again to a still further discovery of lost manuscripts.

On my shelves, since I wrote them in the early Seventies, has lain a large volume of the short stories that I entitled *Traveling*. I wrote these stories, as I earlier said, while living for a year in a primitive medieval town in the mountains of France. It was after a summer spent traveling that my wife and infant son and I settled for the fall and winter into our medieval home. There, I spent the mornings writing, though we spent the afternoons exploring that ancient and forgotten region. The result of my labors was a score of stories based on our travels that summer. Having written the volume and bound it, I have let it rest for these score of years on my shelves.

Among those stories are the two that go back into my war experience, that used details of it: "Honors Due" and "Evening at Abendberg." The first, which you have read, took details from my shell hole experience; the second, details of The Cellar Room. Since these are truly the first and only times I ever came near my war experience in fiction—if I regard my 88 sonnets of the war as scarcely fiction—they have a unique interest for me and I approach them again. What I may write now, in this year 1995, will never recapture the impact of my first approach to that emotionally charged material, and so I find it necessary to here place the second story.

I at first felt I could excerpt the war material from the stories that included it, but I soon see that it is too inextricably part of and emerging from the settings that use it and may have determined in part its unique features. That is what makes these memories short stories: the implication of everything in everything else. "Evening at Abendberg" is a largely contemporary account of a visit to a restored castle hotel in Germany, but the story's study of the new erected upon the old, resurrected from it, probably made the war tale emerge as my first ability to penetrate The Cellar Room. Had I not been living in Medieval France, exploring dungeons and keeps, locating lost ruins and retracing lost histories in that palimpsestual landscape, I doubt that the need to come to terms with "my war" would have emerged. But then, I rather imagine that my being *in* that precise landscape was also an expression of my need to find both the right place and vocabulary for the burial mounds of my own mind. I would write in the early mornings and until noon, and then we would search for fossils in the marn fields and intricately dive into the hidden mysteries of the remote medieval past, intent upon a resurrection of lost lives, lost in forgotten wars and unrecorded battles.

I think "Evening At Abendberg" moves inevitably towards that last scene I describe, for too much is hidden and suppressed there, in that world where I the tourist and his injured host are engaged, and I feel a responsibility to reveal the relations between both sides that were engaged in my war.

And here, in this story, written compulsively one day more than 20 years ago, I think you can see why I offer the story to you now. Far more fiercely than in any objective narrative of events, the story gets at and reveals the depth of affect of my war upon me.

We arrived at Schloss Abendberg in the rain. From a distance the towers of the castle could be seen dominating the town, but when we actually entered the small Schwabian village and began to make our way upwards through the narrow twisting cobbled streets, it disappeared; its walls could not be distinguished from the walls of the houses that pressed about its flanks, and its keep, its dungeon, was hidden behind the skirting walls of municipal buildings and private homes that had chosen to cluster about it. Finally, a fortuitous turn, and we faced a long narrow bridge across a shrub-filled moat; crossing this—it was only a car-width wide—we faced two stone lions rampant on either far bridge abutment: they were pitted by time, deceived by weather; their mouths, undoubtedly sharp-fanged once, were muted and softened now, rounded to ineffectual pitiable gums. The algae-darkened eyes stared blindly, and the device on the shields the blunt paws held had been effaced. Beyond the bridge there was a small external court that supplicated the sharp rain-blackened walls and the half-opened iron gate.

I got out of the car, ran for the shelter of the wall, and quickly pulled the heavy chain cord to the bell. It mystically, hollowly rang somewhere far above me, and I waited. Distances in castles are extreme, and I allowed time for some slow-footed servitor to traverse several imagined halls and courts. But no one came. I waved to my wife and child, who waited for me in the car behind a veil of rain, and dashed through the partly opened gateway, across a spacious inner courtyard and to the first door that looked promising, surely a gatekeeper's entry. Here again no one responded to my knock, so I tried the door, stepped inside and shook myself in the spacious but chilly room, obviously a servant's hallway communicating with apartments and rooms above, kitchen and dining rooms to the right, and what seemed to be caves and dungeons below. I had begun to read a poster stuck on the back of the door I had passed through, incongruously advertising a rock concert to be held somewhere nearby, when there was a sound of a falling spoon or ladle from what I took to be the kitchen.

I swung open the large door to my right and faced a young woman, nervously working her hands in her apron, expectant but embarrassed. I explained: I was sorry to come in without knocking but I *had* rung; I *had* reservations; I had a confirmation letter—actually a note scrawled on a postcard—they had sent me. She nodded, still not speaking, apparently comprehending but still expectant, still apparently needing further communication. Would it be all right to drive in the car; could I be shown our rooms; was there anyone to help me with the bags; could they unlock the gate? Now she startled into response. "But the gate, gate was open." No, I assured her; I had seen the closed hasp and heavy blunt lock that sealed it—it was assuredly locked. "Oh?"—she seemed genuinely bewildered by this information. "But we will open it. Wait." And she turned and hurried from the room into some dark back pantry. Actually, there had been no response as yet to my several requests, no indication that the castle could provide lodgings.

She returned, suddenly, moving quickly now, changed in manner, holding a large key out towards me, thrusting it at me. "Yes, we received your letter; we have been expecting you." Who the "we" was remained mysterious; she seemed so totally isolated, alone, unrelated even to the building she moved in. "Here. This key should work." It was in my hand, and I decided to let mysteries resolve themselves. Meg and Karl were waiting in the car. I wouldn't see the room; we would make do with whatever the place could provide. It was refuge in a storm; I had no further desire to attempt the roads, scan maps, solve the logistics of other lodgings.

Outside the castle and back at the gate I struggled with the huge key and the lock. It seemed to fit but simply would not turn. Again, I made the wet journey to the kitchen. "Oh? But it must. Let me give you another key to try." It was this "other" key that grudgingly turned; the huge iron door swung back in a sweeping arc and I ran for the car. Karl was weeping. After I had left, he had wanted to go with me; Meg had refused, naturally—it would have meant wet feet, mud, complications—and he would not be comforted. Where had I been so long? There was irritation in the question; she had had to absorb the child's temper and noise. But through the gate we drove: myself soaked, a crying child, an irate wife.

But to where? The road before me, obviously a provisional arc that had been devised to sweep in a grand circle about the court and end at the door I had entered, was blocked by a panel truck. I honked once or twice to no avail. Damn. Rather than enter into further elaborate and probably ineffectual negotiations with the kitchen woman, I would grasp the one necessary suitcase, carry that to the distant door and then come back for Karl and Meg. As soon as I started diagonally across the yard, I saw the reason for the new road. They— someone—were installing a swimming pool in the center of the court and its installation meant the truncation of the old graveled path that had run from gate to tower, circumvented now by the dirt arc I had driven. It was interrupted at the pool, even as was my progress, and I had to return to the new path, wetter, muddier, amused at absurdity. I set down the suitcase in the hall, went back and hurried my family across the exposed yard to shelter; I left my car sitting in the road.

In the hallway, the woman, still kneading her hands in her apron, seemed now warmly receptive, sympathetic. She would show us the rooms but first she would get the truck moved out of the way, right away she would do that. While we stood, cool and dripping in the hall—Karl straining to break the grip of his mother's hand, now absorbed in an interest, desire to explore—the woman lifted a crude phone in the corner of the hall and spoke to someone she apparently expected would be sitting at the other end of the wire. I could see it, the one wire only that the phone controlled; it ran directly from the phone, through a hole near the window, and blackly, like an ink tracing, across the yard and through a window on the second floor of the tower across the way. She spoke bluntly, without ceremony, greeting, or any trace of human warmth into the phone. "You have to move the car; it's in the way." She listened for a moment to whatever was said on the other end and hung up; no further word. "Good. Come with me." She seized the bag and was off up the stairs.

Immediately, as we ascended, it was another world. The apartments above were indeed related to the picturesque and historical milieu we had meant briefly to occupy. There was grace in the paneled staircase, style in the furnishings of the halls, of the landings. No armor and stained glass, but old tapestry, fine great chests and armoires, embossed leather chairs, and intricately woven rugs, deserving glass-encased care rather than the use they so obviously still suffered, lying on stone-rippled and wooden-waving floors. The white-washed outer walls were an almost unbelievable three meters in thickness; the beams were huge, darkened by centuries, handsome. Our room, into which she blundered with our bag, was large, probably thirty feet square; it looked out on the pool, whose surface was struck into patterns by the wind and rain that sheered across the courtyard. Beyond the pool, on the high doors of a stable (now a garage) beside the tower, and wrought in massive black iron, was the double eagle insignia of the castle. The screaming mute emblem filled the doors and dominated the court, yet we had not seen it when we drove in. Only now, sheltered and looking down, safely, could we see the ground we had traversed, the relations. I turned to thank the woman, but she was gone.

We collapsed, happily. It might be a weird castle, but it was wonderful in its incongruities. The mixture of regality and discomfort, the antique and modern, humanized it, made it familiar and, like most familiar things, able to be tolerated though absurd. We tried to wash at the sink, but there was no water. This would mean another series of requests, undoubtedly to be followed by vague comprehension and at last a superfluous flow. I saw that the rain had stopped, perhaps briefly, and also that the truck was still standing there in a puddle as though deliberately anchored before me. I would use the dry time to get more things from the car.

In the hall below I met the woman. She saw that I was heading for the door and she hurried behind me, peering over my shoulder through the opening, obviously to note if the truck had moved. When she saw what I already knew, she bustled out behind me, actually partly pushing me aside to get past. Over near the cars, at the foot of the ladder-like stairs to the second floor of the tower and before the emblazoned stable doors, a man stood in the drab green of the standard German war uniform. He was bending over some wood he had chopped and was awkwardly trying to load it under an arm. It took me a moment to see that his awkwardness was unavoidable: he was one-legged and though expertly balancing with one crutch, was trying with one hand to load the severed logs between his crutch and the hand that held it. The woman stopped and, fixed like a halted bull, simply bawled across the yard "Fertig?" The man looked at her, dropped the wood and crutch, then picked up the crutch and hurled himself up the ladder stairs. He went up them three at a time, far more agilely than I could ever have mounted, raising himself like a pole vaulter, his free hand seizing a rope rail to give him the leverage for each successive thrust. Across his shoulder he silently leveled at her a look that I would hesitate to name: a mixture of hatred and contempt. If ever a glance was withering, that one was, and I but saw it at almost the distance of half a castle courtyard.

We had obviously blundered into some tragedy in the making: a personal feud was about to explode among the help in the castle. But even as I tried so to explain it to myself, my mind knew that they were more than "the help": the woman's arrogance in the open court, bawling like a fishwife-proprietor; the rooms on the second floor of the tower—were any rooms above these furnished or even used? There was no sign of it—the negligent clutter of wood, mud, wash, as though there was no one else to oversee the handling of the place. They were, then, probably, state-appointed guardians of the castle, a man and his wife, who had taken over the tower rooms for themselves, letting out only a few rooms, perhaps the only ones still habitable, in the outer wall section of the court. We were probably quartered in what had been once medieval guard's quarters and, later, in the seventeenth or eighteenth centuries, when an absence of brigands meant an absence of fear and a growth of comfort and courtesy, guests' rooms. He was undoubtedly a war amputee and, as one so disabled, especially eligible for such an appointment.

We had already come across, at Schloss Ehrenburg, high above the Moselle, a similar couple: the husband obviously an embittered scarred war veteran, a man who had once been extraordinarily handsome, whose features had been shifted by whatever explosion and healing, whatever shocking head wound or whatever magical plastic surgery, so that they were exactly askew, like a crazed portrait by Modigliani. But that man had not been demonstrably bitter, although, like most veterans whose woundings had deprived them of future experience comparable to what they had once had and to the events that lost it, he was unable to put down the insignias of that war. He was powerful, strong still, and even, to me, formidable—perhaps especially so since I met him as I did there at the end of a narrow dirt road, across a barely passable draw-bridge, behind a great walled Eleventh Century keep. And more especially so, since I knew I had been his enemy, that we had both fought and killed, and his wound was my conscience because of my causing. He had made us welcome; indeed, he had entertained his guests at table exactly like a lord of that ancient castle, while his wife, who was never more seen than as a wrist or the back of a dirndl that were exposed through a narrow slit that communicated with the kitchen, remained throughout our visit like a mechanism behind the walls, a source of the delectation of our palate, but without an image, more god than idol. He had been gracious, as he had made us even royally welcome; he had—though I guessed him to be reasonably uneducated, not an officer, but rather one of those superlatively efficient and handsome noncoms the Germans turned out, a sergeant in a Wappengruppe, who could excel any other man at his specialty, whether of attack or execution—gone out of his way to see that we were comfortable. But behind his split smile on a face that had been tortured was a lingering present torture—the pride of an Abyssinian king in a cage in a European court. So it was at Ehrenburg that I had first felt the urgent hint of heavy fear, inspired by the unadmitted resentment, the unexpended fury of rebellion that burned in that mutilated but unbowed body.

But at Abendberg I had merely seen a man across a court, a torn man disappearing. For all I knew it was streetcar or train, a factory accident which had taken away his leg. I could interpret his retreat as neither pride nor fear. I could only feel that he was struggling against the woman in a distant, silent fury of negation, that he scorned her will, and whether he fled from the woman or not, I know he fled from me, in a fury of rejection or a fury of dismissal. Was I the American visitor expected that he could neither countenance nor deny? Would he deliberately not move his car but only retreat to glower from his upper room? I suddenly realized that I had taken to myself, as directed towards myself, all the impact of the furious and silent exchange between the couple. It was their own silent battle; I had nothing to do with it; let them struggle together as they might wish, caught in their violent or abortive communications. I turned and returned again through the door I had just left; I had no desire to approach the tower.

As I came back to the hall, it was to be met by a steady, throbbing, thumping beat of rock music coming from some deep cellar recess of the castle. The sound led me down the cellar stairs to a landing, and down again towards a spread of white and red lights that glowed upwards from below. As I further descended, the lower room came into view. It was dizzying: one's purchase on time slips, there is distinct vertigo in trying to mesh a discotheque and a 900 year old castle, to place together in one's mind—as one indeed had to place within his spatial memory for the proper execution of turn and in order to proceed and maneuver—the double dimension of the castle. The apartments above were sustained over a lurid hall fronted by a modern bar, a fully stocked bar, facing me with its several shelves of bottles: Punt e Mes, Carpano, Cinzano, Byrrh, Hennessey's Johnnie Walker, Old Crow. There was nothing that I had seen in the castle to prepare me for this: an uncertain yet aggressive woman, a wounded old soldier, a muddy yard.

But now there was someone else I could appeal to: a waiter in boiled shirt and tuxedo coat stood behind the bar wiping a glass. I was aware that a lurid dungeon turned discotheque, a solitary barman wiping a glass, a tower above shielding an isolated solitary wounded man were extraordinarily primitive images. They recommended themselves from some earlier life lived, some demonically-derived dream. I would enter my dream then. And as though I, too, stepped from the wings of some theater upon cue, I lounged down the remaining stairs, drifted to the high stool at the bar, slipped sideways upon it, and asked for a Scotch and soda, Chivas Regal. He turned to search for the bottle, and then turned back to admit that they had had it, but not now; was there another brand? I thought for a moment, savored my own role, my desires, and admitted, no, really, I'd rather have a glass of wine, red. He silently, expertly poured. Our need for roles pacified, we relaxed.

How long had the bar and discotheque been here? Did they really get clientele; was it profitable? He was unmysterious, friendly, and confided that he was constrained to the costume for evenings but had to be up and serving Frühstuck at seven. To run both restaurant and this place was a little much. The whole cellar thing had been *her* idea, but it turned the trick; that was their income. Guests? They never had guests, but the discotheque, which had been going for the last year now, paid over twice and again for the place. Had I seen the swimming pool in the yard? That had been her idea also. Yes, and there are more improvements yet. Wait and see, he urged; in an hour or so you won't be able to get standing room in here. Where did they come from? The whole countryside—where else had they to go, and this was Saturday night. I confided to him that we had no water in our room; could that be remedied. "Yes, I know": he didn't seem concerned. "It's the pool. Whenever we fill the pool, we can't get any water up to the upper floors. You'll have to wait. But it will come, don't worry."

That evening the water ascended, as promised. We bathed hastily and thoroughly, as though given a privilege. When we descended to dinner after Karl had gone to bed, we found the restaurant and were seated in one of a series of low, paneled, connected cell-like rooms lit with low lights. The menu was French, and gave us several options. For a first course I ordered pied de cochon, while Meg had steak tartar. For the main course I settled on coq au vin and Meg vainly tried to decide between tete de veau and ris de veau until our waiter confided that it was head yesterday, ris today. It was an incredible mixture, but we immersed it well in wine, and it all arrived not only well cooked but well served.

When we finished and went briefly back up to our rooms, we found Karl waking and restless, so Meg agreed to read him a story while I would wait for her below, save a place for her at the promised crush in the discotheque. Before leaving the darkened upper room where my wife lay holding the boy beside her, I drew back the closed drapes and shutters. The rain had long ended and it was a clear night of a full moon; the dark clouds that had brought the rain now served to dramatize the sky. All was black except where struck with moon silver—it was like a Ryder or a Blakelock. I saw the moon above me looking back at me from the surface of the swimming pool like the bright pupil set in a black demented eye. Despite its brightness, the eagle on the stable door and beside the tower was in almost total darkness, his doubled head merged into one indistinct black mass.

Below, I came down the last stairs into the red lit rooms to find the Schwabian young so thick in their leather and miniskirts, bell-bottomed trousers and maxis that it was merely luck to find again a single seat at the bar from where I could watch the grinding jazzing bashing bumping crowd on the floor. I ordered wine, red, from my winking friend: "See? I told you," he gloated.

He poured neatly, twisting the bottle swiftly, sharply, to catch the drop that otherwise might have fallen, and I thought of Pagnol's Cesar, who had taught Marius, his son, this art, and it made me inexpressibly sad. Somehow the waiter had sophisticated an economy, had stylized a very simple and very human act. He was teaching nothing; he was competent and expecting applause. I could not meet his eyes or talk to him. Manners were being used as words too callously, too efficiently. And so I used the excuse of the massed dancers to pardon my aversion, the dancers who now swarmed the floor of the subterranean room.

I had been too intently watching or engrossed in the Doré-like inferno, the writhing entwining bodies in the lurid light, now shaking as though electrically wired to the throbbing rock rhythm. They shook in an interconnected shudder of massed bodies in the small low dungeon room as though they were a cluster, a huge family, a vast clot of snakes. And now I had spilled my wine. It had stained my pants leg black and lay on the floor, beneath the high stool I sat on, as a gleaming pool. Instinctively, for whatever reason, I tried to hide my clumsiness, but even as I did so, I saw the waiter stonily watching. "Forgive me," I said in German—"Entschuldige mich!" It was stronger than asking for pardon, for excuse; it carried schuld, guilt, buried within it; it asked for guilt to be forgiven. The spilled wine, the light upon it in the dungeon-like room, the inexpressive face of the German watching: Forgive me! Forgive me!

I had been there before.

He had been the solitary prisoner, and they had brought him there: a corridor, a cellar of grey, blue, green-mottled men. Ghosts of lost battles, a mass grave tilted vertically erect, the eyes all opened. Each wall covered with leaning, propped, holding, standing German wounded; the floor filled with those who had fallen, who could not stand, who now fell, who would fall to fill the floor; and the floor sticky, thick, spattering thick in blood, fresh blood; blood flowing to it, even into the blood that had fallen and lain there. Against the lost guns, the moaning, the abbreviated shrieks from a room beyond a blanket were set in silence—perhaps against the screaming in his own head it was all a silence. It was all eyes and silence. He was propped near the doorway he had entered, and it was as though all the eyes in the dim corridor—eyes like huge white stones in blackened faces fixed on one turning arclight—swiveled towards him. He could see the shattered stump of a leg dripping beside him, a boy holding two remnants of arms vertically from the floor where he lay, a man beginning to slide down from the wall, a sudden rush of blood coming out from his chest. He knew where he was. The blanket pulled aside and he could see the shiny slippery table on which they held one after another under a single large light bulb where, without anesthetic, they cut, they sawed, they hacked, they bound, and did what could be done to stop, to save, for a moment beyond the guns. And the men still held their weapons, still used the guns as crutches, props, and let them hang from shoulders or belts. Then the cloth beside him bellied in, and a mud-made face pushed blackly against and past him, part of its head broken, the P-38 a hand held, still hot-barreled as it touched him. For one second the eyes of a shattered head met his eyes, knew him, saw him as the room saw him in his own singular insulting uniform. It was a room of broken bodies, it was a whole cellar, a dungeon of maimed and tortured men; it was an abattoir; it was all raw and bleeding. Inside his head he screamed Shoot me! Shoot me! Shoot me! Shoot me! Shoot me! But around him it was all slow silence, the drip of silence in perceptible pain. A hand beside him took a cigarette from lips and held it towards him, held the cigarette towards him; there were eyes behind the cigarette in the air and the room was like a compressed steel wall of eyes, unbreathing. And the hand held the cigarette—it was a cigarette in the air before eyes that met his. There was a woman, a woman in boots—what was she doing there? He could see she was a Sister, some order. It was a blood-stained white-winged bonnet she wore, the whiteness like some impossible unworldly color, some unbelievable intrusion, and she came to where he was in the silence and said in the silence of eyes in a broken English, "Is there something I can do for you?" Something I can do for *you*! SOMETHING I CAN DO FOR YOU!

Forgive me! Forgive me!

He waited now like a condemned man, waiting for Meg to descend, to come down to bring him back up. He knew that he would have to wait for her. He was powerless to rise without her, powerless to effect his own rescue.

The Cellar Room

Outside the Door

Now that it was apparent that I was to be handed over, left with others by my sergeant, I was suddenly terribly apprehensive. He had become, during the day we had so intimately spent together, indispensable to me: I felt neither maneuverable nor "safe" without him. He had rescued me from the shellfire in the courtyard but, more than that, he had, I suspected, really rescued me from the threats and intentions of the SS man in Saarbrücken, by getting me so quickly and effectively and on his own initiative, I believe, "out of" there. At every instant I had felt his goodwill and kindness, confirmed during our long and leisured "stroll" on the bicycle into Metz when we had experienced what I now saw was a highly rare and indulgent out of war interlude—the two of us, surrounded by war, nominally "enemies," yet for a fabulous while free from it all.

I recognized that he had undoubtedly been freed from what might have been more dangerous duty by being assigned to me—yet I instantly remember the dash through the gap to Saarbrücken, the courtyard shelling, and I wonder if that is really so. We had rather been released to the human moments we had spent together, when we shared our mutual dilemma of being two rather unmilitary human beings somehow implicated in a war. We had immediately transcended the terminology of enemy or ally and had just been two young men together making their way through the protocols and procedures and instrumentalities of war.

I would miss him. But, immediately, more than that, I would instantly perhaps be in danger without him and need him.

"I will be all right here?" Yes, he had spoken with someone "inside." Here was an advanced aid station—even as we spoke by the door, two German soldiers arrived with what I took to be a dying or already dead comrade on an improvised stretcher. The door was opened and closed after them. Here, inside, they could tend to me, look after me, and then place me with other wounded Americans. He had been assured. It will be all right, he comforted me. "I have to get back." There is no adequate way to ever say thanks. I still to this day carry with me the guilt of an inadequately acknowledged gratitude—for kindness beyond the call of duty.

The Cellar Room

The door was opened, I was helped through the doorway and into the hands of two aid men who advanced up a set of narrow descending stairs on the other side of the door. They arm-lifted me and brought me down those badly lit stairs to the wall at the bottom, propped me to the left of the stairs where I briefly balanced on one foot, and I was in the Cellar Room.

Jesus! God! Mary! and Joseph! How do I begin to describe this? It has been, I now recognize, partly the impossibility of description that has kept me from passing the door I have just passed. The last page or so of "Evening at Abendberg" suggests what I cannot truly describe. There, in that story, it was the whole and enveloping fictional pretense that permitted me the arrogance to try, the vanity of my attempt. And now, at last brought to face the need for a factual account, I find the need to begin, the need for detail or even an approximation of that scene, one I cannot meet. With that knowledge I continue to write.

Here, in the large basement room that opened out at the foot of the stairs, better but starkly and frighteningly lit with candlelight and acetylene torches, was hell itself. Before me, about me, pressing against me on my left shoulder, at my feet and standing, propped as I against all available wall space, lying on stretchers, on the stone floor, almost on top of and against each other, was an army, a defeated army, a ravaged and destroyed army of bodies. Of alive, or barely alive, shattered soldiers.

The floor before me and leading forward towards a blanket and canvas-curtained area beyond was glistening red with blood, the men about me were daubed everywhere, on their torn faces, their wounded or missing arms, about their bodies and smashed or torn legs, with mad scarlet and striking insulting reds—as though a mad painter had swept his demonic brush over all surfaces. The smell was deafening, the smell of blood and bodies and of guns and dynamite and smoke, of every visceral foul smell the world has. It was really, however, as though my eyesight had grown inordinately intense, as though every sensation informed me through my eyes. There was sound—my God!—a steady undertone of moaning, of cries, punctuated by shrieks underwritten by a steady drone of a never ceasing voice, like the needle of a record stuck on a demented chant, coming from behind the curtain wall where, I instantly knew, the "business" of the cellar was being transacted. But I only really saw!

Mostly German field uniforms of infantry soldiers, mud marked and cancelled, but also a wild array of uniforms of those of all branches—engineers, tank corps, artillery—including non coms and privates, officers: All were piled indiscriminately on the stone cellar floor and against the limestone cellar walls of that enormous room. It was at once too large and too small. Everywhere was the mass of writhing, turning, agonizingly moving bodies—striking the air in pain, beating against the floor, or just lying inert and as though for nothing, nothing—so that the room seemed a field or a cellar-full of broken torn men: all waiting for what care they could find. And the numbers that were there, pressed against and upon one another, so that it seemed jammed and filled to bursting with these maimed. Many of them still held their guns cradled, or were lying with or beside them, and most were still clothed as they were when hit, in their stained and clotted and blood-drenched clothing.

Even as I stared, aid men were bringing another soldier down the stairs—a man, his right arm torn away, in tourniquet and shock. And there was another, who came in with him, a grim-faced corporal cradling his machine pistol. Why is it that my memory is of these guns, still seemingly hot to the touch, and, even, smoking? It could not be so, but that is how I remember it, probably because they brought with them the sense of being just minutes from the place of their wounding, moments away from the battle in which they had been hit. I have what must be a false memory but one that is distinctly "there," of, as I stood there at the bottom of the stairs, my arm being touched by the flash protector of a gun barrel and wincing back from its heat.

Going about, as they could through the many bodies on the littered cellar floor, aid men and occasional nurses—German (French?) Sisters of Charity, some in huge incongruous white winged bonnets—moved hurriedly and sporadically. Even as I stood there, the curtain flap raised and I could see the more brightly lit interior of what was the "operating" space or room, with its blood-glistening floor, its glint of light on steel, the doctors, most in regular uniform and others in hospital garb, blood-spattered and drenched white. Screams and shrieks from behind these curtains were intermittently or sustainedly there. Sisters or medical assistants moved in and out from this inner space, and unconscious (or dead?) or stricken, operated-upon men were being moved out on stretchers and away. Where? Others were quickly picked from among those before me and brought in to their own saving or destroying ordeal.

And I, among the others, standing there, waiting. For what? For my turn behind the curtain? For someone to question me, deal with me? I was now weak and laboring to continue standing, propped as I was, trying to keep my weight more on one leg, though there was no pain. I grasped an otherwise useless wall bracket and so took my weight off my legs. I saw the sudden hemorrhaging of a man lying before me, blood pumping out his mouth. I saw the truncated ends of torn away limbs, the torn faces where wads of cloth were held in place where no flesh was. Some were, it seems, young yet hardened veterans of the line, others old men, too old surely for the uniforms they wore, the wounds they bore. Still many, too many more, were boys, no more than fifteen at the best.

Far more incisively I saw the eyes of those who stood propped near me and beside me, of those who lay grim and silent and watching, the faces of broken and dying men whose eyes seemed to strike and probe and come to rest like nails, like bludgeons, like bullets, in me. I saw some, unaware of me, suddenly recognize me, the enemy among them, others who steadily smoked in stoic relentless silence while watching me. And I could not bear it, I could not bear it. Each set of eyes was a sharp hard blow.

And then, the man who stood to my left across the stairs at the foot of the stairs, apparently wounded through his left arm, rummaged in his upper pocket, took out a cigarette with his right hand and placed it in his lips; the man to his left lit it for him, and he deeply dragged, exhaling a cloud of blue-gray smoke. His eyes were watching me watching him, slowly, silently, relentlessly, and the sense I realize I increasingly had was of a great well of silence, an inverted bell-cone of some oppressive sealing force and form, holding us all, in this whole scene like one organism, down in a great wail and shriek of sound that had gone beyond sound, through broken eardrums on into a muffling encapsulating silence. And it was in this great shock of silence that I saw and felt.

The cellar room was like an icon, a sign of ultimate hell. It was a vision of pain and death and terror and violence brought up to a breaking point of intensity: it was *felt* pain, *felt* agony, *felt* madness, *felt* delirium, *felt* death, and, in its fragmented fractured images of dripping and spasming bodies, of sticky pools of fresh blood, of bright lights beyond the blanket bearing down on screaming amputated men, it was one single integrated image of utter devastation. And I saw the faces, like white disks of judging searchlights playing upon me and over me. I saw the young faces, the human faces, the near and comprehended faces of my enemy in agony. And I saw myself, standing there, large and portentous and dominating in that increasingly narrowing closed in space as the single and only source and cause behind their suffering. I saw myself as though I were looking with their eyes, as I stood propped there like an insulting revenging reminder of what had killed *them*, and my mind shrieked "Kill me! Kill me! Kill me! Kill *me*!" I could not bear any more!

Suddenly, the smoking man reached across the interval between us and held out his cigarette to me—to me! to Me! to ME! I felt as though every eye in every head in that convulsed and spasmed room was watching—in a total silence. I reached out what felt like my totally naked arm and took the cigarette from his hand, my eyes not leaving his level eyes, and I took a deep long and unending drag on the cigarette. Then, I kept the smoke in my lungs, letting it fill me, and reached back across to his hand with the returned cigarette. I slowly released the deep draught I had taken: "Danke!" The room reeled. I steadied myself to keep from falling.

A Sister detached herself from somewhere and was before me, touching my arm, the wide-spread flanges of her bonnet reaching up like white wings above me. "Is there something I can do for you?" "Do for you?" "Do for you! " "Do for YOU!" "DO FOR YOU!" It was as though the whole room had risen up in a great bloody wave of concrete and flesh and slapped me in the face: "Do for YOU!" I looked steadily at her through my tear-smashed eyes. "Do for ME?" How would I ever speak again? I could not see, for tears.

"Nothing! Nothing! Nothing! Nothing! Nothing!" How could I answer her?

They were steadily lifting the flap of the canvas to eject and admit those treated and those waiting. Each time it lifted, I looked directly into that bloody abattoir of salvation—the floor rivered in blood, the instruments of resurrection and life like a butcher's arsenal. Was it just that I imagined that those who died there or in my "waiting room" were carried out through the back of that central curtained operating room, and those alive brought out towards me and down a hall to my left? I really do not know, but even as others were carried in under the raised curtain, others were being brought in down the stairs beside me. I saw that what I took to be medical aides or orderlies were just boys, some shockingly young, now 12 or 13 at the most; the majority of the Sisters were in their 30's and 40's.

I have no idea how long this ordeal lasted—the cries, the lament of voices—where I stood like the sole personification of pain before the eyes of a roomful of dying and shattered soldiers, but I was never unmindful of the occasional shrieks and the steady drone of an unrelentingly talking voice coming from behind the canvas-shielded "operating room." And then, again the "curtain" was thrown open, and there stood the surgeon I took to be the officiating doctor in charge of what went on in the space beyond. I immediately discovered that he was the source of the "drone," the steady unending voice that had accompanied the other sounds coming from that "room." His finger was pointing directly at me, and he was saying, in that voice that had never stopped for one moment speaking, as he turned from talking to those within the "tent" to dealing with those outside it, in my room, "Bring *him* to me!"

A pair of aid men or orderlies, approached me, hoisted me between them and swung me from my spot against the wall. I was still so much in the center of my grief, my self imposed guilt, so unable to separate myself from the source of all *their* pain, that something within me deeply rebelled—I wanted to say, "No, take them first. They are dying, can't you see? Take the wounded and the blown apart and those without hands or faces or arms or legs, those with their insides falling out, those who are blinded and ripped apart—take them FIRST! . . . . I'll be all right! I'm all right!" I wanted to assure the surgeon. I'm sure this pain in me that rose to speak was not altruistic in any way, but even perhaps cunning—not wanting to call attention to myself, to be given further insulting and perhaps infuriating priorities and privileges, not in the face of THIS, THIS. What I didn't consider then was that the surgeon undoubtedly had seen me there, been told I was there, and had observed me there again and again, and had recognized the "awkwardness" of my being there, understood the effect I must be having, and that, priorities and emergencies aside, it was best to get me out of that room, away from where I was standing.

He waved my bearers on, never for a moment interrupting his steady and almost uninflected talk: "No. That's it. Bring him in here. That's the way, and over here—here!" And I was swung under the canvas and blanket-covered entrance—the sound of feet sticking to, walking through, pools of blood, the smell and stench of blood and so much else—and up and onto the edge of a large table. The light came from sizzling field lanterns, wall torches.

"Now, I understand you speak German, some German?" he went on, never suggesting he might be able to speak English. About us, at two other tables, a bustle about what was there going on—other doctors, other wounded, two blood-spattered Sisters, elaborately painted with stigmata.

"So, you are wounded. In the leg. When?" Even as he was speaking, they had stripped my trousers, cut away the splint and dressing. I tried to tell him the extent of my injuries, but he was waving me off: "Does this hurt? This? He was suddenly turning and twisting—"Christ, Yes!"—and striking across surfaces of my legs and feet with something metal. "How long have you been frozen like this? How many days?"

Even as he was probing and trying to get response or feeling from my legs, then assessing my hands, I was aware of the emergency going on at the adjacent table, where they were desperately urgently working to stop a full hemorrhaging from the chest of a boy who lay there unconscious. At the other table something horrible was going on. I was embarrassed for the "unseriousness" of my wound, the survivability of my hurt. Look, get me out of here. Let someone else have your table, your help! But at the same time I was fascinated by my unfeeling feet which seemed not to belong to me—far more enormous than I had remembered them, and bluish dark gray and even black where they weren't, occasionally, red and bone white.

He went on steadily talking, refusing even the interruption of my attempted answers. "Yes, you are a long time frozen. That is worse than your wound. You don't know what pain is yet. Your leg is broken, but that is nothing. Your legs, I do not know what can be done. Look, we will give you what we can, now, but we will have to wait and see. There are others here, others of your Kameraden. I will send you there"—he had never for one moment stopped moving, attending, disinfecting, washing, wrapping bandaging—"Here we have nothing, nothing, Nothing, NOTHING!" His rage built with this. "You understand, we have NO electricity, NO morphine, NO anesthetics, NO plasma left. We have no running water! You know what it is like to operate without anesthesia? Without morphine?" And, even as he was so raging, he was speaking to others, "Here, give him a shot!" and to me, "Take this, swallow it!" Then, without an interruption in the stride of his running discourse, turning to others: "Here, take him away! Get this leg stabilized, . . . and bring me something interesting! Schnell! Why are we wasting our time?" I doubt that the whole "operation" had taken five minutes.

I was being carried out the door, as I was, fresh from "the table," out under the "tent" flap and to the right and— again the eyes! the room! my consciousness again of the vast river of sound and the torrent of pain there—down a hall, darker, but away from the room. A bench. They sit me down and give me into the hands of a Sister and her assistant, and the new ones quickly apply a splint-like contraption on either side of my leg and, as it is being tied tight and rigid against my leg, she speaks. In German, "You are from where? . . . I have relatives there, Verwandten: Meine Tante und Onkeln." She gestures with her head towards the room I have come from. "You see the war you make? You see? You children."

"Here! Call Franz!" She was speaking to her aide. He disappeared and then reappeared, a stocky limping man coming back with him, the first indicating me with his glance, "Noch ein Ander!"

"Ja. So!" As they together picked me up, she put her hand on my arm, studied my face, her white wings framing her aging but lovely face like a radiance: "You will be all right. You! You! You!"

They swung me between them, my arms locked about their necks, Franz lurching, and I was taken further down the yet darkening hall.

Our Prison Room

Towards the end of the long dark cement corridor, damp and smelling of wet cold stone, a doorway yawned darkly, and there they turned and brought me to a standstill just inside. For a moment I could see almost nothing—the interior room was too dark. After the corridor with its occasional torches, this was a room lighted by four or five low small flickering candles. And then a voice just beside me in what I could see was a bed to the left of the doorway, startled: "Hey, Look what we have here!" In loud emphatic southern American. "Hey, Mac, Welcome to the Club." A man there had raised himself on his right elbow from his blankets and was turned, eagerly staring up into my face. He, candlelit, was in sharp chiaro-scuro, like a Caravaggio, or a Goya in a dungeon.

The room beyond him (1) seemed a long rectangle that advanced forward towards a cement/stone wall. In it I could make out another bed to my right with a dark shape in it (2), and then three additional beds, two several feet further in the room along both left (3) and right (4) walls of the room and a bed along the far wall (5), two of these beds with a bedside table with its own candle. The right wall ended at the foot of the bed to my right (2) where a large entryway opened out to what seemed a very small room to the right, and then the wall with bed #4 along it continued beyond this break to the far wall. I could see one candlelit bed (6) on the far side of that opening and yet another bed in darkness parallel to and across from it (7).

This assessment was an instant's impression, while I and those who carried me took in the room's response. Creakings, turnings, the room awakening into darkness. We three—my two bearers and me—we must have been to those inside the room one large multi-legged creature fused together in a grotesque silhouette in the doorway. We stood there, hearing the creak of bodies shifting on metal frame beds, as though leaning up or twisting in the darkness.

"Where you from, Bud? . . . You the Fifth or the 95th?" This from #3. And simultaneously from #4: "What the fuck's going on out there?" No movement from #2, #5, #6 or #7. I answered: "95th, 379th." "How close are we?" This from southern voice (#1). But #4 was, in a hard northern voice, saying "Give him a break."

They seemed to lapse back while my briefly halted carri-ers continued on with me into the room and into the small alcove room to the right where, I now saw, the bed on the far wall (7) was empty and apparently to be mine. No stirring from #6, a dark shape under dark blankets in darkness. The head of my bed was against the far wall, while my companion sleeper in the parallel bed had his head and bedside table near the alcove opening. My bearers carefully sat me on my bed, then made me lie back as they arranged my legs and loosened and then covered me with a blanket. Franz lighted a candle near my head from the other candle. "Nun?" They were turn-ing to leave me. Suddenly, I spoke out to them: "Vielleicht hast du etwas zu essen . . . zu trinken? Für lange Zeit ich habe nichts." They continued on their way out without indicating they had heard.

As they left, there was a great surge of voices from three of the beds in the dim candle-lit gray-dark room:

"What company, Mac? I'm 379th too."

"How're you hit?"

And, from the first voice I had heard, nearest the door, "Where'd you pick up the Deutsch? What were you saying?"

I gave them the sort of name, rank, and serial number they were after. The 379th man wasn't from F Company, and I explained that my high school German had really saved my life, which I was going to lose if someone didn't feed me. I was nervously aware that the soldier in the bed beside me hadn't moved but just lay there staring up at the darkness of the ceiling, while the questioning came from others in the outer larger room. The voices came from beds 1, 3 and 4, while I heard nothing from 2 and 5.

"We're mostly Fifth here." This from the man nearest the door who had first spoken, and then his repeated question, "How close are you guys?"

I explained that I hadn't any idea, that I'd last seen my outfit some several days ago now and a good ways south of where I imagined we now were, and I hadn't any idea where the division was or what it was up to. I minimized my wound: "broken leg and frozen feet."

Me: "What do you know? Where's the Fifth?"

"We don't know shit. All I know is it's somewhere out there."

The man in bed 3 said, "Christ, we can use your Deutsch sprechen. No one here has any. Try to get us some anesthetics, or morphine. Clint here's suffering"—I thought he indicated the man lying at the foot of his bed—"he's got a gut wound."

The man in #4 spoke so his voice leaned into the alcove: "They won't give us any morphine—the fuckers. Snake— he's the guy next to Tex—he indicated the two flanking the door—"he's got his feet off. He needs it bad."

Number 3 was speaking through him: "Look, Tex is the only one of us who can maneuver. He's got a million dollar wound. He can hop around. We can get water sometimes, through orderlies—they've given us a couple of kids—but we

can't make them understand much. We need you. I'm Sam
the man from Illinois, but I've got a shattered hip now, and
we've gotta depend on them."

I let them know I would do what I could with what German I had. When would they be back? When did they feed
us? When would we get water? Did doctors come by? When?

"When they feel like it." (#4)

Tex (#1) took over and in a reasonably leisured fashion he
let me know that he, Tex, was from Tennessee, that #4 was
Arnold, who had a chest wound and couldn't sit up, and that
#6, the man beside me, was Horse, who wasn't speaking
much, who had some sort of head wound, and not to worry if
he didn't say anything much. That's his way now, but it's not
the way he was, and if my German could get the doctors to
tell us something more.

It was while we were talking in this fashion that the
young aide who had brought me to the room came in with a
tray on which was a bowl of very simple hot broth and a piece
of hard granular bread. The others in the room had eaten
earlier—so Sam the man from Illinois explained. While I was
wolfing down the bread and drinking the almost cold soup, I
tried to talk with the orderly but he brushed away whatever I
tried to say with "Später. Später" and was gone.

"Fuck you, Jerry!" followed him out—from Sam.

Tex explained about the bed urinals, "ducks," and the bed-
pans, "But you may not need the pans. Everything's clogged
up for most of us and we don't eat enough for deer turds."

I can't remember anyone coming for the tray or what
others in the room may have said because I either passed out
from exhaustion or just passed out and slept unaware of time
or day or night. I must have simply let myself go, safe among
buddies for the first time in several days. I awoke once in
the darkened room, with only a dim light in the hall, to hear
someone sobbing and then apparently groaning and weeping
from pain. But it was as though I were sliding down a chute
into darkness and I was asleep again before I could really
react, and I knew nothing until, probably several hours later,
I awoke with the most unbelievable shooting stabbing searing
pain in my legs, in both of them: like fire, like an acetylene
torch turned on my feet—like needles being inserted steadily
and without letup into my veins. My eyes were open and

staring up into a gray room. Although it was gray rainy day outside—as I could gauge by a dim and ugly light which filtered through a high rectangular metal-screened window over my bed—the room was mostly dark and without candles after the remaining ones had been allowed to gutter out. I heard movement in the other room.

"Christ, can we get something? Can we get someone. Christ!" I was trying not to cry out, not to alarm the others. "Can we call a medic? An orderly. My legs are on fire."

Tex was sitting up. It was him I saw most clearly as I looked out into the outer room as he sat up near the light from the hall. "Well, hell no—and hell, yes. You never can tell." It was almost as though he was playing with me. "We can get them and they will come if they want to and then again maybe they won't."

I was aware there was a steady, low, droning moan coming from my neighbor. No words, just a low moan as though from beneath sleep. Outside, somewhere I could hear firing.

Arnold spoke from the other room, "Horse! Horse! They're off at Pimlico! They're running at Saratoga!" No response.

"Can't you just call "Medic!"?

Quickly Tex raised himself and leaned around the door frame towards the hall: "Hey, Fritz!" "Hey Heintz!"

This time Snake, who had never moved before, leaned up and mimicked Tex's call: "Oh fucking Fritz! Oh fucking Heintz!" mocking Tex.

There was a scuffling sound down the hall and sounds of someones approaching. Then, there absurdly framed in the doorway were two small young boys, perhaps 13, maybe even just 11, one taller than the other, and both wearing enormous over-large white tunics crossed with a giant red cross. They looked like grammar school pageant players in a skit on the Crusaders and the Middle Ages.

"Ja?" One had spoken.

While Tex was replying "He wants something," I was speaking from where I was, "Ich müss etwas haben. Ich habe viel viel viel . . . I couldn't find a word for pain: Leid? No, that was sorrow. "Es Schmertzt!" Was that it? "Meine Beinen sind am Feuer. Ich muss etwas haben. Morphine? Hast du Morphine? Und hier, die Andere, sie müssen auch etwas haben für. . . . "—again the word for pain eluded me. "Diese Männer benutzen etwas für Schmertzen." Was that it? It didn't sound serious enough, commensurate enough with actual pain.

Snake: "Tell them I'll stick their friggin heads up their ass if they don't bring me something."

Me: "Kannst du mit der Doktor sprechen und Ihr hier bringen? Bitte. Bitte!"

Oh Christ, my feet were being acetylene torched, they were unbelievably filled with extraordinary searing stabbing and flashing pain. "Bitte!"

Snake: "Bitte hell. Tell them I'll break their fucking Kraut necks if they don't get me something."

The two boys had, hearing my German, maneuvered to the side of my bed, and they stood there like two Christmas pageant costumed angels staring large-eyed at this German-speaking American. One was a blonde advertisement for Hitlerjugend, the other a dark thin ascetic-looking antithesis. Looking at them closely, I saw they were surely no more than 12.

"Du bist Fritz?" I asked the blonde short one. "Und du bist Heintz?" I asked the second.

"Nein." It was the taller dark boy: "Er is Josef, und ich bin Hartmund."

The smaller blonde boy was stammering: "Aber wir haben nichts. Kein Medizin! Verstehst?"

"Kein? Aber hier ist ein Lazaret. No?"

"Nein. Hier ist eine Schule, und viele dass sind schwer verwundert. Es gibt nichts. Willst du etwas essen?"

"Nein! Nein! Nur etwas für Schmerzen, für mich und die Andere." There were on the instant two large crashing explosions beyond our headwall, seemingly just in the courtyard outside. Something was getting close.

I had told the boys our need, and they were declaring they had nothing in this school become hospital where many lay wounded.

Tex: "What do they say?"

"That they haven't anything."

"Is this any way to run a hospital?"—this coming from Arnold—but Snake: "Shit! Shit! Shit! Shit! Shit! Shit! Shit!."

The steady droning moan was coming again from Horse, and then Arnold: "It's all right, Horse, it's OK. You'll be OK," and then his chanting from the next room, "Hialeah! Hialeah! Hialeah!" as though he were singing the Hallelujah chorus.

From Joseph: "Willst du Wasser? Essen?"

Me: "They want to know if we want water or food."

Snake: "I want some fucking brandy . . . and fucking caviar. I want a goddamned steak. Tell them to bring me a steer and I'll tear it apart with my bare hands and eat it raw, hoofs and horns—the whole shebang. Tell them . . . go ahead, tell them."

Me: "Hey, Mac, I don't have enough German for that."

"Well, you've got a fucking lot of it. Enough of it to cozy up to them."

Arnold: "You hear those, before? Maybe we're getting close. Maybe we'll be here any time?"

Tex: "Yeah, and what happens then? Do they shoot us or move us back?"

"Don't even mention it"—a new voice: Sam. "But they've gotta have something—maybe even aspirin. Something."

Me: "But what have they been giving you? "

Tex: "Well, when most of us got here, they gave us shots, and they had some morphine, then. And they gave us pills. But this last day before you got here, we've had nothing, and they seemed to be saying what the boys say, that they have nothing no more. And Horse needs something, and also Clint."

"Wasser?" It was Hartmund, prodding.

"OK," I said. "Ja, Wasser ist gut. Aber kannst du der Doktor hier bringen?"

Sadly, the boys left.

"Well?" It was Arnold.

"I've asked them to bring the doctor here so he can explain, and they've gone to get water at least, I think."

"Fucking water." It was Snake.

Outside, at an indistinguishable distance, there was the sound of a firefight somewhere: the muffled ripple of guns and machine-guns, punctuated by the small explosions of grenades and larger ones of bazookas and the sudden quick slam of 88s responding.

"Hey! Hey! Hey! They'll be here for dinner! Our boys are coming in!"

A shadow fell black into the room. I could see it was a Sister, her bonnet like some great ship riding on her head.

"Wer ist er?" She was asking. "Es gibt hier ein Mann das spricht Deutsch."

"Ja. . . . hier!" I called. She came through the outer room and into my alcove. "Was ist's?" Apparently Joseph and Hartmund had told her something. I repeated our requests and became more detailed with her about Horse and Clint and my pain—that these were very real urgent needs.

Suddenly, Snake: "Tell her we'll fuck her up sideways and flying, all of us; that she can take that hat and stuff it, and she knows where."

I cut away from her. "Hey, Mac, would you mind? She may have enough English for that."

Snake: "Hey, Tex, Lover Boy over here wants a nun in his bed. Who the fuck does he think he is?" Then, to me, "Hey, Lover Boy, there's' enough for all of us. Don't get greedy. Go ahead, I'll take sloppy seconds. Tell her she can suck my rosy cock any time she . . ."

Tex: "Shut the hell up, Snake."

"Well, who the fuck does he think he is? Probably a fucking collaborator they planted here with us. What the hell is he telling her anyway?"

I went on talking to her, trying to screen out the increasingly enraged obscenities of Snake. He had one of the foulest mouths I'd ever heard. But now, with the sounds outside mounting, I was concerned. What were they going to do with us? What would happen when we, the Americans, took the hospital?—and we would. "Listen, we really need to talk with the doctor. Two of the guys in here don't talk any more, and we don't know how badly off they are. That other one, who is talking all the time, he probably does it out of his pain—don't mind him."

We were interrupted by the arrival of Mutt and Jeff, Josef and Hartmund, Fritz und Heintz, carrying in a huge heavy-for-them bucket of water—that is, Hartmund carrying it with Joseph behind him with a ladle and extra cups. They went from bed to bed filling the cups. They were just kids, smiling nervously, laughing awkwardly, trying to make jokes and be pleasing. Concerned.

"Hey, Lover Boy, tell her to take off that robe and she can fuck the boys. We'll watch!" You know who.

Quickly, as the boys reached my bed, she bobbed and turned and left, after saying, "Ich will was ich kann . . . und Ich weiss nicht" to most of my other questions. Meanwhile, I could hear Snake and Tex arguing, Tex saying, "You know, you're an obscene son of a bitch," and Snake saying, "As far as we know he's an enemy agent."

The boys were on her heels out the door, Arnold sending them on their way with "Mach schnell, Krauts."

I lay there in my pain—it was really something now— trying not to make special demands when the others were more badly off than I was, but terribly needing something to knock me out. Additionally, I was trying to sort out the range of emotion and turmoil inside me. Here I was, with my buddies, trying to become part of an "us" again, trying to relax back into the security of having them around me, trying to be safe in my own space, defined as ours and mine by them, but something was wrong. Talking to the Sister while listening to the steady steel voice of Snake cutting through was like a tearing. She—I could tell from her eyes, from her voice—was on the edge of hysteria, was worried and intense and frightened, of us—of us!—and she had come in trying to see if she could do something for us. And the boys—they were kids who would be better off playing somewhere, were worried and in a mess of confusion, not knowing what they could do and feeling lousy that they couldn't do anything. And there was Snake. And there was Arnold.

A lot of stuff was coming in. Every so often there was the slam like the dropping of a ten-ton truck from the sky, or a hit on the building somewhere above, and the whole place would shudder. I guess we were afraid it would come down on us. Most often it was the occasional explosion out beyond our two small visor-like windows high in our outer wall, like mortar rounds keeping the playground deadly. Always, somewhere far off was the sound of real battle. We held our breaths, wondering.

Shortly after the Sister left with our two kids, the boys were back with coffee and bread. They sort of enjoyed being our "orderlies," you could tell. They were in a stammering confusion of manner over not being able to really understand except through me, or to do anything for us. So they were always asking if they could get us more water, even when we had enough. They loved each other, that too you could tell:

they were always pushing and shoving and joshing with one another, communicating the way kids do with one another. They were kids.

But in the background was Snake: "Hey, Heintz, you getting any of those Sisters? Don't let the praying stuff get you. They keep them in those black robes all the way down because they're really fish: they have scales for tails but they fuck like rabbits." And there was Arnold. No matter what the kids did, as they left, "Fucking Krauts."

About an hour later the doctor came in, the one who had taken care of me. He came breezing in at a fast clip, didn't stop at the door and came right over to where I was—the Sister must have told him.

"All right. Wass kann ich machen? Was ist los?"

I tried to tell him, the best I could, the range of our questions and needs. How Horse and Clint weren't talking, or even moving, really. What was wrong with them? What could be done? How Clint and even Snake, I guess, were in great pain, and that I was too. My legs suddenly, after several days of being numb, were now torched by fire, with stabbing steel. Could we have some morphine, some codeine, some anesthetic, some pain killer, even some aspirin. And what was going to be done with us? Were they going to move us? When? And if so, since things were so bad here, wouldn't it be wise to get us back where we could get care and medicine soon? But since Metz was going to fall—there was no doubt about that—what were their plans for us and the building? We could help negotiate with the Americans. Given the noise in the courtyard, how close were things?

All during this, while he was tolerating my German and the time it took for me to get it out, he was busy, undoing my legs from the blanket and the bandages and splint, checking, moving—Oh Christ! Oh Christ!—and tolerating the steady garbage coming from Snake by the door. At one point, as I went on, he went over to Horse, lifted his head and tried to get his response, to see into his eyes. It was the first time really, when he lifted Horse's head, that I saw Horse, how he was: like a staring inert emotionless drained body.

When I was through, he set me aside like a package, and began:

"Listen! We have nothing here. We have nothing for our own soldiers, our own. Nothing. You can see. There is no electricity, no anesthetic, we operate with nothing for pain. Yes, you Americans will take the building. I don't know when. We will pull back before then and move you back with us or leave you here. You will get better treatment from them, your own. You, you have everything, and you will be all right. Meanwhile, we do what we can for you. The Sisters will be in to change bandages, to clean. You have the two boys, they are good boys. And listen, we have no running water here, inside. When the boys get you water, they go out and across that courtyard, all the way across to the other side, where there is a well, and back. But it's dangerous, very very dangerous. You should know that."

While he was speaking there were additional hits on the building above us, and in the couryard two or three shells or mortar-bursts, to make vivid the urgencies. He went on:

"As to this man, here"—he indicated Horse—"we can do nothing for him. When he was brought in, he thought he had had a miracle wound, a grazing wound. A bullet had come through his helmet and hit his head. He couldn't believe it, just a scratch. But it isn't a scratch. The bullet is in there, in his head, and we don't have the place or equipment to operate. The best thing that can happen to him is to have this building be captured by you soon. That man there by the door"—indicating by an inclination of his head Snake—"has lost his feet. He is not talking. It is his grief and his lost feet talking. He's all right. He will be all right. The man out there with the stomach wound, again, we cannot treat: just hope and give him sulfas as long as we have them. The rest of you are just casualties, and in time you will recover. Your feet—yes. It hurts now?" he smiled—"Of course it hurts. What did you think? That is a good sign. The best sign. It means you are alive. The feet are alive. As long as we are alive we hurt, Nuh?"

He turned to go. "I'll send in the Sisters."

He quickly spun into the outer room and went from bed to bed, looking, checking. When he came to Snake, he studied his stumps of feet and said, in German, "You, you have a big wound, and you have a big mouth now." Then, just as he was about to leave, he came back over to me:

"Look. A question. A purely theoretical question. This hospital unit, we here, we are going to pull back, but let's say, let's just say as a question, what if we were not to pull back, but rather to surrender to you, to your Army? If I were a prisoner, would I still be allowed to go on inside your Army prison being a doctor? Could our other doctors do that? Would we still be allowed to treat our sick and wounded?"

I assured him, lying through my teeth—I had no idea!— that of course he would be well treated and certainly allowed to continue to practice inside the camps. I argued with all my power as persuasively as I could that they *should* surrender, arguing the obvious superiority of our Armies, describing them as fresh and many, the deteriorating situation in Germany—as though I knew anything really about it!—and the wisdom of ending this war, just getting it over with.

He listened quietly—the first time I had seen him still since I first saw him—then he began to leave but stopped again, and turned:

"Listen! These two boys you have, Josef and Hartmund. Whatever we do, if we leave you here for your own medicine and soldiers, I would like to leave them here with you, here in the room here, so they can be captured when you are, IF you are—how do you say it?—repatriated. And they will be well cared for? Well looked after? They are good boys, and they are very young."

I assured him that I understood and that they would be OK.

He was gone.

Tex was out of his bed in a flash and hopped over to me, grasping this and that to help him along. He sat at the foot of my bed beside my fire-feet.

"OK. What'd he say? "

Arnold and Snake were calling in from the other room.

Snake: "Don't talk to the cocksucker. He's one of them. You heard it. He talks like one of them. He's a fucking collaborator, or he's really a German. Anything he says is shit."

Arnold: "What's going to happen?"

I told them, except about Horse and Clint. "The Sisters'll be along."

"The fucking . . . . or not fucking Sisters!"

When Tex pressed me about Horse and Clint, I, seeing Horse's open ceiling-staring eyes, lied, "They're OK. They'll be OK. Especially if they decide to leave us all here when they pull out."

Arnold: "When our guys come, I wish to Christ I could have my BAR, and when the Krauts come in the door, I'll sweep the hall." He imitated the Tak-tak-tak-tak-tak-tak-tak of his brave gun.

Tex went back to his bed and the villifying cesspool filth of Snake. I didn't have the doctor's compassion.

The Sisters came and went, undressing our wounds, cleaning, swabbing, and re-bandaging. Josef and Hartmund stood beside them, holding things and helping. After they had gone, I slept, and then when I woke in what I think was the afternoon, I woke to an apocalyptic whump and crash above. I saw that Horse was asleep still, or at least I guessed him to be, and I waved Tex over to me. He hopped on across.

"Look, I whispered. Horse has a bullet in his head, but they can't operate here." I explained about Horse and Clint. He listened wide-eyed; then, "Horse kept saying, when he was talking, that it was so crazy—he had this scratch on the back of his head. He'd felt a whunk in the head and he'd taken off his helmet and stared at a hole in it, and he felt his head and there was just this cut, really a grazing wound. What luck! . . . . . Shit!"

Somewhere in the afternoon, a man came bustling into our room, all bandoleers and machine pistol, a line soldier. "Wer is Guy-du-scheck. Gajdusek?" he asked the room. I sat up. "Hier!" He came over.

"You are from Vienna? Ja?"

"How can I be from Vienna? Ich bin ein Amerikanische Soldat."

"Aber du hast Eltern in Wien?"

I had to acknowledge that I did. And on the spot we learned what he had guessed from my name on a prisoner roster, that I was related to the Cristyl Gajdusek who ran an Apothek in Vienna, the Cristyl with whom he "used to go skiing before the war." It was all very emotional, his amazement being almost childish delight, as though somehow he had come upon his salvation. Maybe he thought me being related to the man he knew would guarantee his safety. He wanted to hug me, to grasp me in his arms—you can imagine how that went down with Snake!—and I kept pushing him off and saying, "Yes, it was probably the same Cristyl, my father's brother and his skiing buddy. Crazy things happen in war.

Liberation:
I Am Recaptured

I really cannot now remember how many days we spent in that cellar "hospital room." Was it three? four? or only two, before the hospital was taken by storm by the Fifth Division? And during those days the pain mounted in my feet until it was all I could do to suppress groans and screams of pain. And during all that time Clint, who was consciously alert, so I was told, though from my bed I could not see him, said nothing. Horse surfaced occasionally to protest that his head hurt, and whenever he broke through into consciousness, Arnold was chanting "They're off! At Pimlico, Hialeah, Churchill Downs, Tanforan," or singing "Hialeah! Hialeah! Hialeah!" Tex was the island of rationality, and Sam the man from Illinois spent his time imagining postwar idylls when he wasn't plotting revenge against a sergeant he had had and describing in ever more intricate detail new ways he had designed for his torture/killing. Snake was as he was, unrelenting in his hatred of me, especially when the tale of my speaking German brought in on the coattails of the Viennese skier other Germans who wanted to ask what would happen to them if. . . . He raged like a madman at my supposed treachery, my ability to speak German, and at the "whoors" who were in the uniforms of Sisters—at anyone and everything. All of this while the battle outside was intensifying and increasing in volume and ferocity.

One thing that did not change was the unaltering childish eagerness of Josef and Hartmund to help us as they could.

They never lost their stammering embarrassment for being inarticulate and unable to do anything more than they could. They were always offering to get us water, though now that I knew what the water journey meant—especially when it seemed that mortar fire had almost become regular and grid-zeroed-in on the courtyard—I tried to drink less and never to ask for it. But Snake, "Fucking Krauts! They need the exercise. Think what a well-placed tree-burst might do!"

The doctor returned several times, to look at Horse and Clint, and to talk with me, ever more trustingly—about how I felt the war was going, truly—and I would talk truthfully but as though I knew something about it, telling him our reserves were depthless, our divisions fresh, and that all that mattered was to get it all over with—they really, really should surrender. Then, one morning, just before it *was* all over, he came in to reflectively and wearily ask again if I could assure him that he and his staff would be able to continue their medical work as POWs IF, IF, IF they decided to surrender.

By then, they were obviously in a standoff fight to keep the school-hospital, defending it, as far as we could tell, against gunfire from almost directly across the court. There was a steady stream of gunfire both from the building and at it, and "our" bullets were slamming into the walls and whatever above. And during all of this, continuing as it did, we ran out of water, and Snake and Arnold were demanding that we have water, but I told them they would fucking well have to do without it. They knew the "story" from what they could hear, and it was only a matter of time before it would be over. But before I knew it, Josef and Hartmund were gone, running off together as though to play tag.

A little while later the aid man and two Sisters appeared at the door: he was screaming in at us, "You Barbarians! You Barbarians! You Barbarians! You Dregs! You Pig-dogs! [Schweinhunde!] If I had a gun I would shoot you . . . all of you!!!!" The Sisters were trying to pull him back, to hold him back, to bring him off. And at last they did. And when Tex dragged in one of the Sisters to ask her what was going on, what was wrong with *him*, she was stone cold and filled with large hatred.

"YOU. Your men, they shot them. They shot the boys. The boys. Josef. Hartmund. They were there with only buckets for water, and with their huge huge HUGE red crosses over their white tunics—"they" couldn't have *not* seen them. Boys. Just boys, you understand. And trying to get water for YOU! Water, for YOU! And they shot them, with their machine-gewehr. Just shot them. And kept shooting them! What kind of people are you? You are not people! You are not people!"

So Josef and Hartmund would not be going back with us. And when, after a battle-royal somewhere in the corridors above, some GIs from the Fifth came roaring into our room, breathing fire, their guns hot, astounded to find us there, I really had very little welcome for them. Actually, I had become like Clint but more like Horse. I had a wound somewhere in my head and I didn't, I really didn't want to talk to anyone. Anyone, ever again.

Postscript

Many many years afterwards, out of nowhere, when I was a professor teaching at The George Washington University in Washington, D.C., I received a letter from a doctor in Leipzig, inside Red Germany, who wanted to thank me, to tell me that he had taken my advice, and had urged his unit to surrender. They *had* surrendered and he had been a POW, and now, after the war, he had a family and a home and a medical practice in Germany. He would like to thank me. ME!

THAT NIGHT after having been re-captured, we were transferred to stretchers and moved up into the outer courtyard where there were ambulances to meet us. It was raining, and I remember in that rain and the light shining on dark surfaces and cobblestones, our aid man, now a prisoner, breaking away from where he was being held and throwing himself on my stretcher and pleading, pleading pleading to be allowed to go along with us. He was terrified of being shot if the ambulances left without him, and my German must have seemed the one rope to cling to that could save him from what would happen after we left. I DID come out of my funk long enough to argue for him, saying "Why not?" and that he was a good guy and all that, but they tore him away and when we drove off, he was with the other prisoners in the falling rain in that place of stone.

We were taken back to a behind the line field hospital, and from there to a larger field unit where, a day or so later, two doctors who were captains convinced me that my legs couldn't be saved. "Look at them! They are black!" They *were*

207

black, in places black as coal tar, black as black leather shoes, much of the way well above my ankles. "And the gangrene is already set in. Can't you smell it? If we don't amputate, we can't save YOU!" I couldn't disagree. What did I know? And it seemed true; it was obviously the case.

I suppose it was because of all I had been through in the shell hole that I felt the loss of my feet something I had already come to terms with. And so, when they wheeled me into an operating area in a large tent for the operation, and marked places just below my knees with Merthiolate to indicate where the amputations were to be, I knew there was nothing to be done.

Then, just as an assistant was lowering the ether mask over my nose, someone came into the tent, someone official and because of his rank being allowed to attend. The nurse took away the mask and I just lay there like one already anaesthetized and observed while the two captains explained to this visiting major the operation about to be performed and the reason for it. The major came to where I lay, prepared for what was to happen, and carefully probed my feet, studied them intricately. "You know," he said, "I have seen gangrene as far advanced as that recede. I have seen cases like this, where there is as much damage, suddenly reverse themselves. I know it's rare, and you are probably right and the operation probably should be done, and will have to be done, but isn't it worth a chance to watch it a day or two more, to simply wait and see? Then, if you're right, you can go ahead." I could see he had taken the wind out of the captains' sails, and that they were suddenly bewildered, but he had the rank, he had the authoritative position of being a field hospital observer, and they were intimidated.

The immediate result was that they canceled the operation on the spot and wheeled me back out of there and to my improvised ward. The subsequent result of that is that I have been dancing and racing and roaring about for fifty years since then; and the final result is that I have a great and unshakable respect for rank, believing that it pretty generally stands for something worthy of note. I have also a rather low opinion of captain surgeons.

I guess gratitude is what it is all about, my writing of this war chronicle now, after 50 years of it unspoken, unrevealed inside me. There are some things that before I die I need to acknowledge and pay respect to, and among these are that visiting major, those Sisters, Tex, that doctor, Joseph and Hartmund, my Luftwaffe sergeant, the sergeant on the hill, and a whole host of the living and the dead who accompanied me on my escape journey back into life.

———————>➤●◄—————————

I want very much to let what I have said say what it has to say—the rest is silence—but I have been urged by several, including one of my editors, to append some comment on the effect of this writing: what it may have finally meant, for me. It may be important for some to know the psychological effect of "all this," all that I passed through as well as this recovery process of the writing. Apart from the narrative itself, is there something I can and should say about what I may have learned.

First of all, the title *Resurrection* is not literary but essential. It was liberating—the experience—and I have lived for these fifty years since it all happened within that liberation. Upon being back with my own army and in the Army hospitals, I was already an utterly changed person. Who I had been— somewhat of a childish, jejune romantic and certainly both a prig and a pseudo intellectual—had been, in my war experience, fully called in question and rejected as absurd: not by others, but by myself, at a very fundamental level. I *had* been resurrected, I had risen from my shell hole no longer the person I was when wounded into it but someone "other," reformed in the crucible of the decisions there made, the necessary confrontations and realizations, especially within the reductions and renunciations, into a new and, to me and others, very altered person.

The first and most obvious change was one of energy. From being a somewhat reflective and quiet young man I had been catapulted into outrageousness: I can remember breaking my leg twice again while in hospital—once in a head-on crash at 60 miles an hour while on convalescent furlough, and once when a crutch slipped out from under me while engaged in a crutch race while still in cast in the corridors of my General Hospital. Within a year after being released from the Army, despite a 100% disability rating, subsequently revised down to 50%, I had taken a bicycle with me to Europe, on which I bicycled unaccompanied from Paris to Prague—en route exploring my territories of war and wounding. I found my way back to my shell hole—though it meant pushing my bicycle through undergrowth, woods and bogs and fields and up forested hillsides—and then back through Switzerland, during which I crossed several Alpine passes: all that, on a no-speed cycle. In those immediate postwar years, I was liaison for the Algerian Black Market in Paris; I attended a communist youth festival in Prague; I cycled covert dispatches here and there for the US military while living in bunkers under the streets of Vienna; and I worked in Zurich on a Hoch und Tief-Bau construction company as a laborer—between whiles zipping back to continue with a Princeton education. The energy has never deserted me—I knock on wood—whether throughout my 42 years of teaching (as my colleagues and students can attest), or in my traveling: I have driven across the country by car some scores of times and I doubt there has been a year I haven't widely traveled. This year, at 71, I am delivering a dozen talks and papers at national and international conferences, and I am working simultaneously on several book length manuscripts: one of these details Hemingway's Italian experience and fiction, and meant the photographing of every image from every line of *A Farewell to Arms* in the landscape of Yugoslavia, Italy, and Switzerland, and of *Across the River and Into the Trees* in Venice, and the details from all the short stories and biographically established events from his Italian life; another, on Hemingway's Cuban backgrounds, has, since 1959, brought me back to Cuba five times, in 1982–3 driving almost 3000 miles of Cuba, to record and track the legend of the man. These are some of my activities.

I record all this because I have always known that my energy was a unique combination of my inheritance and my experience, that I rose from that shell hole invested with life as I had never understood life before. This is not brag or swagger, it is rather awe-filled and I hope humble acknowledgment of what was given to me, partly by a descending white bird, and partly by a reenacted rite of passage in my shell hole, where I descended into death and the earth and rose again. I am and shall always be an ardent supporter of primitive rites of passage—that have passed from our feebly rational attempts to educate youth without bringing them through sensualized and mystically and religiously charged moments of apprehension and discovery. Primitive cultures still understand the essential need for these. They understand instinctively far more than we do about the necessary education of the young, and in the Western world, I best see this ongoing process in Latin cultures, where in the subtle languages of movement, dress, manners, dance, song, religious ritual, and the aesthetics and poetics of desire, enormous and vital information about life, death, sex, and social living is transferred. Nothing is more inhibiting and stultifying and ultimately destructive than rational and impersonal "unmystical" classes in sex education or social graces. One dance in which eyes meet and hands touch or do not touch is worth a million lectures. One night in a shell hole waiting for death educates more profoundly than a lifetime insured and assured.

Energy, I have come to believe, is a concomitant of problem solving: it uniquely flows from a profound and authentic encounter with forces, always more incomprehensible than we can name, where a victory, in survival or understanding, in recognition or fusion, grants us the singular benefit of power that flows to us, of mystery that becomes part of our unlocked capacities. Forces unlocked in nature merely unlock the reciprocals of themselves, which are always within us to be unlocked. Nature may merely be the externalized visualization the mind and spirit must have of all that they unknowingly are. Emerson once said that eloquence belongs to him and flows to him who has made the authentic contact with nature, not with its human abstractions. But he was a transcendentalist, who well understood the spiritual meaning of nature.

Part of the fortunate nature of my war experience, granted me by Fortune, Fate, and by immanent forces I cannot name, was that I was in that experience allowed to be alone: I had to deal with it and understand it, endure it, and survive it on my own, unaided by others (except my captors) who might have taken unto themselves the job of explaining it or determining its outcome. Instead of society, or buddies, I had my adversary, with whom I had to deal, and the adversarial nature of Nature and its weathers and cold and its informing reductions.

Necessarily dealing with it alone granted me a respect for my mind and sensibility and the fortunes of war and those qualities and capacities within whatever met me and confronted me. I do know that there has seldom passed a day since those days on those fields outside Metz when I have not rejoiced at the sun on my body, the winds on my cheeks, the thrust of the earth back against the weight of my advancing step, the overbowing sky, the enrounding unknown and waiting to be experienced various world. Selfishly, less frequently but consistently, I have mourned all those who there died too young, who did not survive their battle.

Well, then, what was the immediate result of my writing of this war account? Immediately, I recognized that I had simultaneously with the writing unlocked parts of myself in an exhilarating and wonderful sense of truth and release. I knew that I had rid myself of false myths and spurious half truths and, actually in the writing, come upon unknown history. I almost instantly started out writing *North of the City*, a book I have now finished, trying to extricate and learn for the first time about my childhood years, from three till about 16, when I was growing up north of New York City in Yonkers, New York.

The writing of "my" war was actually a recapitulation of the war experience itself, because in both art and life I was necessarily locking back my language and words in one instance and my sensibility and nature in the other upon the rough and crude and basic facts of life that a rifleman cannot avoid knowing. It all has to do with authentic possession in the place of false possession, of the way an artist comes upon his style by way of a mastery of his medium, during which he encounters the sources of his language in its experiential factual occasions. It has much to do with love and with belief, as the lover replaces love in his heart of his beloved with the sure sense of her or himself, and as his gods become God or the living vitalized fact of the essence of living life. As I elsewhere said, a god or God can be a radiance, a cloud, a shower of gold, a tree, a descending bird.

For some years after the war I was constantly afraid, at some level beneath consciousness, that all that I called life, the life I had been returned to and was living, was but a dream being dreamed in my shell hole, and that at any moment I might wake from that dream and find myself in that shell hole still and at the very moment before my death. That did not seem impossible. Though that fear has faded, due to all that I have received—a long dream or a long life—I am not without the feeling that, before my death I may well be reduced to, or find myself experiencing, whether in coma or medical dependency or stages of advanced senility, the position of one who is able to feel only the sense of the turning changing stages of the sun or the fine drift of soft wind over my cheeks as, deaf or blind and inert, I live out my death. If that should be, I hope I may have the grace to accept that with a smile of benediction, with happiness in my heart for life.

Both war and the memories of war have been here my subjects of concern. No one passes through that fire without carrying beyond it embers in his soul and sensibility. I remember after the war discovering how sensitized my infantry experience had made me to the earth and landscape: for several years after being honorably discharged from the service, I reacted to all terrain that I passed through in terms of defilade and cover: I knew on every instant walking just how many advantageous feet I was from land I could regard as parapet and paradose and how effective my concealment might be in it, and how secure it might leave me from lanes of fire. The earth had become sensualized, dramatized, and more intimate to me—indeed, I had dug into it, been sheltered by it, had hidden in it, had covered myself with it and rubbed it upon me that it might be both my warmth and camouflage; and in basic training, I had sculpted it in Georgia clay foxholes and learned how its warmth and shelter meant life itself to the infantry soldier. This intimacy with gross and basic nature was for me an unpredictable gift; and no one receives such a gift without coevally receiving the gift of a certain eloquence when nature, which is the source of our imagery and language, informs and pours itself full-bodied into our abstractions and thoughts.

My experience also allowed me to see my "enemy" up close, to be able to evaluate and judge him even as I needed to cajole him and influence him to my survival while remaining loyal and not betraying my trusts—not that I had anything to betray: what did I know? And so I think I was able to see the two faces of war fortuitously and uniquely. Remarkably, I had been sensitized to "my enemy" by a strange experience I had had while behind the lines moving as a replacement closer and closer to the front. When we were finally placed in "barracks" on a hill at Jarny/Conflans, we would sit on the hill at night and watch the muttering of big guns in the distance, the electric sky flickering and flashing at skyline with what seemed an immense short circuit; and on certain nights we could watch the exploding German shells in the rail yards below us in the valley—we were engaged and involved with and yet detached and spectators to the war that we were rapidly approaching.

One day there I wandered off alone behind our barracks and found on a lane nearby on the hilltop a primitive German military cemetery for German soldiers killed in the First World War. It was small, ringed by dark granite low walls and fronted with an intricate iron gate. I had my rifle slung, and with curiosity and some temerity I explored inside the gate where a few hundred graves were fixed under their headstones, some bearing elaborate funereal sculpture, others a plain stone marker. The graves were scattered about and under dark cedars and occasional pines and other deciduous trees almost stripped of their leaves. It had been an ominously slate gray day with brooding darker blue clouds and occasional bursts of rain, and I somewhat nervously advanced into the burial ground to read the legends and information set there in stone. The buried soldiers of that earlier war had died uniformly amazingly young, and there was a grave to a 17-year old German nurse who was buried there among her compatriots. I read the inscriptions on other graves, and they equally saddened me: this lost youth of that earlier age, still lost here in this island in enemy territory.

The day and the weather made the experience enormously sad, painted with a gloom and foreboding and given a lament by a suddenly gradually increasing wind bringing heavier rain—not falling but seemingly thrown in bursts. And then it was almost hysterically upon me, a quickly rising intense and heavy wind coming from the back of the cemetery towards me and bowing some trees and tossing others, as though a rage had come into nature and a vengeance. I instantly "read it" as aimed at me, having risen to drive me, the enemy intruder, from that sacred and singular plot of alien ground in the midst of France. It seemed sinewed with malice and designed to drive me, a contaminating presence, out— and out I went, slowly, backing towards and through the gate and away from that place where I felt myself so thoroughly suddenly The Intruder. The sky raged, the trees whistled and roared, and what few leaves were left seemed being stripped and flung after me. As I went backwards through the gate, still facing the great darkening wind and rain, I again read the legend I had somewhat ignored over the gate when I entered: "Hier Ruhen Helden. Bitte, Fremde, stören Sie nicht," or something like that: "Here rest heroes. We beg you, stranger, do not disturb them."

I was profoundly moved by the experience. It was, to me then, electrifying, leaving me feeling that I had been singled out for that colloquy with the dead and their protective spirits. I could not easily return to barracks or rejoin others. I was at once deeply shocked and changed. I KNEW that it was a singular message I had received and one that would leave me never. I now know, only after having written what you have read, that that experience had sensitized me to "my enemy," had invaded me, imploring my compassion and understanding—a message across time, binding me to the dead of other wars and also to my enemy. If I was singularly responsive to that cry, I imagine that it prepared me to meet, in the flesh, the soldiers, my captors, I was later to meet. Some years later when I went back to Jarny/Conflans, I found the graveyard being dismantled, the graves dug up and strewn about. I found no trace of the grave of the 17-year old nurse who had been buried there.